SHELLEY: A voice not understood

To the memory of my father

TIMOTHY WEBB

SHELLEY:
A VOICE NOT UNDERSTOOD

HUMANITIES PRESS

Atlantic Highlands, New Jersey

Published 1977 in the U.S.A.
  by Humanities Press
  Atlantic Highlands, N. J. 07716

Library of Congress Cataloging in Publication Data

Webb, Timothy.
  Shelley : a voice not understood.

  Bibliography : p.
  Includes index.
  1. Shelley, Percy Bysshe, 1792–1822. 2. Poets,
English – 19th century – Biography.
PR5431.W4   821'.7   77–24903
ISBN 0–391–00757–2

Printed in Great Britain by
WILLMER BROTHERS LIMITED
Birkenhead, Merseyside

CONTENTS

CONTENTS

PREFATORY NOTE

Definitive texts of Shelley's poetry and prose have yet to be established. For the purpose of this study, I have cited the poetry from my *Shelley: Selected Poems* (Everyman's University Library, 1977); in the few cases where the poem or passage in question is not included in my own selection, I have used the Oxford edition by Thomas Hutchinson, making corrections wherever this seemed necessary and possible. *A Defence of Poetry* is cited from the edition by H. F. B. Brett-Smith; Shelley's prefaces are cited from Hutchinson's editions; other essays are cited, with some emendations, from *Shelley's Prose*, ed. D. L. Clark. Full details of these and other primary sources can be found in the list of Abbreviated Titles.

This book includes a number of prose passages, cancelled readings, jottings, and quotations from Greek literature, most of which are derived from the Shelley MSS. in the Bodleian Library, Oxford. For permission to consult and quote from these manuscripts I am very grateful to the Delegates of the Clarendon Press; to them I also owe my thanks for permission to quote from *The Letters of Percy Bysshe Shelley*, ed. F. L. Jones, 1964. My thanks are also due to the Keeper of Western Manuscripts and the staff of Duke Humfrey's Library at Oxford for their unfailing courtesy and efficiency.

I should like to acknowledge a general debt to the pioneering work of K. N. Cameron, the late Earl Wasserman, Donald H. Reiman, Harold Bloom, Neville Rogers and Geoffrey Matthews, without whose example and inspiration this book could not have been written. My graduate class at Michigan State University provided a stimulating opportunity to explore *Prometheus Unbound* in informed but enthusiastic company. A debt of gratitude is also due to Mrs Winifred Leonard who prepared the typescript with admirable accuracy and expedition. Finally, I should like to record a debt to my parents who have encouraged me over the years and to my wife Ruth whose critical understanding, advice and generous support have always proved invaluable.

ABBREVIATED TITLES

Clark, *Prose*   *Shelley's Prose: or The Trumpet of a Prophecy*, ed. David Lee Clark, corr. ed., University of New Mexico Press, Albuquerque, 1966.

Defence   *A Defence of Poetry* cited from *Peacock's Four Ages of Poetry, Shelley's Defence of Poetry*, etc., ed. H. F. B. Brett-Smith, reprinted ed., Blackwell, Oxford, 1953.

Hogg, *Life*   T. J. Hogg, *The Life of Shelley* cited from *The Life of Percy Bysshe Shelley as comprised in The Life of Shelley by Thomas Jefferson Hogg, The Recollections of Shelley and Byron by Edward John Trelawny, Memoirs of Shelley by Thomas Love Peacock*, ed. Humbert Wolfe, 2 vols., Dent, 1933.

Journal   *Mary Shelley's Journal*, ed. F. L. Jones, University of Oklahoma Press, Norman, 1947.

K.–S.J.   *Keats–Shelley Journal*.

K.–S.M.B.   *Keats–Shelley Memorial Bulletin*.

Letters   *The Letters of Percy Bysshe Shelley*, ed. F. L. Jones, 2 vols., Clarendon Press, Oxford, 1964.

Letters of M.W.S.   *The Letters of Mary W. Shelley*, ed. F. L. Jones, 2 vols., University of Oklahoma Press, Norman, 1944.

P.W.   *The Complete Poetical Works of Percy Bysshe Shelley*, ed. Thomas Hutchinson, 1904, reset ed., Clarendon Press, Oxford, 1943.

Shelley and his Circle   *Shelley and his Circle: 1773–1822*, vols. I–IV ed. K. N. Cameron, vols. V–VI ed. D. H. Reiman, Harvard University Press, Cambridge (Mass.) and Oxford University Press, 1961–73.

S.I.R.   *Studies in Romanticism*.

CHAPTER ONE

ANGELS
AND CRITICS

We are a review-and-newspaper ridden people; and while we contend clamorously for the right of thinking for ourselves, we yet guide ourselves unconsciously by the opinion of censors whom we know to be partial or incompetent.

W. S. Walker in *Knight's Quarterly Magazine* (1824)

(*i*)

We can begin with an incident which is supposed to have taken place at Pisa in the early months of 1822. The narrator is Edward Trelawny, that disengaged man of action, who was hovering around Shelley and Byron, in the hope of recording the divine idiosyncracies of genius:

I was bathing one day in a deep pool in the Arno, and astonished the Poet by performing a series of aquatic gymnastics, which I had learnt from the natives of the South Seas. On my coming out, whilst dressing, Shelley said mournfully,

'Why can't I swim? it seems so very easy.'

I answered, 'Because you think you can't. If you determine, you will; take a header off this bank and when you rise turn on your back, you will float like a duck; but you must reverse the arch of your spine, for it's now bent the wrong way.'

He doffed his jacket and trousers, kicked off his shoes and socks, and plunged in; and there he lay stretched out on the bottom like a conger eel, not making the least effort or struggle to save himself. He would have drowned if I had not instantly fished him out. When he recovered his breath, he said,

'I always find the bottom of the well, and they say Truth lies there. In another minute I should have found it, and you would have found an empty shell. It is an easy way of getting rid of the body.'[1]

Though one detects an authentic Shelleyan ring in the extraordinary singlemindedness and self-possession of that retort, this highly coloured story is as likely to be a fabrication of Trelawny's as it is to be true. This concerns biographers more than critics, or so one might suppose; yet because Trelawny set down this unforgettable story, imaged Shelley to us as a conger eel curled up in the well of truth, this incident with all its implications has become an ineradicable fact of Shelley biography, an imaginative reality which no weighing of historical probabilities can erase from our consciousness.

Clearly this does matter to critics; those who have written on Shelley have shown themselves peculiarly susceptible to legend. From this incident alone one might deduce several significant facts about Shelley and then apply them (if one wished) to his poetry, or (more circumspectly) read the poetry and 'discover' in it those very tendencies pointed up by the anecdote. Take for instance that unworldly neglect of the elementary principles of self-preservation, that infuriating passivity in the face of challenge or danger. This might lead the suspicious to interpret Shelley's death by drowning as a fate which if not deliberately courted was, at the least, acquiescently embraced:

Shelley was drowned near here. Arms at his side
He fell submissive through the waves, and he
Was but a minor conquest of the sea:
The darkness that he met was nurse not bride.[2]

Such a death and such a posture imply an unwillingness to bare the knuckles, to counter the assaults of life in vigorous fighting terms. Where Thom Gunn suggests Shelley lacked the pugilistic muscle which might be expected of a true poet in a violent time, the nineteenth century critics spoke of his effeminacy and his 'lack of robustness'. For proof in poetic terms they pointed to declarations such as 'I fall upon the thorns of life! I bleed!' or 'I die! I faint! I fail!' Thus, the passivity evidenced in Trelawny's story might be linked on the one hand to a kind of escapism, a reluctance to come to grips with daunting realities and, on the other, to a kind of licensed swooning in the poetry which could be equated with sentimentality, self-pity and other unmanly and unaesthetic practices. One might, if one wished, go further. Shelley's behaviour at the bottom of the pool might be interpreted as emblematic not only of an attitude to life and a philosophy but also of a whole literary method. What is Shelley doing here if not practising a kind of negative capability (or incapability, if you prefer)? For those who do not want to believe that Shelley the poet exercised intellectual control over his material, here is a convenient illustration from the life:

Shelley stretches himself on the sands of the river-bed as palely and meekly as he prostrated himself before the wayward winds of inspiration; he offers his face to the ripples of the Arno as supinely as he opened his mind to the stream of association.

I offer this interpretation as a paradigm of the complicated and dangerous ways in which biography and criticism can interlace. I do not know of any evidence that this story was used directly in any of the ways I have indicated; yet it seems certain that it is on this story and others like it that such critical response to Shelley has been based. Even the most circumspect of critics, even those who hold themselves aloof from any biographical response, scrutinising the poetry in the most antiseptic conditions, have been influenced by the various legends of Shelley the man, so that their investigations of Shelley the poet have been contaminated by alien matter, whether they recognise it or not. This in itself would be bad enough: what makes the situation far worse is the fact that all the standard biographies and memoirs are, in a variety of ways, misleading. Trelawny's anecdote, for example, might just be true or it might be a highly embroidered version of what actually happened: yet even if it *were* true, it could well be dangerously suggestive since it emphasises one aspect of Shelley's character at the expense of others which must be obvious to any one who has read all the poetry with care and without preconceptions. There *was* a passive side to Shelley's nature, a need to submit himself to influence, but he was also a man of strong will, resolute in his beliefs and determined to suffer for them if that were necessary. The two lines of 'Ode to the West Wind' which give evidence of weakness are more than counterbalanced by the strength and drive of the other sixty-eight. The heroic resistance of Prometheus is infinitely more significant than the conventional pallor of 'The Indian Serenade'.

Given this confused situation, it will be necessary to devote some space to exploring the ramifications of biographical influence before we approach the poetry. Why are the biographies so misleading and in what ways do they misrepresent the truth? How have the best known biographical interpretations affected criticism? And have these problems been complicated by others, such as political prejudice, or editorial misrepresentation, or textual difficulties? Not till we have answered these questions will it be time to examine the poetry itself.

(*ii*)

The roots of the biographical problem were evident as early as August

1822, a mere month after Shelley had been drowned at Lerici. An anonymous critic in *The Paris Monthly Review* analysed the situation with great clarity:

Never did the remorseless deep engulph so gentle, so angelic, so melodious a Lycidas, as Percy Bysshe Shelley; and yet never was there a name associated with more black, poisonous, and bitter calumny than this.[3]

We can see here not only two ways of looking at Shelley which are radically opposed but also the extravagance of both reactions. It seems that one either had to be violently for Shelley or violently against him. Only the alignments were sometimes puzzling. The pacific Charles Lamb, while salivating over the delights of frogs dressed in parsley and butter ('Imagine a Lilliputian rabbit!'), modulated abruptly into righteous wrath: 'Shelley the great Atheist has gone down by water to eternal fire!';[4] yet the cynical Byron was moved to say, 'You were all brutally mistaken about Shelley, who was, without exception, the *best* and least selfish man I ever knew. I never knew one who was not a beast in comparison.'[5] Already, in 1822, Shelley's reputation was being squabbled over with varieties of possessiveness, rancour, hate and unqualified adulation, much as his charred remains and the water-logged *Don Juan* were to be jealously ransacked for relics—heart (or was it liver?), waterstained volume of Sophocles (was it Aeschylus?), Hunt's copy of Keats '*open* and doubled back, as if it had been thrust in, in the hurry of a surprise'.[6] The process of canonisation began early; so too did the ritual vilification of the class traitor, the aristocratic revolutionary, the atheist, the adulterer, the immoralist.

Poetry might seem to have little to do with this but that unfortunately is not the case. Shelley's reputation was largely created out of factors which had little direct connection with poetry but that reputation soon transferred itself from the realms of biography, ethics and politics to the realm of literary criticism. If Shelley's views on politics were dangerous, then Shelley was a bad poet; if his attitude to sexual morality was unacceptable then so was his poetry; if his philosophy did not conduce to the stability of the *status quo*, then it followed that his poetry had little aesthetic merit. Leigh Hunt understood this better than anyone:

They dare not say a word till they know a man's connexions and opinions. If his politics are not of the true cast, they cannot discover his poetry. If his faith is not orthodox, how can he have any wit in him? Before they admit a thought respecting his odes, they must learn what are his notions respecting the Mosaic Dispensation. The question is not, 'Has he genius?' but 'Is he one of us?' . . .

Hunt's courageous and perceptive reviews in *The Examiner* were intended to explore the poetry with a more dispassionate eye than that of the *Quarterly* or *Blackwood's* (the *Edinburgh Review* expressed *its* view by keeping contemptuous silence). Though his articles are splendidly direct and outspoken, he can also respond with tact and insight to the complexities of Shelley's greatest poetry. Nor is he afraid to criticise Shelley's predilection for metaphysics at the expense of men and things. Yet, although the nineteenth century produced no criticism of Shelley which was more inward, Hunt sometimes displayed an understandable tendency to romanticise Shelley, a tendency which developed considerably after Shelley's death. Most important of all, Shelley and Hunt were in agreement politically.

What all of this amounts to is a situation in which, for a variety of reasons, almost everybody took sides and, having taken sides, invested their opinions with the rhetorical emphases of their adopted positions. In so far as they can be separated, this applied to 'critical' opinion almost as much as to political or moral opinion. Without contraries is no progression, but the road of excess does not always lead to the palace of wisdom. Both sides idealised—those who hated Shelley or who feared him concentrated on all that was bad in his work, morally and poetically, while those who admired him focused their attention on what they considered the best. Both sides exaggerated, both selected unfairly, both ignored evidence (biographical or poetic) which did not fit in with their preconceptions. Thus, we are confronted with Shelley the pale and bleeding martyr or Shelley the persuasive adulterer, the 'sweetest singer of our saddest woe' or the man 'whose writings tend to make our sons profligates and our daughters strumpets'.[8] Needless to say, neither version is the true one. Yet the selections from Shelley's poems in popular anthologies, his critical reputation and the whole way in which we respond to his work have all been profoundly influenced by one or other of these traditions, sometimes by both.

For this reason, it is worth examining in greater detail how these two versions of Shelley came about and their particular consequences for criticism. To begin with, the main biographical sources in the nineteenth century, those few people who had known Shelley well and were prepared to make public their memories, were influenced by various considerations which an objective biographer would do well to avoid. Partly because of pressure from Shelley's sensitive father Sir Timothy, who felt that the family name had already suffered enough, and partly because of her own reluctance to face the difficult facts, Mary Shelley never attempted a full-scale biography of her husband. Instead she produced several pioneering editions of his works, notably the *Posthumous Poems* of 1824 and the collected editions of 1839 and 1840, in which she published from the manuscripts many poems which Shelley had left unfinished (the results of these excavations were not, on the whole, helpful to Shelley's reputation, as we shall see later).[9] Mary had the wisdom to see that a correct and complete edition was a more fitting memorial than a biography. However, she supplemented the poems with long editorial notes in which she examined the genesis of each of his major works and offered some limited biographical background and a little elementary criticism. In addition she provided a general note for the shorter poems of every year from 1814–1815 till 1822 and two brief prefaces. Together this constituted an immensely valuable body of material which, though it did not aspire to the completeness of a formal biography, offered an extensive picture of the poet at work, particularly during the years in Italy (1818–1822). Whether because of various external pressures or through a due regard for reticence, Mrs Shelley directed her focus on the work rather than the man: 'I abstain from any remark on the occurrences of his private life, except inasmuch as the passions which they engendered inspired his poetry.' Had the other biographers observed the same priorities, the history of Shelley criticism would be very different.

For all her reticence, however, Mrs Shelley was not in a position to be objective. For one thing, a wife is not qualified to be a dispassionate biographer and this problem was exacerbated by the fact that after Shelley's death she bitterly reproached herself for the estrangement of the last years, the painful failure to communicate which led Shelley to lament in one of his notebooks, 'My dearest M[ary] wherefore hast thou gone / And left me in this dreary world alone[?]'[10] Now, too late, she hoped to make amends by claiming for her husband his rightful place in the pantheon of English poetry. Such an aim and such a motivation naturally led her to idealise the character of Shelley:

He died, and his place, among those who knew him intimately, has never been filled up. He walked beside them like a spirit of good to comfort and benefit—to enlighten the darkness of life with irradiations of genius, to cheer it with his sympathy and love. Any one, once attached to Shelley, must feel all other affections, however true and fond, as wasted on barren soil in comparison. It is our best consolation to know that such a pure-minded and exalted being was once among us, and now exists where we hope one day to join him;—although the intolerant, in their blindness, poured down

anathemas, the Spirit of Good, who can judge the heart, never rejected him.
(Preface to the 1839 edition, *Poetical Works*, p. xi)[11]

The facts of Shelley's life bear much of this out but it is not the whole picture. One notes also the strategic softening of Shelley's own heterodox views on religion into a pious hope which would have been acceptable to the most conventional Victorian believers (excepting those like Lamb or Gilfillan who felt that Shelley was a candidate for eternal damnation). Perhaps more damaging was Mrs Shelley's own critical view, widely expressed in her editorial notes, that his poetry was too concerned with the unreal, with 'huntings after the obscure' as she put it. She even hinted that some of the poetry was about nothing at all: 'The luxury of imagination, which sought nothing beyond itself (as a child burdens itself with spring flowers, thinking of no use beyond the enjoyment of gathering them), often showed itself . . .' (*P.W.*, p. x).

Some of the possibilities hinted at by Mary Shelley were made explicit by the first official biographer, Thomas Jefferson Hogg, who had been sent down from Oxford with Shelley as co-author of *The Necessity of Atheism*. As a biographer, Hogg suffered from three grave disadvantages. First, ever since his departure from Oxford he had been growing more reactionary, more devoted to Greek literature as a hermetically sealed escape from the harsh realities of the pre-Reform era, more crudely derisive at the expense of things he did not understand. One result was that he reshaped various events in which he and Shelley had been involved, exculpating himself when possible and safely transmuting Shelley's revolutionary ardours into something closer to eccentricity. Although he was a lawyer, Hogg did not stop short of falsifying documents when necessary. Thus, notoriously, he changed the pronouns in some letters in order to transfer some of his own feelings and actions to the innocent Shelley.[12] The family were so displeased with Hogg's misdemeanours as biographer that they withdrew their official approval, so that Hogg only published two volumes, taking Shelley up to the age of twenty-two. Hogg's second disqualification was his quite amazing egotism. He seems to have resented the fact that Shelley was more talented than he was: the consequence is that Hogg's *Life of Shelley* is not so much a biography as an autobiography. There are long stretches where Shelley does not appear at all. This is how Hogg justifies his biographical procedure:

Shelley was fugitive, volatile; he evaporated like ether, his nature being etherial; he suddenly escaped, like some fragrant essence; evanescent as a quintessence. He was a lovely, a graceful image, but fading. vanishing speedily from our sight, being portrayed in flying colours. He was a climber, a creeper, an elegant, beautiful, odoriferous parasitical plant; he could not support himself; he must be tied up fast to something of a firmer texture, harder and more rigid than his own, pliant, yielding structure; to some person of less flexible formation; he always required a prop. In order to write the history of his fragile, unconnected, interrupted life, it is necessary to describe that of some ordinary everyday person with whom he was familiar, and to introduce the real subject of the history, whenever a transitory glance of him can be caught.[13]

There is more than a hint here of one of the most enduring Shelley legends, Shelley as the sensitive plant, the anaemic poet without a backbone. Shelley also bears a distinct resemblance to the cloud as characterised in one of his most popular poems. It's amusing to note Hogg's suggestion that Shelley was in need of support, if one has read the letters which passed between Shelley and Hogg, or if one remembers how in the most tangible of all senses, Shelley supported so many of his friends. The egotistic implication of superiority in this passage is highly significant for an understanding of Hogg's biography. Hogg's need to patronise his gifted friend, to loosen Shelley's hold on reality, to exaggerate his weakness, can be traced not only to his own egotism and his crude standard of common sense but it also connects with Hogg's latent homosexuality.

The Hogg–Shelley letters as we now have them leave little doubt that, consciously or not, there was a homosexual attraction between the two. After one of their separations, Shelley writes to Hogg more like a lover than a friend and the tone of the correspondence around the time of Shelley's marriage to Harriet is distinctly emotional in the circumstances. We may add to this Shelley's habit of inviting Hogg to form a *ménage à trois* (how much he acted from communistic principles and how much from more emotional considerations, it is impossible to say) and Hogg's eagerness to accept these invitations, even to insinuate himself more tangibly than may have been intended. Hogg involved himself in turn with Shelley's sister and his two wives, Harriet and Mary: to bring the series to a satisfying conclusion, he finally settled down with Jane Williams, the object of Shelley's affections during his last days and the focus of some of his most beautiful poems ('To Jane: the Recollection', 'Lines written in the Bay of Lerici' etc.). Translating this knowledge back into our reading of the biography, we discover a distinct tendency to feminise: 'As his port had the meekness of a maiden, so the heart of the young virgin who has never crossed her father's threshold to encounter the rude world, could not be more susceptible of all the sweet domestic charities than his ...' Or, take this passage, which presents Shelley's genuine distaste for vulgarity or obscenity, which he regarded as 'blasphemy against the divine beauty of life':

Bysshe was serious, thoughtful, enthusiastic; melancholy even, with a poet's sadness: he loved to discourse gravely of matters of importance and deep concernment; the unceasing jests, perpetual farce, and profane and filthy ribaldry of the comic Master of the Rolls he found wearisome, puerile, and worse. In behaviour, modest; in conversation, chaste; like some pure, innocent young maiden, the gross and revolting indecency of an immoral wit wounded his sensitive nature.[14]

The comic Master of the Rolls is John Philpot Curran, the Irish barrister and patriot, father of the sweetheart of the romantic revolutionary, Robert Emmet, who was executed by the British in 1803. Shelley had written an early poem on the subject (in the style of Thomas Moore) and he was, of course, directly involved in Irish republican politics. His disillusionment with Curran was produced not so much by a maidenly disposition to be shocked as by his discovering the real character of a man who had once been associated with stirring deeds in the name of liberty. Call this childish innocence, if you will; let the sober eye of experience smile knowingly at the enthusiasm of youth— but do not put it down to a prim objection to dirty stories. For comparison here is the real Shelley commenting on the statue of an athlete in the Uffizi: 'Curse these fig leaves; why is a round tin thing more decent than a cylindrical marble one?'[15] So much for maiden modesty.

From the sensitive plant and the blushing miss it is but a short step to the unworldly angel: as Geoffrey Matthews put it, 'Turn but a petticoat and start a luminous wing.'[16] Shelley, said Hogg, had no idea of time or space but that was quite forgivable when you understood why: '... no human being, no poet was ever less punctual; he had no perception, no notion of time, a divine nature lives not in time, but in eternity.'[17] One result was an inability to tell the truth:

He was altogether incapable of rendering an account of any transaction whatsoever, according to the strict and precise truth, and the bare, naked realities of actual life; not through an addiction to falsehood, which he cordially detested, but because he was the creature, the unsuspecting and unresisting victim, of his irresistible imagination.[18]

Hogg seems to be divided between the urge to deride Shelley for his lack of common sense and the urge to applaud him for indulging in the higher inaccuracies in which all losses are restored and sorrows end. As a man, he hints, Shelley was awkward, perhaps inconvenient to know; as a poet, he could be excused, even admired. If he didn't keep appointments, or left the room suddenly, that was understandable; after all, he had been admitted to the society of the Muses, and he must be about his business. This showed in his appearance: 'Bysshe looked, as he always looked, wild, intellectual, unearthly; like a spirit that had just descended from the sky; like a demon risen at that moment out of the ground.'[19] (Here we have that very ambivalence which was to trouble the nineteenth century and then our own; was he angel or devil?) And, of course, it showed in his poetry:

Shelley is the only modern poet whose verses uniformly appear to be inspired; no other poet of recent times is so completely and universally under the influence of inspiration. The earliest, the most hasty, the least finished, the most unformed and irregular of his poems have, notwithstanding their manifold defects, something superhuman about them. They seem to have been breathed, not by a mere mortal, but by some god or demon.[20]

While Hogg respected and probably envied these superhuman talents, he also made vigorous efforts to drag Shelley out of the company of the Muses and face to face with reality. Presumably he intended to make a man out of the maiden. Here is one graphic example:

I led him one summer's evening into a brick-field; it had never occurred to him to ask himself how a brick is formed; the secret was revealed in a moment; he was charmed with the simple contrivance, and astonished at the rapidity, facility, and exactness with which it was put in use by so many busy hands. An ordinary observer would have smiled and passed on, but the son of fancy confessed his delight with an energy which roused the attention even of the ragged throng, that seemed to exist only that they might pass successive lumps of clay through a wooden frame.[21]

A similar note was struck by another of Shelley's early biographers, Edward Trelawny, whose story about the swimming lesson we have encountered already. Trelawny is quite explicit:

I never lost an opportunity of . . . giving the dreamy bard glimpses of rough life. He disliked it, but could not resist my importunity. He had seen no more of the working-day world than a girl at a boarding-school, and his habit of eternally brooding on his own thoughts, in solitude and silence, damaged his health of mind and body. Like many other over-sensitive people, he thought everybody shunned him, whereas it was he who stood aloof.[22]

This generalisation follows an account of how Trelawny took Shelley to the docks at Leghorn and pointed out a Greek ship where the crew 'squatted about the decks in small knots, shrieking, gesticulating, smoking, eating, and gambling like savages'. Trelawny inquired if this realised his idea of Hellenism : 'No,' said Shelley, 'but it does of Hell.'[23] After this he was introduced to the Greek captain and, not surprisingly, disappointed by the Captain's view that the Greek revolution was an obstacle to trade. A Yankee skipper who offered him weak grog was more acceptable because of his associations with George Washington and American republicanism. Here again, if one looks below the surface, it appears that Shelley's recoil from realities was caused not so much by a reluctance to soil his hands as from strongly held and passionately advocated political principles.

In fact, Trelawny's book (or books, since there were two, the second an elaboration and more romanticised version of the first) is a much subtler and less egotistic narrative than Hogg's and many passages in it seem to carry the ring of truth. He also had the advantage of knowing Shelley at the end of his life, when he was undoubtedly more mature than in the Oxford period and shortly after, when Hogg had known him best. He describes Shelley as falling from his boat and shrieking with delight as he floundered in the water; on another memorable occasion he images Shelley appearing naked and dripping at a dinner party to the amazement of the guests : 'To confine Shelley within the limits of conventional or any other arbitrary laws of society was out of the question; he retained his simple, boyish habits.'[24] We see him reading and writing in a variety of outdoor settings; he is discovered composing a draft of 'With a Guitar, to Jane' in a pine forest ('it might have been taken for a sketch of a marsh overgrown with bulrushes, and the blots for wild ducks'); he reads Plato on board the Don Juan and has his hat knocked overboard when the sail shifts suddenly. Underneath all the exaggeration and the pointing of anecdotes one senses what one rarely senses in Hogg, the presence of a real human being, complicated and sometimes contradictory. Hogg presents a caricature, Trelawny an imaginative recreation. Where Hogg regards Shelley's eccentricities as laughable deviations from the norm of sensible behaviour, Trelawny presents them as credible manifestations of an exceptional personality. And yet even Trelawny succumbs to the fatal temptation of romanticising.

It is important to recognise that Trelawny's portrait of Shelley is not presented in isolation : in its second version it was called *Records of Shelley, Byron, and the Author*. The title is revealing, since what the book presents is not simply records or recollections of Shelley and Byron, Trelawny looking on with pencil in hand; it does offer us portraits of both men but they are seen as the opposing poles of a dialectic, a dialectic in which Trelawny himself is engaged. Trelawny was, in some respects, similar to Byron—a man of action, a man of the world, a romantic traveller, an autobiographical teller of tales. Each presented a challenge to the masculinity and prowess of the other; to his discomfort, Trelawny soon found that Byron was almost a match for him in the sphere of action. To make matters worse, he was not properly romantic as one might have expected from the author of *Lara*, *The Corsair*, and *The Giaour*. 'Byron disenchanted me' said Trelawny, who did not like being patronised, and who did not understand Byron's sense of humour. In this situation, Trelawny tended to align himself with Shelley, who in his turn idealised the retired buccaneer (see the Pirate in Shelley's 'Unfinished Drama'). The result was that Trelawny prized Shelley for those qualities which differentiated him from Byron and did not pay enough attention to other aspects of his personality. If Byron was an unpoetic poet, then Shelley was eminently poetical; if Byron was too addicted to humour then Shelley 'did not laugh, or even smile'; if Byron was a man of action and a man of the world, then Shelley was not; if Byron was ruggedly masculine (indeed challengingly so) then Shelley was appealingly feminine. Some such process is at work in Trelawny's memoirs, where Shelley is transformed into 'the ideal of what a poet should be',[25] the archetypal Poet usually honoured with a capital P.

A famous passage in the *Records* illustrates this very clearly. Trelawny has just arrived in Pisa and is talking to Edward and Jane Williams when he is 'rather put out by observing in the passage, near the open door . . . a pair of glittering eyes steadily fixed on mine'. The apparition turns out to be Shelley:

With the acuteness of a woman, Mrs Williams's eyes followed the direction of mine, and going to the doorway, she laughingly said,
    'Come in, Shelley, it's only our friend Tre just arrived.'
    Swiftly gliding in, blushing like a girl, a tall thin stripling held out both his hands; and although I could hardly believe as I looked at his flushed, feminine, and artless face that it could be the Poet, I returned his warm pressure . . .
    [Shelley is then asked what book he has in his hand. It turns out to be Calderón's *El Mágico Prodigioso* and he is invited to read aloud.]
    Shoved off from the shore of common-place incidents that could not interest him, and fairly launched on a theme that did, he instantly became oblivious of everything but the book in his hand. The masterly manner in which he

analyzed the genius of the author, his lucid interpretation of the story, and the ease with which he translated into our language the most subtle and imaginative passages of the Spanish poet, were marvellous, as was his command of the two languages. After this touch of his quality I no longer doubted his identity; a dead silence ensued; looking up, I asked,

'Where is he?'

Mrs Williams said, 'Who? Shelley! Oh, he comes and goes like a spirit, no one knows when or where.'[26]

The configurations should be familiar by now: the poet is noticeably feminine in appearance, he prefers the ideal world to the real one, he is more like a spirit than a man. Shelley soon makes another appearance, this time in the company of his wife:

Presently he reappeared with Mrs Shelley. She brought us back from the ideal world Shelley had left us in, to the real one, welcomed me to Italy, and asked me the news of London and Paris, the new books, operas, and bonnets, marriages, murders, and other marvels. The Poet vanished, and tea appeared.[27]

Shelley's behaviour here seems to bear certain similarities to his behaviour as described by Hogg. The problem is that, for their own purposes, both Hogg and Trelawny romanticised some quite recognisable and not characteristically poetic social traits such as a habit of withdrawing from uncongenial society. Hogg would have it that Shelley was periodically assumed into Helicon without warning. Trelawny does not like Shelley to walk: 'gliding' is a more spiritual form of locomotion, and appropriate for a man who was known to his friends as 'the Snake'.[28] We can't of course *prove* that Shelley walked rather than glided but we *can* observe Trelawny at work on facts which are verifiable and draw our own conclusions.

The test case is his account of the drowning and cremation of Shelley and Williams, a climactic series of events of which he wrote no less than eight versions, each less realistic than its predecessor. During this process the physical details became gradually less gruesome. In one early version Williams' body is discovered deprived of hands, one leg and the foot of the other leg; the eyes are eaten out by fish, the scalp torn from the head and the flesh separated from the face.[29] In the final version, Williams becomes, much less specifically and less offensively, 'a shapeless mass of bones and flesh'.[30] Finally, the romantic setting which originally had been the backdrop to the cremation of Williams, was later transferred to the cremation of the Poet, to whom it was more appropriate.

I have dwelt on Hogg and Trelawny at some length because both of them were such potent mythmakers and because the images of Shelley which they offered to the reader and the critic have been so influential. Other biographers might be mentioned—Thomas Medwin, who drew on Hogg for the full-scale version of his *Life* in 1847, a gossipy writer, inaccurate but full of fascinating detail;[31] or Thomas Love Peacock, who reviewed Hogg's assertions with his own brief *Memoir* (he, like Hogg, never saw Shelley after the spring of 1818). Peacock had a real understanding of certain facets of Shelley's personality as he had already shown in the thinly disguised character of Scythrop Glowry in *Nightmare Abbey*, a character, thought Shelley, 'admirably conceived & executed'.[32] Unfortunately, the main drift of his *Memoir* is that Shelley was subject to hallucinations, and several delightfully amusing episodes are devoted to Peacock's *proving* to his satisfaction, though not to a quite unpersuadable Shelley, that certain events could not have taken place. It so happens that the evidence we now possess concerning the most celebrated of these episodes, the mysterious shooting incident at Tan-yr-allt, tends to indicate that Shelley may have been telling the truth.[33] But neither Medwin's *Life* nor Peacock's *Memoir* excited the same influence as Mrs Shelley, Hogg and Trelawny.

There were other forces at work, too, which operated to thin the poet's blood and to idealise his memory. Notorious among these were two—the standard portrait by Amelia Curran and the behaviour of Jane, Lady Shelley. Amelia Curran was the daughter of the ribald Master of the Rolls who had disconcerted Shelley on his first visit to Dublin; she did not like the portrait and had been on the point of destroying it when Mary had written to ask for it. It resembled Shelley, said Leigh Hunt's son Thornton, 'about as much as a lady in a book of fashions resembles real women'.[34] To make matters worse, this idealised version was further idealised by the Victorian artist, George Clint. Contemporary descriptions make it clear that the real Shelley had touches of grey in his hair, was somewhat stooped from his continual reading, had a 'little turn-up nose' and 'a look of active movement, promptitude, vigour and decision, which bespoke a manly, and even a commanding character'.[35] Miss Curran's Shelley was noticeably feminine, which is not surprising if (as Richard Holmes has suggested) the portrait was influenced by Guido Reni's picture of Beatrice Cenci which Shelley had commissioned her to copy in September 1819. This portrait, or versions of it, still provides the standard image of Shelley with which we are all familiar.[36]

The influence of Jane, Lady Shelley is also widely acknowledged.[37]

She was married to Shelley's son Sir Percy Florence, a harmless eccentric, more interested in yachting, amateur theatricals and the Bournemouth Bicycle and Tricycle Club than in 'me old father'. It was her duty to look after the reputation of her father-in-law, a duty which sometimes involved the suppression or even the destruction of manuscript evidence. She it was who commissioned Hogg to write his biography and she it was who withdrew the commission. Much later it was she who edited the *Shelley Memorials* and who presided over the first complete biography, which was compiled by the Dublin professor, Edward Dowden. All of these activities were forms of worship; it was no surprise when, as the centre of this cult, she created a shrine at Boscombe Manor. Here she kept the poet's hair, his manuscripts (limited access for true believers only), his books and his heart (or was it liver?) which had been rescued from the flames at Viareggio. Before you could enter the shrine you had to remove your hat. The religious flavour was maintained by the marble monument which Lady Shelley commissioned from Henry Weekes—a *pietà* obviously based on Michelangelo's, in which an idealised Mary supported a pallid Shelley, drowned and naked. One can almost sympathise with Charles Kingsley who associated Shelley with the depravities of Roman Catholicism, worshipped as he was by 'a mesmerizing, table-turning, spirit-rapping, spiritualizing, Romanizing generation who read Shelley in secret, and delight in his bad taste, mysticism, extravagance, and vague and pompous sentimentalism. The age is an effeminate one . . .'[38]

For all these reasons, the image of Shelley was soon etherealised, with disastrous consequences for an understanding of his poetry. Of course, the biographers could not have been completely wrong; they were responding to elements in Shelley's nature which were undeniably *there*. Unfortunately, for a variety of reasons, many of which had to do with the needs of the biographer rather than of his subject, these elements were exaggerated at the expense of the compensating factors in the character of real Shelley. Briefly, let us consider the evidence of two more witnesses.

First, there is Leigh Hunt, who was of course closely attached to Shelley and who had reason to be grateful for his generous financial assistance. Hunt recognised the qualities which are celebrated by the early biographers: 'He was like a spirit that had darted out of its orb, and found itself in another world. I used to tell him that he had come from the planet Mercury.'[39] This might serve to remind us that Shelley was variously known to his friends as Oberon, the Elfin Knight and Ariel and that he took a special interest in the child-god Mercury and translated the Homeric *Hymn* which celebrates his adventures. But Shelley was also known as the Snake, and if Hunt was responsive to the angelic side of his character, he was also well aware of its tougher, more active manifestations. For example, he gives a detailed account[40] of how one Christmas night Shelley came upon a poor woman lying at the top of Hampstead Hill; it was snowing and she was having convulsions. He went for assistance but nobody was willing to give it or to take the woman in. Finally, he accosted an elderly gentleman as he descended from his carriage: the gentleman was suspicious and affronted: 'Impostors swarm everywhere: the thing cannot be done; sir, your conduct is extraordinary.'

'Sir,' cried Shelley, assuming a very different manner, and forcing the flourishing householder to stop out of astonishment, 'I am sorry to say that *your* conduct is *not* extraordinary; and if my own seems to amaze you, I will tell you something which may amaze you a little more, and I hope will frighten you. It is such men as you who madden the spirits and the patience of the poor and wretched; and if ever a convulsion comes in this country (which is very probable), recollect what I tell you: you will have your house, that you refuse to put the miserable woman into, burnt over your head.' 'God bless me, sir! Dear me, sir!' exclaimed the poor, frightened man, and fluttered into his mansion.

This may be slightly hysterical, it may even demonstrate a naive ignorance of the way of the world, but surely it is not effeminate, surely it does not demonstrate an angelic detachment from everyday realities? Indeed, Shelley's righteous indignation with its fairly explicit hints of violent retribution matches ill with those images of the visionary poet offered us by Hogg and Trelawny. Yet this anger was a constant feature of his life as far back as those desperate days when he was bullied at Eton and it provides the animus and drive of much of his political poetry.

Hunt also envisaged Shelley as a practical man:

His charity, though liberal, was not weak. He inquired personally into the circumstances of his petitioners, visited the sick in their beds (for he had gone the round of the hospitals on purpose to be able to practise on occasion), and kept a regular list of industrious poor, whom he assisted with small sums to make up their accounts.[41]

The second witness is Leigh Hunt's son, Thornton, who knew Shelley as a child but remembered him vividly:

The outline of the features and face possessed a firmness and *hardness* entirely inconsistent with a feminine character. . . . [His countenance] changed with every feeling. It usually looked earnest—when joyful, was singularly bright and animated, like that of a gay young girl,—when saddened, had an aspect of sorrow peculiarly touching, and sometimes it fell into a listless weariness still more mournful; but for the most part there was a look of active movement, promptitude, vigour, and decision, which bespoke a manly, and even a commanding character. . . . The impulsiveness which is ascribed to him is a wrong expression, for it is usually interpreted to mean the action of sudden motives waywardly, capriciously, or at least inter- mittently working; whereas the character which Shelley so constantly dis- played was an overbearing strength of conviction and feeling, a species of audacious but chivalrous readiness to act as promptly as possible, and, above all, a zealous disposition to say out all that was in his mind.[42]

This description provides the balance that seems to be missing in the more popular versions of Shelley's character. Certain aspects of his appearance may be feminine, but he is not effeminate. His spirituality is balanced by vigour and decisiveness. He is not a dreamer, or rather he is a poet *and* a man of action. Above all, his character is unified.

It was necessary to establish these facts before proceeding to the next stage, an investigation of the ways in which these widespread biographical myths, these distortions and castrations of the real Shelley, affected the course of Shelley criticism and the appreciation of his true merits. It would be foolish to suggest that the biographies had sole responsibility for all these misinterpretations. After all, Shelley's critics did read his poetry, or some of it. Undoubtedly, there are elements in the poetry which, when isolated from other significant elements, might seem to justify some of the biographical assumptions: for example, moments of almost ritualised weakness, the use of spirit voices in poems like *Prometheus Unbound* and the tendency of some of the most cele- brated works to concentrate on 'beautiful idealisms of moral excellence' rather than gritty social realities. However, this kind of reading was generally selective—it read what it wanted to read and noticed what it wanted to notice, both within the individual poem and within the work as a whole. One of Shelley's most extraordinary achievements, his wideness of range and scope, has hardly ever been acknowledged. This myopia has been caused in part by the difficulty of Shelley's poetry, the bewildering diversity of his intentions and the originality of his achievement. There is also behind much of the poetry an easy access of reference to the history of philosophy, scientific discovery, politics ancient and modern, the facts of nature, and almost the whole range of European literature from the Greek and Latin classics through Dante, Calderón and Goethe, including most of English poetry and drama. For even the well-informed reader this can be taxing and it is undoubtedly more comfortable to assume that Shelley means nothing in particular than to admit that he is saying something specific which is beyond our range. In these circumstances, the biographical emphases have been very helpful to the less adventurous reader, with the result that, between them, biography and rudimentary criticism have narrowed the range of Shelley's achievement and diluted the essence of the poetry. This is something close to a vicious circle. The first step towards breaking it has been to analyse the development of the biographical legend. We must now examine in greater detail the subtle and often unsuspected ways in which this has contaminated criticism. The remaining chapters of this book will be an attempt to put Shelley together again and to suggest what we might look for in his poetry and how we might go about reading him.

(iii)

A significant fact about most Shelley criticism is that many of its basic assumptions are shared both by those who approve of Shelley and by those who do not. Until very recently the vast majority of those who have written on Shelley have subscribed to the biographical distortions which have just been analysed. As Blake remarked of the story of Satan's fall from heaven: 'this history has been adopted by both parties.' To some extent it is true that Shelley is admired by some people for the very same reasons which cause him to be despised by others. And very often his friends turn out to be his enemies; when Palgrave selected his *Golden Treasury* he paid Shelley the compliment of including twenty-two poems, but that selection has done great damage to Shelley's reputation.[43]

First, there is the widely held belief that Shelley never grew up, that he was in effect a retarded genius. That implication is clear enough in Hogg's account of his pranks in Oxford and London, his reluctance to leave the sweet society of the Muses so that he had to be dragged to brickyards as part of his education. This view of Shelley was sufficiently common in nineteenth-century criticism: Gilfillan, for example, referred to him as the 'Eternal Child'.[44] This particular incarnation reached its climax in 1889 when Francis Thompson responded to 'The Cloud' with this notorious purple passage:

Coming to Shelley's poetry, we peep over the wild mask of revolutionary metaphysics, and we see the winsome face of the child ... his play is such as manhood stops to watch, and his playthings are those which the gods give their children. The universe is his box of toys. He dabbles his fingers in the dayfall. He is gold-dusty with tumbling amidst the stars.

This is the presiding image in André Maurois' fictional biography *Ariel* (1924), which became the first Penguin book in 1935 and which has had such a wide and unfortunate influence on twentieth-century readers. Such visions of Ariel are celebrations of Shelley or are intended to be; Shelley's childishness has been less attractive to twentieth-century critics. Here are two instances.

... his problems were peculiarly those of an adolescent personality displayed with all the complexity and vigour of a man of genius. (Humphry House)

The ideas of Shelley seem to me always to be ideas of adolescence—as there is every reason why they should be. And an enthusiasm for Shelley seems to me to be an affair of adolescence ... (T. S. Eliot)[46]

Both of these judgements are, in fact, *ex cathedra* condemnations delivered with a patronising arrogance which is almost worthy of Hogg. Little or no attempt is made to justify these assertions; the adolescence and the immaturity are taken for granted. Indeed, Eliot goes on to make further unjustified assumptions about incoherence and shabby ideas which will be examined later. What is important here is the ease with which it can be suggested that so profoundly subtle, intelligent and thoughtful a poet as Shelley was a mere child. Humphry House is on the verge of a point of some importance : but if by adolescent problems he means the complications of emotional involvement and sexuality, it won't do to dismiss these as 'adolescent' and therefore beneath the superior interest of the normal, well-adjusted adult. Shelley's contribution to the literature of sexual love is significant, perhaps even revolutionary, and this should be to his credit, rather than an index of his immaturity.

There is another element in his work which might be described as 'adolescent', though it is only a 'problem' in the sense that he found it difficult to adjust to. That is his refusal to take for granted the deplorable state of the world as he found it in those grim years of poverty and unrest after the French Revolution, during and after the Napoleonic wars and before even a modicum of reform had been achieved. Shelley looked on this world with an eye of accusing innocence :

And much I grieved to think how power and will
In opposition rule our mortal day—

And why God made irreconcilable
Good and the means of good . . .
(*Triumph of Life*, lines 228–31)

To put this feeling of puzzlement into words, so unequivocally and so forcefully, is to do a service to our better feelings. If this is adolescent immaturity, it is infinitely preferable to the mature, coherent and adult philosophy of Wordsworth, who was able to write, 'Almighty God! / . . . Yea, carnage is thy daughter.'[47]

As a student of history and an observer of contemporary politics, Shelley understood only too well the expedients and necessities of power, but he never learnt to accept them with resignation or equanimity. In that sense, it is true to say that he never grew up: instead, he took with him into the world of experience a fundamental innocence which could be disillusioned but which could never be dislodged or shaken. His radicalism was in part the radical innocence of the child, whose eyes have not been clouded by the film of familiarity but to whom 'Familiar [things] are beautiful through love' (*P.U.*, IV. 403). What Coleridge said of Wordsworth could certainly be applied to Shelley, if to the world of nature we add the moral world, the world of human actions: 'To carry on the feelings of childhood into the powers of manhood; to combine the child's sense of wonder and novelty with the appearances which every day . . . had rendered familiar . . . this is the character and privilege of genius.'[48] In the case of Shelley, that sense of wonder and delight extended from a delight in the varieties of the daedal world of nature to an open-eyed and often critical attention to the ways in which men behave.

The childish element in Shelley is not so much childish as child-like (an important distinction made by Charles Lamb when discussing the poetry of Wordsworth). The child-like quality in Shelley is one of his great strengths, but it has been misunderstood, turned into a deficiency and generally held against him. A closely related image and one with much greater consequences is the best known of all images of Shelley— that of the beautiful angel. We have already seen that Shelley's contemporaries, even those who might have been expected to be more objective, frequently thought of him as a seraph, a spirit from another world, a divine messenger, an Ariel in a cloven pine, an angel. The critics followed suit. To De Quincey Shelley was 'an angel touched by lunacy'; to David Masson he was 'some fluttering spirit of a lighter sphere, that had dropped on the earth by chance, unable to be in happy relation to it as a whole, though keenly sensitive to some of its beauties';

to Matthew Arnold he was a 'beautiful and ineffectual angel, beating in the void his luminous wings in vain'.[49] This may be a charming image but it did much to obscure what Shelley was really like and to soften the real drive and thrust of his poetry.

The general acceptance of this image cannot be explained in any simple way, or attributed to any single cause, but it is difficult not to recognise that it served a very useful purpose for those Victorians who did not want to listen to what Shelley was saying. Again and again in Victorian criticism one comes across the idea that Shelley's poetry must be distinguished from his ideas: the ideas, when one can understand them, are at best foolish, at worst dangerous, but the poetry is pure and beautiful. Reviewing *Posthumous Poems* in 1824, a highly perceptive and sympathetic critic suggested that his ideas were often misrepresented and hit upon the following convenient formula:

... his peculiar opinions in politics and theology, instead of being interwoven with the texture of his poems, appear rather as excrescences on the surface, disfiguring them in parts. . . . It is, indeed, remarkable, that the worst parts of his poems are those which are devoted to the promulgation of the controverted points; his theory hangs like a leaden weight on his fancy.[50]

This is a very dubious piece of criticism; when writing about contemporary politics Shelley is sometimes shrill and often violent, and his admirers may sometimes wish that he would unsay some of his high language; but his sensibility was unified and his views on politics cannot be ignored or dismissed because we do not like to see them disfiguring his poems. It is his political views in the widest sense which inform such beautiful idealisms as *Prometheus Unbound* and which provide their directing energy, but those political views cannot be separated from his views on nature, religion, philosophy, love, art and literature. Each of these was related to each of the others and together they constituted a matrix of rich complexity which lies behind all of his major works and most of the minor ones.

W. S. Walker's review is symptomatic and the more disturbing in that it was written by a professed admirer of Shelley's poetry. The implication here is that we should close our ears to what we do not want to hear. Soon critics were misreading 'To a Skylark' and Shelley had been transformed not so much into an airy minstrel who sang from Heaven or near it as into a beautiful bird in a gilded cage. Palgrave's *Golden Treasury* was substituted for *Prometheus Unbound*. *Julian and Maddalo*, *The Cenci* and *The Triumph of Life* were more or less forgotten. *Queen Mab* was widely read by the Chartists and also

B

by Bernard Shaw but not by many others. *Adonais* was the next best thing to Christianity (he would have been among the Christians had he lived, said Browning confidently)[51] and its attacks on the literary establishment were quietly ignored.

There are three consequences here of enormous significance. First, there is the suggestion, which soon became a received opinion, that Shelley was an inspired singer—he 'outsang all poets on record but some two or three throughout all time' said Swinburne, who went on to add 'He was alone the perfect singing-god; his thoughts, words, deeds, all sang together.'[52] The second half of this sentence suggests an interesting qualification which is overbalanced by the rhapsodic appreciation of the larger assessment. Somewhat later A. C. Bradley was to compare him to Schubert, a parallel which is singularly inappropriate if one is thinking of the works rather than the life. For Bradley 'he made immortal music' but he lacked the criticism or interpretation of life which might have made him a symphonist rather than a song-writer.[53]

The second consequence was that, if Shelley was a muddled thinker but an immortal singer, a shift in critical attention was obviously called for. So, from about the middle of the nineteenth century, Shelley was regarded primarily as a writer of lyrics. This new approach to reading Shelley operated in two ways. First, it generally involved a concentration on the shorter poems, many of which had never been published during his lifetime and some of which were fragmentary or unrevised: alternatively, it focused on lyrical passages in longer works, such as the two famous choruses in *Hellas* or 'Life of Life' in *Prometheus Unbound*. Such an emphasis on lyricism was subtly undermining. Almost everyone was (and still is) agreed that Shelley had rare gifts as a lyric poet (Bradley rated him above Shakespeare in this department). Even critics who questioned his ultimate stature were ready to acknowledge that he had a rare lyrical faculty (or facility, as they might have put it). Indeed, this lyrical ease was often related to their own critical attitudes, since it was Shelley's fatal fluency, his uncontrolled emotionalism, his habit of going on 'till I am stopped' which produced those results which they found so irritating. 'The effect of Shelley's eloquence is to hand poetry over to a sensibility that has no more dealings with intelligence than it can help,' wrote Dr Leavis, notoriously.[54] For Shelley's admirers the poems often provided a similar experience, but their conclusions were exactly the opposite—for them the lack of 'meaning' was a positive virtue, a sign of the highest poetic achievement. For critics such as these, Shelley (like Blake) moved in a world of pure poetry, uncontaminated by realities, insulated from the harsh necessities of meaning.

The main result of this unholy alliance between those who despised Shelley and those who adored him was that, between the two extremes, the real Shelley was persistently neglected. To concentrate on Shelley's lyrical poetry was to ignore the poetry by which he would have wished to be judged and remembered, the long and complex poems which grapple with the problems of politics, society, philosophy, love, art and religion. To assess Shelley's achievement on the basis of 'The Indian Serenade' was to exhibit a seriously distorted perspective, as if one were to base a final judgement of Shakespeare on the songs from the plays (at the same time reading biographical significance into lines such as 'I am slaine by a fair, cruel maid'). All of this may be traced back in one way or another to the image of Shelley as a beautiful angel or to the alternative version of the fragile but pure-throated songbird.

There is a third consequence which helped to take the sting out of Shelley, attracting some cautious readers, no doubt, but fundamentally turning the poet into an insipid and mawkish figure. As we know from Milton and elsewhere, angels transcend the distinctions of sex, and it is not difficult to make the same assumptions about skylarks, whether in or out of a cage. Yet, anyone who reads Shelley with attention would recognise that there is a challenging sexuality about some of his writing. Take for example the erotic dream of the poet in *Alastor*; the intimations of pregnancy in *The Revolt of Islam*; the love scenes between Laon and Cythna; the closing invitation to Emilia in *Epipsychidion*. Shelley even writes about the poetic process itself in terms which are explicitly erotic: poetry 'strips the veil of familiarity from the world, and lays bare the naked and sleeping beauty, which is the spirit of its forms'.[55] This, of course, was hardly acceptable in the drawing-room and so it was ignored in a number of ways: by concentrating on the less challenging pieces, the album verses rather than the serious achievements; by neglecting the precise meaning as much as possible; and finally, and treacherously, by suggesting sometimes that Shelley was a sexless angel and sometimes that he was a woman. This necessarily eliminated any suggestion of eroticism.

At first, Shelley's enemies used to accuse him of being *unmanly*; for reasons too complex to examine here, the nineteenth-century often resorted to this form of abuse when defending the *status quo*, notably in matters of immorality. In 1820 *The London Magazine* while recognising the great poetic gifts displayed in *The Cenci* lamented that they were 'closely connected with the signs of a depraved, nay mawkish, or rather emasculated moral taste, craving after trash, filth, and poison, and sickening at wholesome nutriments'.[56] Thirty-three years later, Charles

Kingsley was even more explicit:

... Shelley's nature is utterly womanish. Not merely his weak points, but his strong ones, are those of a woman. Tender and pitiful as a woman; and yet, when angry, shrieking, railing hysterical as a woman. The physical distaste for meat and fermented liquors, coupled with the hankering after physical horrors, are especially feminine. The nature of a woman looks out of that wild, beautiful, girlish face...[57]

Once again, Amelia Curran's portrait, based on Beatrice Cenci, seems to have had its effect and to have influenced Kingsley's reading of the poetry. What is really interesting here is that the womanly and womanish qualities which *The London Magazine* and Kingsley largely deplored and which they regarded as indications of a corrupt and depraved sensibility, a basically immoral view of life, were gratefully accepted by some of Shelley's admirers, so that his lack of masculinity was turned into one of his greatest and most attractive virtues.

The de-sexualising of Shelley was assisted by what might be regarded as a publishing accident. Having translated Plato's *Symposium* in July 1818, Shelley realised that it could never be acceptable to the British reading public without a sympathetic explanation of the social mores of the Athenians, more specifically of their attitude towards homosexuality. Shelley had no illusions about Athenian democracy: 'All the virtue and wisdom of the Periclean age arose' in spite of 'personal slavery and the inferiority of women...' Women were regarded as second-class citizens and so they 'possessed, except with extra-ordinary exceptions, the habits and the qualities of slaves'.[58] Shelley approved neither of the social circumstances associated with homosexuality nor of its physical implications but he was prepared to regard it sympathetically and he did not feel that it should be an obstacle to an appreciation of the achievements of the Greeks or the doctrines of Plato. His essay *A Discourse on the Manners of the Ancient Greeks Relative to the Subject of Love* investigates these matters with flexibility and insight; unfortunately, when Mary Shelley published it in 1840 she deleted the most important sections, thus destroying the whole point of the undertaking. It was not until 1931 that the complete text was available and then it appeared in a privately printed edition which was limited to one hundred copies.

Shelley's translation of the *Symposium* suffered a similar fate when it appeared in 1840. With the help of Leigh Hunt, Mrs Shelley removed those passages which were relatively explicit about physical matters and rewrote a number of other passages to the great detriment of the translation in terms of readability, directness and stylistic momentum. At the present moment, the only edition of the translation which is generally available is based on this distorted and censored version of Mary Shelley: the complete and authentic version can only be found in a scholarly edition which is not available in most libraries.[59] The great irony here is that this censorship has been held against Shelley, not against his editors. More than once, it has been said that Shelley could not bring himself to face up to these sordid physical realities, either because he was a homosexual and didn't realise it or because he did realise it and didn't wan't to acknowledge it, or, more generally, because he found all varieties of sex distasteful.[60] It should be obvious how convenient this was for those drawing-room readers of Shelley who had turned him into a versifying pet lamb. It would not have been easy to acknowledge that in its true meaning even Platonic love must 'descend / T'affections, and to faculties, / Which sense may reach and apprehend': according to the *Symposium*, as Shelley translated it, it has its origins in operations which are only too obviously not 'Platonic'.

(*iv*)

It is time to examine more carefully the influence of this elaborate process of distortion, suppression and mythmaking on the critics of our own century. The general trend of that influence should already be obvious. It is very difficult to live in the literary environment and to remain uninfluenced by potent and widely accepted biographical myths. Even those critics who sternly withdraw themselves from any suggestion of partiality and who claim to base their judgements on a fearless and dispassionate scrutiny of the work itself apparently have succumbed to the subtle and insinuating atmosphere. I am thinking here in particular of critics such as T. S. Eliot, F. R. Leavis, Yvor Winters and Cleanth Brooks. Most of them would deny the influence of Hogg and Trelawny: some may not even have read these biographies.

What is much harder to escape is the general attitude of nineteenth-century biography and criticism which I have tried to analyse in the earlier sections of this chapter. This affects not only one's view of the poet himself but one's view of what is significant in his poetic achievement. Thus, the leading critics of the modern movement in English literature have tacitly accepted the premises of the Victorians and the Georgians against whom they are in revolt. Dr Leavis, for example, advances the following proposition as if it were an undisputable fact in literary history: 'it is . . . universally agreed that . . . Shelley's genius was "essentially lyrical".'[61] So obvious is this, that in Leavis's vocabulary *Shelleyan* may be substituted for *lyrical*: writing of T. S. Eliot, he speaks of 'his poetic, Shelleyan impulse'.[62] What he assails, then, in his wrongheaded but vastly influential essay is not so much the real Shelley as the Victorian or Georgian substitute. Hence, the otherwise inexplicable concentration on Shelley as a lyricist, the solemn attention to the supposed infelicities of so minor a work as 'When the lamp is shattered'. There would have been little point in breaking this butterfly on a wheel had not Shelley's reputation been grounded on the flutter of lyrics rather than on the metaphysical and political complexities of poems such as *Prometheus Unbound* and *The Triumph of Life*. And where are *they* in Leavis's essay?

The virtue of this approach is that it refuses to take Shelley for granted. Had Leavis devoted more attention to Shelley's more challenging achievements, had he not accepted so readily the nineteenth-century valuation, then his essay might have been a serious and significant contribution to Shelley criticism. In fact, it could almost be said that it is part of a social or cultural critique, rather than a literary one: what Leavis has so vigorously assailed is not so much Shelley as the Shelleyans, not so much the poet as his cult. Above all, his approach deserves our respect because it assumes that Shelley ought to be saying *something*. Many distinguished twentieth-century critics and scholars have refused to take this line, some deploring Shelley's lack of meaning, others apparently rejoicing in it, but few of them ready to initiate even a cursory search for meaning:

On no poet is criticism so unsatisfactory as on Shelley, because in none is the poetry so pure, so independent of subject, so mere a harmony in the early Greek sense of the word. Analysis of it is nearly impossible, and of little value when it can be made. (George Saintsbury (1925))

To comment on *Arethusa* is like trying to describe a waterfall. (Douglas Bush (1937))[63]

It is a good thing that neither Leavis nor the American New Critics were satisfied with this, whether as appreciation or as dismissive criticism. However, in their various responses, not only did they devote most of their attention to the shorter, and usually the slighter, poems but they were also imbued with some of the very misconceptions which they were fighting against. To put it bluntly: where Saintsbury detects a kind of pure poetry, floating free from the trammels of specificity and meaning, Leavis and the others assume that he did not know what he meant or mean what he said. This gives rise to a very captious kind of literalism, which might lay the critics open to charges of stupidity or bad faith, were they not so obviously distinguished. T. S. Eliot, for example, appears to be incapable of seeing that 'winter weeds' in 'The world's great age begins anew' from *Hellas* refers to widow's weeds rather than the gardener's despair. Leavis, too, allows himself the following severity concerning 'Ode to the West Wind':

The appropriateness of the Maenad, clearly, lies in the pervasive suggestion of frenzied onset, and we are not to ask whether her bright hair is to be seen as streaming out in front of her (as, there is no need to assure ourselves, it might be doing if she were running before a still swifter gale . . .)[64]

Not to ask, indeed, since the answer is available in the poem with enough specificity to satisfy most of us:

> Like the bright hair *uplifted* from the head
>
> Of some fierce Maenad, even from the dim verge
> Of the horizon to the zenith's height,
> The locks of the approaching storm.   (My italics)

The italicised word is undoubtedly there and, once one has seen it, the rest of the passage makes perfect sense. One final, and even less excusable, example, brings us back to T. S. Eliot. In his celebrated dismissal of Shelley, Eliot takes exception to the ideas put forward in a passage of *Epipsychidion*, ideas which bear a very close similarity to certain passages in Plato and which may have been derived even more directly from Eliot's much admired Dante. Eliot didn't take to this passage, probably because he thought it was putting forward an argument in favour of free love, but what he actually said was that the lines in question 'gravelled' him. This is not surprising since, as he prints them in his essay, they are in the wrong order and might have confused even Shelley himself.[65]

This leads us to two final points. First, these critics appear to have approached Shelley's poetry with the assumption that he might not know what he was saying. There *are* difficulties in his poetry but for the most part the critics seem to have imposed their own confusions upon it. It can be no accident that this tendency is confirmed and buttressed by the history of the Shelley text. Just as those people who believed that Shelley could not face up to sexual reality accepted the evidence of the censored version of the *Symposium* and actually used it to prove their case, so those readers who believed that Shelley had a brilliant but confused intellect and paid no attention to words were happy to find in the confused texts of the poetry a confirmation of what they had always known. Here again we are faced with a vicious circle. The history of Shelley's poetry is particularly sad, with jumbled and unrevised first drafts accorded a status only slightly inferior to that of the poems which Shelley actually published; the collected works are full of insignificant fragments, thousands of verbal errors, stanzas printed in the wrong order, false and misleading punctuation. Most of this has been accepted without comment: few people expect Shelley to make sense and even those who do are not particularly surprised when it appears that he does not.[66]

The second conclusion follows directly from Eliot's misreading of *Epipsychidion*. What we have here is not only a preconception that Shelley is muddleheaded but a preconception that he is morally dangerous. Throughout this chapter I have concentrated on the more positive interpretation of Shelley, the view which etherealised him as angel or singing-god and which effectively drew his sting, so effectively indeed that it was ultimately possible to ignore his major works and to suggest that most of his poetry was beautiful or meaningless, or alternatively that it did have a meaning but was too confused to be taken seriously. The other interpretation and the less subtle one was the view which was formulated with such vituperative force by the *Quarterly* and *Blackwood's*, the view that Shelley was mad, bad and dangerous to know. As the *Literary Gazette* put it in 1821: 'That any man who insults the common order of society, and denies the being of God, is essentially mad we never doubted.'[67] It therefore follows necessarily that the poetry is bad, worthless even as literature. Sometimes, especially during his lifetime and shortly afterwards, the beautiful and ineffectual angel became a fallen angel with considerable powers for doing harm. 'Yon man Shelley was a scoundrel, and ought to have been hangèd' growled Carlyle.[68]

The same view was embodied in a number of nineteenth-century novels. A long succession of fictional characters either bore some resemblance to Shelley or explicitly subscribed to his ideas on sex, marriage and free love: the most obvious example is Hardy's Sue Bridehead who bases her views on *Epipsychidion*. Characters such as these usually damage themselves and others by trying to flout the conventions of society. More frequently the Shelleyan character is portrayed as dangerously immoral, a threat to society and all its most hallowed institutions. The emphasis here is on sexual morality since the political dedication of Shelley and of his own heroes (Lionel, Laon, Prometheus) made less of an impression on the novelists (though the political note is very evident in Will Ladislaw). These Shelleyan surrogates were sometimes the victims of an avenging fate: the same sense of divine justice which took pleasure in imagining how Shelley's boat had set forth with its sails 'gallantly unfurled, and glittering in the sun' and how 'in the twinkling of an eye, the boat had disappeared, and the atheist had sunk to the bottom of a fathomless abyss'[69] contented itself too with the image of James Steerforth, who had betrayed another Emily, palely washed up on the beach at Yarmouth.

These, making allowance for the intellectual sophistication, are essentially the views of T. S. Eliot. Eliot admitted that Shelley had poetic gifts of the first order but regretted that he did not put them at the service of more tenable beliefs. He believed that poetry could not be separated from the ideas it expresses, a concept which Shelley certainly would have endorsed; the view of life presented in a poem had to be one which the reader could accept as coherent, mature, and founded on the facts of experience. Shelley failed this test: he 'borrowed ideas—which . . . is perfectly legitimate—but he borrowed shabby ones, and when he had got them he muddled them up with his own intuitions'.[70]

Eliot is honest enough to acknowledge that both his reading of the poetry and his response to the ideas are conditioned by biographical influences. 'I find his ideas repellent . . . And the biographical interest which Shelley has always excited makes it difficult to read the poetry without remembering the man: and the man was humourless, pedantic, self-centred, and sometimes almost a blackguard.'[71] An even more egregious example can be found in Yvor Winters who reacts with great suspicion to Shelley's poem 'To Night':

The poem is a prayer to Night to come quickly, but we are not told why. I have heard it said that Shelley wished to hasten an assignation with a lady, and this is possible; for one thing, Shelley is the author, and, for another, the imagery is erotic. But it may be merely an expression of the common romantic love of night, the home of mystery and the stars.[72]

We may observe here yet another example of disingenuous literalism; we may observe too how Winters contrives to smear Shelley's character while at the same time admitting that the biographical reading is irrelevant.

In conclusion, let us return to Leavis, whose reading of Shelley has been so influential in this country, if not in America. Although he claims that 'it is strictly the "poetry" one is criticizing', this does not appear to be the case. For instance, on the one hand he does resort to the life to underline his criticism of *The Cenci* while, on the other, he claims that, although 'the consummate expression' of 'Ode to the West Wind' is 'rightly treasured', the poem is 'disablingly limited'. His essay is full of innuendo, laden with biographical assumptions: '. . . surrendering to inspiration cannot, for a poet of Shelley's emotional habits, have been very distinguishable from surrendering to temptation. . . . His need of loving . . . comes out in the erotic element that . . . the texture of the poetry persuasively exhibits.'[73] Faced with such evidence we may find it hard to believe Donald Davie when, twenty-seven years later, he tells us:

We dislike Shelley's eroticism, in the end, because it seems a vicious attitude, morally reprehensible; but we dislike it in the first place only because it produces a vicious diction, a jargon. . . . It is best to think . . . that we condemn Shelley's eroticism (as we do) because it produces a jargon, and not because we dislike it 'in itself'.[74]

There is a suspicious circularity about this formulation, combined with a symptomatic lack of certainty. Perhaps it is best to resist the inclusive gesture which is designed to implicate us in this judgement.

Notes to chapter one

1   Trelawny, *Records of Shelley, Byron, and the Author*, ed. David Wright, Penguin Books, Harmondsworth, 1973, p. 106.
2   Thom Gunn, *Fighting Terms*, Faber and Faber, 1954.
3   Newman Ivey White, *The Unextinguished Hearth: Shelley and his Contemporary Critics*, 1966, p. 327.
4   Sylva Norman, *Flight of the Skylark: The Development of Shelley's Reputation*, 1954, p. 22.
5   *Letters and Journals*, ed. R. E. Prothero, 6 vols., Murray, 1898–1901, vi. 99.
6   For the general details, see Norman, *op. cit.* For Sophocles, see Timothy Webb, 'Shelley's Sophocles: A Legend Re-examined', *K.–S.M.B.*, XIX (1968), pp. 47–52. For Keats, see White, *op. cit.*, p. 322.
7   R. Brimley Johnson, *Shelley–Leigh Hunt: How Friendship Made History*, 1928, p. 61.
8   Hugh Sykes-Davies, *The Poets and their Critics: Blake to Browning*, Hutchinson, 1966, p. 153.
9   For an account of her attitudes, see P. D. Fleck, 'Mary Shelley's Notes to Shelley's Poems and *Frankenstein*', *S.I.R.*, VI (1967), pp. 226–54.
10 *P.W.*, p. 582.
11 cf. 'It is not with you as with another. I believe that we all live hereafter; but you, my only one, were a spirit caged, an elemental being, enshrined in a frail image, now shattered' (*Journal*, p. 183).
12 For full details, see *Shelley and his Circle*, especially III. 50–6.
13 Hogg, *Life*, I. 301.
14 Hogg, *Life*, I. 83, 337.
15 Clark, *Prose*, p. 346.

16 'Shelley's Lyrics' in *The Mortality of Art*, ed. D. W. Jefferson, Routledge & Kegan Paul, 1969, p. 196.

17 Hogg, *Life*, II. 73. See also I. 152.

18 Hogg, *Life*, I. 313.

19 Hogg, *Life*, II. 59, I. 364.

20 Hogg, *Life*, II. 44.

21 Hogg, *Life*, I. 135–6.

22 Trelawny, *Records*, p. 127.

23 Trelawny, *Records*, p. 125.

24 Trelawny, *Records*, p. 149.

25 Trelawny, *Records*, p. 55.

26 Trelawny, *Records*, pp.67–8.

27 Trelawny, *Records*, p. 68.

28 Trelawny, *Records*, p. 103. In Goethe's *Faust* Mephistopheles refers to 'My aunt, the renowned snake'. When Shelley translated this, Byron said, 'Then you are her nephew'. The name stuck.

29 Cited in Trelawny, *Records*, p. 314.

30 Trelawny, *Records*, pp. 169–70; Leslie Marchand, 'Trelawny on the Death of Shelley', *K.–S.M.B.*, IV (1952), pp. 9–34.

31 See Ernest Lovell, Jr., *Captain Medwin: Friend of Percy Bysshe Shelley*, MacDonald, 1963.

32 *Letters*, II. 98.

33 See discussion in Richard Holmes, *Shelley: The Pursuit*, 1974.

34 K. N. Cameron, *Shelley: The Golden Years*, 1974, p. 73.

35 See Cameron, *Shelley: The Golden Years*, pp. 58–63; *Letters*, II. 114; Thornton Hunt, 'Shelley [by one who knew him]', *Atlantic Monthly*, XI (1863), p. 203.

36 Holmes, *Shelley: the Pursuit*, p. 517.

37 Norman, *Flight of the Skylark*, p. 215 ff.

38 Norman, *Flight of the Skylark*, p. 204.

39 *The Autobiography of Leigh Hunt*, ed. J. E. Morpurgo, Cresset Press, 1949, p. 331.

40 Hunt, *Autobiography*, pp. 272–3.

41 Hunt, *Autobiography*, pp. 266–7.

42 Of the twenty-two poems published by Palgrave, only seven had appeared in print during Shelley's lifetime. These included 'To a Skylark', 'Ode to the West Wind', a truncated version of 'Lines Written among the Euganean Hills' (which omitted over one hundred and forty lines, including the long political section), and two passages from *Prometheus Unbound*, labelled *The Poet's Dream* ('On a poet's lips I slept') and *Hymn to the Spirit of Nature* ('Life of Life'). Among the fifteen poems which had never been published, there were several fragments, though a larger number had obviously been completed and were printed from fair copies.

43 Cited in Cameron, *Shelley:The Golden Years*, pp. 61–2.

44 Thomas Medwin, *The Life of Percy Bysshe Shelley*, revised ed. by H. B. Forman, Oxford University Press, 1913, p. 332.

45 Francis Thompson, *Shelley*, [1889] 2nd ed., Burns & Oates, 1909, pp. 45–6.

46 *All in Due Time*, Hart-Davis, 1955, pp. 58, 70; 'Shelley and Keats' in *The Use of Poetry and the Use of Criticism*, [1933] 2nd ed., Faber & Faber, 1964, p. 89. See too Edward E. Bostetter, *The Romantic Ventriloquists*, University of Washington Press, Seattle, 1963, pp. 193–7. Bostetter detects in *Prometheus Unbound* 'an unhealthiness of perspective, an emotional immaturity, a kind of infantilism which is prominent in much of Shelley's early writing' (p. 195).

47   'Ode 1815' original version, later altered by Wordsworth. Contrast Shelley's disillusionment in the following fragment: 'Alas! this is not what I thought life was. / I knew that there were crimes and evil men, / Misery and hate; nor did I hope to pass / Untouched by suffering, through the rugged glen. / In mine own heart I saw as in glass / The hearts of others' (*P.W.*, p. 633). For an extended parody of Wordsworth's views on the sanctity of carnage, see *Peter Bell the Third*, ll. 634–52.

48   *Biographia Literaria*, ed. J. Shawcross, Oxford University Press, 1967, I. 59.

49   Norman, *Flight of the Skylark*, p. 166; Sykes Davies, *The Poets and their Critics: Blake to Browning*, pp. 180, 178.

50   W. S. Walker in Theodore Redpath, *The Young Romantics and Critical Opinion 1807–1824*, 1973, p. 404.

51   See *An Essay on Percy Bysshe Shelley* (1852). Hawthorne must have agreed with Browning, since in one of his essays he imagined a visit to London in 1845 in which he met Shelley, who was miraculously undrowned and who had recently 'taken orders, and been inducted to a small country living in the gift of the lord chancellor' (*The Writings of Nathaniel Hawthorne*, 1900, V, 181–4).

52   Sykes Davies, *The Poets and their Critics: Blake to Browning*, p. 176.

53   A. C. Bradley, 'The Long Poem in the Age of Wordsworth' in *Oxford Lectures on Poetry*, MacMillan [1909] 1965, p. 197.

54   F. R. Leavis, *Revaluation:Tradition and Development in English Poetry*, Routledge & Kegan Paul, 1936, p. 210.

55   *Defence*, p. 56.

56   White, *The Unextinguished Hearth*, p. 190.

57   Sykes Davies, *The Poets and their Critics*, p. 173.

58   Clark, *Prose*, p. 220.

59   In J. A. Notopoulos, *The Platonism of Shelley: A Study of Platonism and the Poetic Mind*, 1949.

60   Eustace Chesser, *Shelley & Zastrozzi; Self-revelation of a Neurotic*, Gregg/Archive, 1965, p. 39; Edward Carpenter and George Barnefield, *The Psychology of the Poet Shelley*, Allen and Unwin, 1925, pp. 94–8.

61   *Revaluation*, pp. 206–7.

62   *New Bearings in English Poetry*, Chatto and Windus, new ed., 1950, p. 89.

63   *A Short History of English Literature*, Macmillan, 1925, p. 671; *Mythology and the Romantic Tradition in English Poetry*, Norton, New York, 1963, pp. 135–6.

64   *Revaluation*, p. 205.

65   Eliot, *The Use of Poetry and the Use of Criticism*, p. 89. Eliot quotes lines 160–1 and 149–53, divided only by suspension points at the end of 161, so that the six lines appear to be in sequence. He goes on to quote lines 121–3 which he identifies as 'a few lines later'.

66   See my introduction to *Shelley: Selected Poems*, Everyman University Library, 1977.

67   White, *The Unextinguished Hearth*, p. 289.

68   Roland Duerksen, *Shelleyan Ideas in Victorian Literature*, Mouton, London/The Hague/Paris, 1966, p. 124.

69   White, *The Unextinguished Hearth*, p. 103.

70   *The Use of Poetry and the Use of Criticism*, p. 89.

71   *Ibid.*

72   *Forms of Discovery*, Swallow, New York, 1967, p. 178.

73   *Revaluation*, pp. 230, 216, 222.

74   *Purity of Diction in English Verse*, [1953] 1967, pp. 146–7.

CHAPTER TWO

POETRY AND THE PRINCIPLE OF SELF

(i)

'To have lived to be thirty is to know that we have failed in life,' said Saki. To have died before thirty in interesting circumstances, having lived a short, passionate and sometimes melodramatic life, against an exotic background and at odds with authority, is to put one's poetic reputation in jeopardy. Even the well-informed reader tends to confuse Shelley's life with his poetry. The usual consequence is that the poetry is either invested with spurious glamour or ruthlessly decoded as a document which might help us to understand the life. So frequently does Shelley's work allude to the life, or appear to be drawing directly from it, that it is only too easy to assume that what we are reading is essentially autobiographical, at times almost a direct transcript of actual events in the life of a man who lived with such intensity that he could say, on the eve of his death a month before his thirtieth birthday, 'If I die to-morrow, I have lived to be older than my father.'[1] Yet this is not the poetry of self-expression nor is it autobiographical in any simple sense.

In fact, Shelley's views on the separation between poetry and personality were firmly held and firmly expressed: 'The poet & the man are two different natures: though they exist together they may be unconscious of each other . . .'[2] His devotion to the principle of reticence where personal matters were concerned would have found approval from even the sternest of eighteenth-century theorists. Yet most critics persist in believing otherwise. T. S. Eliot's celebrated shudder at the self-revelations of the Romantics ('Poetry . . . is not the expression of personality, but an escape from personality') may be matched by Cleanth Brooks's distaste for 'Shelley's sometimes embarrassing declarations'.[3] The biographical identification is often made with a lack of hesitancy which would do credit to a police witness. Ellsworth Barnard, for instance,

interprets 'Epithalamium' as a celebration of Shelley's imagined consummation with Emilia Viviani, while he reads the sad lyrics as a
reflection of Shelley's grief that it was only imaginary:[4] yet, the
'Epithalamium' is totally unspecific in its references and many of the
lyrics, though undeniably sad and seemingly personal, belong to a
recognised convention.

Indeed, the most serious weakness of the literal biographical reading
is that it regularly fails to acknowledge the existence of literary genres.
An instructive example is provided by *Epipsychidion*, a poem which
undoubtedly presents us with an autobiography of love, although
alchemised and transmuted after the fashion of Dante in *La Vita Nuova*.
Here Shelley describes a temptress and her effects on the narrator in
terms which have suggested to many readers that he may have been
referring to venereal disease:

> One, whose voice was venomed melody,
> Sate by a well, under blue night-shade bowers;
> The breath of her false mouth was like faint flowers,
> Her touch was as electric poison ...   (lines 256–9)

One biographer has commented: 'It is possible that, despairing of
Harriet Grove, he did have a first experience of sex with a woman
encounted by a well; but the evidence as to a disease seems to me
slender.'[5] In this interpretation false assumptions about the relations
between poetry and biography have been compounded by an inability
to recognise that Shelley's enchantress has a long, if dubious, lineage
in the history of literature. The precise source or sources are unim-
portant: what does matter is that Shelley is employing a literary convention which ought to be recognisable to his readers. We take him
literally only at our peril.

Exactly the same kind of error was made by the biographers Edward
Dowden and Newman Ivey White in their interpretation of a passage
from the Dedication to *The Revolt of Islam*. In the following lines
Shelley recreates the moment in which he was first impelled by a sense
of vocation, a mysterious intimation that he was specially marked, a
spirit dedicated to the pursuit of liberty:

> I do remember well the hour which burst
>   My spirit's sleep: a fresh May-dawn it was,
>   When I walked forth upon the glittering grass,
> And wept, I knew not why; until there rose
>   From the near schoolroom, voices, that, alas!

Were but one echo from a world of woes—
The harsh and grating strife of tyrants and of foes.

To this Dowden and later White responded by pointing out that this experience could not have taken place at Eton since, if it had, there would have been no 'glittering grass' so near to the schoolroom. This confuses the distinction between poetry and biography, applying a very rigid standard of factuality which is quite inappropriate; furthermore, it makes no allowance for the special features of the convention which Shelley is employing, the poetry of religious dedication. What is evoked here is a spiritual experience, a mystical moment of intuition comparable to the climax of 'Hymn to Intellectual Beauty', where Shelley records how 'Sudden, thy shadow fell on me; / I shrieked, and clasped my hands in ecstasy!' In poems such as these the particularities of biography do not apply. Shelley's concern is not with the playing fields of Eton, nor with the view from one classroom window, nor from outside the classroom window looking in. 'Art is art because it is not nature' said Yeats, borrowing the saying from Goethe: if many readers of Shelley have been reluctant to acknowledge the difference, it is not simply because they are unaware of the literary conventions involved (though in some cases that may be true) but also because of their preconceptions about Shelley. Since Shelley famously acknowledged the necessity of inspiration in the *Defence of Poetry* and since he is popularly associated with a kind of poetry which has all to do with inspiration and nothing to do with art, it is not surprising that his readers suppose him innocent of a knowledge of literary tradition. The intensity of much of the poetry seems to corroborate the general belief that the poetry emerges directly from the life, 'comes native with the warmth'.

The clearest example of this is the lyric usually known as 'The Indian Serenade', of which this is the second stanza:

The wandering airs they faint
On the dark silent stream—
The champak odours fail
Like sweet thoughts in a dream;
The nightingale's complaint—
It dies upon her heart—
As I must die on thine
O beloved as thou art!

Received critical opinion of this poem may be represented by the reaction of Cleanth Brooks and Robert Penn Warren:

Quite overcome by his passion, he half swoons away, and appeals to his mistress to revive him, or at least (though the poem is not too clear here) to allow him to die upon her breast. ... An almost inevitable accompaniment of sentimentality is this obsession with one's own emotions—an exclusive interest which blinds the person involved to everything except the sweet intensity of the emotion in question.[6]

This is forceful and seemingly cogent but it is based on a fundamental misapprehension. It is closely related to the biographical tradition which was traced in the first chapter, the tradition which concentrates on certain feminine elements in Shelley, his emotionalism, his pallor, his weakness, his incapacity for aggressive response to the terms of life. That tradition, as I have tried to show, is generally misleading and the critical response of Brooks and Warren is an excellent example of how it can unbalance even those who would claim to be open-minded. For all their acumen when faced with other kinds of poetry, Brooks and Warren are guilty here of an elementary blunder. Knowing what they think they know about Shelley, they have assumed that this poem is autobiographical and that the speaker is Shelley himself. How like Shelley to go wandering in the night like this, how like the ineffectual angel to swoon on the grass. Above all, how weak, how effeminate and how characteristic that *he* should die on the breast of his beloved, weakly clinging for support.

It can't be said that this reading is entirely wrong. The emotionalism and the feminine behaviour are undeniably there in the poem. But what Brooks and Warren have failed to recognise is that the speaker is not Shelley but a woman, and that the poem is not autobiographical but dramatic. Like so many of the poems on which his critics have chosen to concentrate, this slight piece was not published during Shelley's lifetime; though it has appeared under various titles, the only holograph fair copy is headed 'The Indian girl's song'. Details in the poem corroborate the implication that the speaker is not Shelley but a girl. The mysterious line about the champak odours refers to the scent of a species of magnolia (smelling somewhat like a jonquil, said Captain Cook) which Indian women wore in their hair, a fact mentioned both by Thomas Moore and Sir William Jones. Not only is Shelley employing a dramatic voice here: there is also good reason to think that this song may have been intended as part of a play (the 'Unfinished Drama' perhaps, with its Indian Enchantress and Indian Youth and its oriental setting). Once this has been recognised, it is easy to see what an injustice we have been doing to Shelley. Although the poem is emotional, it is carefully structured, and the relation between the

Indian girl's emotions and the corresponding manifestations in nature is adroitly, even wittily, managed. 'The champak odours fail / Like sweet thoughts in a dream' is a characteristic Shelleyan synaesthesia, marked as usual by the clarifying simile; this is not a switching off of intelligence, an abandonment to voluptuous delight, but a careful and conscious deployment of effects to create the impression of losing control. The whole poem is an example of what Shelley himself once described as 'intense but regulated passion'.[7]

(ii)

Behind much of Shelley's poetry it is possible to detect a variety of literary traditions centred on religion and religious experience. His reputation as an atheist has tended to obscure the fact that, though his opinions were heterodox, his sensibility was profoundly religious. 'Hymn to Intellectual Beauty', for instance, suggests by its very title where we should look for analogues, while 'Ode to the West Wind' is both a hymn and a prayer. The postures and attitudes are recognised when we find them in Crashaw or in Cowper's *Olney Hymns* but we do not see them in Shelley because we don't expect to encounter them in such an unlikely context. Yet the parallels are undoubtedly there, once we are ready to see that for the received notion of God, Shelley substituted 'the interfused and overruling Spirit of all the energy and wisdom included within the circle of existing things'.[8] There can be little doubt that Shelley was a poet who, in his own way, was acquainted with the varieties of religious exeprience.

Consider these lines from the 'Ode to the West Wind':

I fall upon the thorns of life! I bleed!

A heavy weight of hours has chained and bowed
One too like thee: tameless, and swift, and proud.

This cry of despair is deplored by most contemporary critics, who see it as symptomatic of a radical weakness. Leavis, for example, makes the following accusation:

. . . the emotional luxury he invites others to share involves and propagates a self-indulgence that feels itself noble but is blindly and dangerously egocentric. 'Shelley's characteristic pathos is self-regarding, directed upon an idealized self' and 'for all his altruistic fervours and his fancied capacity for projecting his sympathies, Shelley is habitually his own hero'. . .[9]

It will be observed that Leavis's objection here is founded on Shelley's dangerous self-regard, a kind of monstrous egotism in which Percy B. Shelley is the focus of all attention. This criticism is the result of a complete misunderstanding of Shelley's intentions. The kind of poem which Shelley is writing is no more egotistical than the Psalms or the *Olney Hymns* and the personality, the focal identity of the speaker, is no more relevant to the 'Ode to the West Wind' than it is in either of these cases. In all three, the emotion is highly personal and emerges from a profoundly realised personal dilemma but in all three the personality of the poet is transcended, so that he becomes a bard, a *vates*, a prophet through whom the spirit may speak and whose personal experience is archetypal or representative for the whole community. Here the poet is only a poet in so far as he speaks to and for that community. As an individual he has ceased to exist.

Not only is Shelley working within a tradition of prophetic poetry in which the individual counts for nothing but his terms of reference are also identifiably part of that tradition. Just as Shelley switches from a sense of overwhelming joy to a sense of overwhelming sorrow, so does the Psalmist: 'Over against the ecstatic apocalypse, in every prophetic tradition, there stands the despondent psalm; over against the power of the divine afflatus, the weakness of uninspired humanity.'[10] Compare the offending lines in 'Ode to the West Wind' to this passage from the Psalms:

> I am troubled; I am bowed down greatly; I go mourning all the day long.
> For my loins are filled with a loathsome disease; and there is no soundness in my flesh.
> I am feeble and sore broken: I have roared by reason of the disquietness of my heart ...
> My heart panteth, my strength faileth me: as for the light of mine eyes, it also is gone from me.
>
> (38: 6–8, 10)

Or, take another example, which many readers will recognise, from Wesley's 'Jesu, Lover of My Soul':

> Wilt thou not regard my call?
> Wilt thou not accept my prayer?
> Lo! I sink, I faint, I fail!

Thus, Shelley's exclamation is a highly-stylised cry of despair which must be seen as the culmination of a long tradition of prophetic poetry. This tradition insists on the weakness of the supplicant, which is contrasted to the strength of the god to whom he calls for assistance: 'For thou art the God of my strength; why dost Thou cast me off? why go I mourning because of the oppression of the enemy?'[11] Like the Psalmist, Shelley staggers under the burden ('A heavy weight of hours has chained and bowed / One too like thee'); like the Psalmist, his hope of deliverance is centred in a mysterious and powerful divinity.

The religious implications are even clearer in Shelley's image of the thorns of life: here there is more than a suggestion that the poet's experience can be equated with Christ's just as it is in *Adonais* (lines 305–6) and just as Christ's image is sometimes fused with that of Prometheus in *Prometheus Unbound*. This is not heresy, an incendiary device planted *pour épater les bourgeois*: it derives from Shelley's profound and life-long admiration for Christ, whom he regarded as a reformer whose doctrines were so revolutionary that, if they were put into practice, 'no political or religious institution could subsist a moment'. Yet these benevolent doctrines had been misinterpreted, Christ had been misunderstood and had suffered crucifixion. Thus, as recipient of 'benignant visitings from the invisible energies' and as agent in the ultimate regeneration of society, the outlawed poet waiting for the spring can see himself 'despised and rejected' as Christ had been. Both Christ and the poet, in his role as promulgator of the doctrine of love, can be regarded as the 'unacknowledged legislator[s] of the world'. There is no question here of Shelley's egotism putting him on a level with Christ. What he is suggesting in 'Ode to the West Wind' is an overlapping of experience in so far as the poet, like Christ, is a prophet, a vehicle of the spirit, a voice crying in the wilderness.

There is yet another variety of weakness in Shelley's poetry which is very frequently attributed to his own shortcomings of character: that is, the acknowledged failure to complete a poem or to sustain inspiration. It is generally accepted that this kind of weakness is related to Shelley's theory of poetry, according to which 'the mind in creation is as a fading coal, which some invisible influence, like an inconstant wind, awakens to transitory brightness'. But it is not generally recognised that this view of poetry, although Shelley gives it an unforgettable formulation, is a traditional one and that Shelley's protests in some of his poems are ritual exclamations rather than symptoms of poetic collapse. Take for example the closing lines of the invitation to Emilia in *Epipsychidion*. Here Shelley rises to a great climax as he prophesies the unity and perfection of their love:

One hope within two wills, one will beneath

> Two overshadowing minds, one life, one death,
> One Heaven, one Hell, one immortality,
> And one annihilation.

Like the word *forlorn* in the 'Ode to a Nightingale', *annihilation* tolls him back to his sole self and to the limitations of his poetic powers for the high enterprise of expressing the nature of true Love. The abyss is glimpsed, the poem sinks, the fading coal is extinguished:

> Woe is me!
> The wingèd words on which my soul would pierce
> Into the height of love's rare Universe,
> Are chains of lead around its flight of fire—
> I pant, I sink, I tremble, I expire!

A characteristic response to these lines is provided by Edward E. Bostetter, who attempts a literal reading:

Like Icarus he falls to his death. There is no struggle except the convulsive reflex. He makes no effort to live in the imperfect world. He simply gives up. Perhaps Shelley's greatest weakness is revealed in the lack of embarrassment with which he describes his weakness, the unawareness finally that it is a weakness.[12]

This implies that there is no division between the poem and the poet, that the weakness of the one necessarily signifies the weakness of the other. Yet, the ending of *Epipsychidion* is not an episode of autobiography or an embarrassing piece of exhibitionism but a conscious and stylised recognition of the difficulty of penetrating to the heart of the matter and the impossibility of maintaining inspiration. That it is not an involuntary loss of control but a calmly deployed technique should be obvious from the coda which immediately follows:

> Weak verses, go kneel at your Sovereign's feet,
> And say:—'We are the masters of thy slave;
> What wouldest thou with us and ours and thine?' [etc.]

In these lines Shelley is employing a tradition which he must have encountered in a number of European poets: in this case his debt is directly to Dante, whose address to his own poem he had translated in the Advertisement to *Epipsychidion*: 'My Song, I fear that Thou wilt find but few / Who fitly shall conceive thy reasoning, / Of such hard matter dost thou entertain.' The sinking and expiring which immediately precede this do not come from Dante (though in the *Paradiso* he does admit that he cannot find words to convey the radiance of Beatrice as she appears in heaven; indeed, like Shelley, he is struck dumb by a vision of love).[13] However, the conjunction of these lines on the flagging of inspiration with the traditional author's address to the completed poem should be enough to show that they too are the product of a highly calculated approach to poetic art. The whole of *Epipsychidion* is a self-conscious and highly wrought piece of art; indeed, to a much greater extent than most of Shelley's other poems, it is a poem about the difficulties involved in its own composition. The ebb and flow of inspiration is deliberately exploited as a structural principle; the apparent lack of unity is the result of a calculated attempt to reproduce the very process of creation.

Shelley is equally self-aware in other poems, where he often uses this idea of poetic collapse. A good instance is the elaborately developed pattern of the final stanza of the 'Ode to Liberty':

The solemn harmony

Paused, and the Spirit of that mighty singing
    To its abyss was suddenly withdrawn;
Then, as a wild swan, when sublimely winging
    Its path athwart the thunder-smoke of dawn,
Sinks headlong through the aërial golden light
    On the heavy-sounding plain,
    When the bolt has pierced its brain;
As summer clouds dissolve, unburthened of their rain;
    As a far taper fades with fading night,
    As a brief insect dies with dying day,
My song, its pinions disarrayed of might,
    Drooped; o'er it closed the echoes far away
Of the great voice which did its flight sustain,
    As waves which lately paved his watery way
    Hiss round a drowner's head in their tempestuous play.

This extraordinary *tour de force* can only be properly understood when it is related to the opening stanza where the poet describes the onset of inspiration:

        My soul spurned the chains of its dismay,
    And in the rapid plumes of song
    Clothed itself, sublime and strong;
As a young eagle soars the morning clouds among,
    Hovering in verse o'er its accustomed prey;
    Till from its station in the heaven of fame

> The Spirit's whirlwind rapt it, and the ray
>   Of the remotest sphere of living flame
> Which paves the void was from behind it flung,
>   As foam from a ship's swiftness, when there came
>   A voice out of the deep: I will record the same.

It is evident that we are dealing with a poem which is extremely formal and which has been organised with very great care. Both of these stanzas refer to the poetic process: the first stanza endeavours to recreate the feeling of elation which comes with inspiration, while the last attempts to suggest the corresponding feeling of deflation, which Shelley elsewhere calls the 'vacancy' of the spirit. In both stanzas the poem itself, or rather the poetic process, is imaged as a bird: in the first it is an eagle triumphantly hovering over its prey, while in the last it is a wild swan, an image which Yeats recognised as a symbol for the solitary soul and which is particularly appropriate here because of its more usual poetic connections with death. Both stanzas make use of the image of water: in the first the poem gathers speed and impetuously rides the waves, while in the last the glow of inspiration is fading and ordinary uninspired consciousness is returning (or as Shelley put it in the *Defence of Poetry* the 'poet becomes a man, and is abandoned to the sudden reflux of the influences under which others habitually live'). One might compare this final collapse with the end of *The Ancient Mariner* where the ship suddenly sinks and the mariner's body is found floating in the sea 'Like one that hath been seven days drowned'. Another parallel can be found at the end of *The Love Song of J. Alfred Prufrock* where 'human voices wake us and we drown'. In both of these cases, as in the 'Ode to Liberty' the departure of the spirit of inspiration and the return to normal everyday consciousness is a sudden and painful wrench imaged in terms of drowning or physical collapse.

Perhaps the most important analogy to Shelley's simulation of poetic collapse is with Pindar, the great master of the ode, whom Shelley admired so greatly that he copied into his notebook a number of phrases and passages from his *Odes*.[14] These poems which are, in part at least, models for Shelley's 'Ode to Liberty' are highly self-conscious works of art, for all their obeisance to the mysterious breath of inspiration. One highly characteristic image is the eagle; for example, in one of the *Nemean Odes* Pindar uses it to compare his own poetry to that of his rivals:

Among birds the eagle is swift.

Pondering his prey from afar, he plummets suddenly to blood the spoil
  in his claws.
Clamorous daws range the low spaces of the sky.[15]

This proud declaration may well be the primary source for Shelley's
impressive simile. Yet quite apart from the strong probability that there
is a specific debt here, both in detail and in general sprit, the 'Ode to
Liberty' is distinctly Pindaric both in the elevation of its tone and in
the self-awareness of its approach to poetry. Pindar frequently comments on his poetic intentions, referring to his poems as buildings or
chariots or ships driven by a following wind. It is possible that Pindar's
ship may have helped to suggest the watery context which encircles
the beginning and the end of Shelley's poem but the device of looking
at the poem from the outside is a more pervasive and significant debt.
The collapse at the end of the 'Ode to Liberty' is not, of course, specifically Pindaric, but it is managed as carefully and as artfully as the
rest of the poem.

On other occasions, Shelley overtly denied the necessity of collapse
when this seemed poetically appropriate. At the end of *Adonais* his boat
sails on—this reverses the conclusion of the 'Ode to Liberty' but the basic
image is similar:

The breath whose might I have invoked in song
Descends on me; my spirit's bark is driven
Far from the shore, far from the trembling throng
Whose sails were never to the tempest given;
The massy earth and spherèd skies are riven!
I am borne darkly, fearfully, afar . . .

(*iii*)

Any suggestion, then, that these passages are an indication of Shelley's
personal weakness would be ill-advised. Clearly Shelley was attracted
to letting himself go (see for example the fondness for floating and
allowing himself to be carried away that helps him to imagine a boat
'sailing pleasantly / Swift as a cloud between the sea and sky').[16] On
the other hand, his approach to this experience is often analytical and
in many passages he is observing his own reactions with detachment.
Much misreading of Shelley results from a failure to recognise this,
often compounded by a failure to recognise the genre or tradition in
which he is working.

Many of these misreadings imply that Shelley was egotistical or narcissistic: Leavis sees Shelley as incurably self-regarding, while some of the nineteenth-century critics attributed his literary misdemeanours to pride or vanity. Such criticism would have been very surprising to Shelley since his whole poetic theory involved the avoidance of self-projection. Indeed, Shelley's views on the dangers of introducing the purely biographical into poetry would have been largely acceptable to such rigorous observers of decorum as Thomas Gray and Dr Johnson. Mrs Shelley is quite specific about this in her preface to the *Collected Poems*. She divides her husband's poems into three classes: there are the poems 'sustained by a lofty subject and useful aim', then the 'purely imaginative' and finally 'those which sprang from the emotions of his heart'. Shelley regarded the first group with 'most complacency' (i.e. satisfaction) because of its practical intentions. Of the third category, Mrs Shelley remarks: '... he was usually averse to expressing these feelings, except when highly idealized; and many of his more beautiful effusions he had cast aside unfinished, and they were never seen by me till after I had lost him.' She also mentions that she found 'Lines Written among the Euganean Hills' and *Rosalind and Helen* among his papers 'and with some difficulty urged him to complete them'.

These remarks are very interesting both because they give us an insight into Shelley's attitude and because they give us some idea of why a poet who believed so firmly in reticence has been so widely misrepresented as a poet of self-expression. An important factor in this false identification is that a high proportion of the poems by which Shelley is best known were not published by the poet himself but were collected by his wife after his death and revealed to the world with all their imperfections on their heads. Many of these poems were unfinished and many were also intensely private. For example, 'To Edward Williams' is a detailed discussion of Shelley's domestic problems, and was accompanied by instructions which could hardly be misunderstood: 'If any of the stanzas should please you, you may read them to Jane, but to no one else,—and yet on second thoughts I had rather you would not.' Of another poem he writes to Jane Williams, 'I commit them [these lines] to your secresy and your mercy ...' The manuscript of 'The Magnetic Lady' is marked 'For Jane & Williams alone to see' and that of 'Remembrance' bears the injunction 'Do not say it is mine to any one'. Again, Shelley's intentions for the *Letter to Maria Gisborne* are perfectly explicit: 'The enclosed must on no account be published'.[17]

As these instructions might suggest, Shelley himself published very few poems which could be regarded as personal. If one excludes the *juvenilia*, he published eleven volumes of verse between *Alastor* (1816) and *Hellas* (1822). These eleven volumes included only four poems which could be regarded as personal: 'Stanzas—April 1814', 'Hymn to Intellectual Beauty', 'Lines Written among the Euganean Hills' and 'Ode to the West Wind'. Of these, both the Hymn and the 'Ode to the West Wind' were highly stylised and Shelley actually had to be persuaded to finish 'Lines' and to publish it in its complete version. He also contributed ten poems to periodicals, all of which were published anonymously: none of these could be classified as personal and two of them ('Sunset' and 'Grief') had the personal passages removed before publication. In addition to this, there is some evidence that Shelley wanted his publisher to omit the self-portrait from *Adonais*; certainly he cancelled in the preface 'the whole passage relating to my private wrongs'. Shelley did attempt to include in the projected *Julian and Maddalo* volume 'all my saddest verses raked up into one heap'.[18] But this was never published.

The poems themselves provide further interesting evidence of Shelley's beliefs in this matter. The two stanzas from the 'Ode to Liberty' which we have just considered make it clear that the personality of the poet himself is of no significance. He is a vehicle of the Spirit, which in this case may be equated with the Spirit of Liberty, inspirer alike of poetry and of political action. The opening stanza suggests that the poet is lifted above the ordinary limitations of mortality —'the chains of its dismay' refers specifically to the political condition of the pre-revolutionary world but it also implies that these sad realities are a clog and an obstacle to the poet who has to rise above them to the heights of poetic prophecy where he can 'behold the future in the present'.[19]

As he rises above the limitations of mortality, he casts off too the chains of individuality and becomes open to larger influences. The voice we hear in the 'Ode to Liberty' from stanza 2 until the beginning of the last stanza, when the Spirit withdraws to its abyss, is not the voice of Percy Bysshe Shelley but 'A voice out of the deep', the 'great voice which did its [the poem's] flight sustain'. This voice has obvious Biblical resonances[20] and it seems that one of Shelley's analogues here is the Biblical prophets, whom we know he admired and assiduously reread throughout his life. The whole concept should be related to the reverberating affirmations with which Shelley closes the *Defence of Poetry*:

Poets are the hierophants of an unapprehended inspiration; the mirrors of the gigantic shadows which futurity casts upon the present; the words which express what they understand not; the trumpets which sing to battle and feel not what they inspire; the influence which is moved not, but moves.[21]

There is no room for personality here, no room for verse which is simply confessional. The poet is not expressing himself but performing a sacred duty: he is a 'minister' of the spirit of good, a hierophant, an acolyte of 'that imperial faculty, whose throne is curtained within the invisible nature of man',[22] since for Shelley the power of inspiration comes equally from within and from without, or more precisely there is no distinction between the two.

The idea of the poet as attendant upon an oracle occurs quite frequently. It is here in an unused passage from the draft of *Epipsychidion* which does not refer specifically to poetry but which may be taken to include it:

> alas what are we? Clouds
> Driven by the wind in warring multitudes
> Which rain into the bosom of the earth
> And rise again—and in our death and birth
> And restless life, take as from heaven
> Hues which are not our own—but which are given
> And then withdrawn and with inconstant glance
> Flash from the Spirit to the countenance—
> There is a power, a love, a joy, a God
> Which makes in mortal hearts its brief abode
> A Pythian exhalation, which inspires
> Love . . . only love
> There is a mood which language faints beneath . . .[23]

Here Shelley underlines the helplessness and insignificance of the individual, coloured as he is like the cloud by 'Hues which are not our own, but which are given'. The burden too is emphasised, the dependance on involuntary energies, the fallings, the inadequacy of language. For all its exultation, the central definition is cautious and scrupulously defined ('a power, a love, a joy, a God' since the Spirit might manifest itself in any of these incarnations): but there can be no doubt about the effects of the 'Pythian exhalation', that Delphic oracle from which

> the oracular vapour is hurled up
> Which lonely men drink wandering in their youth,
> And call truth, virtue, love, genius, or joy—
> That maddening wine of life, whose dregs they drain
> To deep intoxication, and uplift,
> Like Maenads who cry loud, Evoe! Evoe!
> The voice which is contagion to the world.
>
> (*P.U.*, II, iii. 4–10)

Here again though Shelley hints at the impossibility of definition, all the images indicate a going out of oneself under the impulse of the spirit. Here too the irrationality and the divine insanity of inspiration are emphasised, together with the fact that the ministers of this inspiration are the enemies of the illiberal and repressive world we live in and have learned to accept. All of these images present the poet to us as in himself nothing but, when inspired, a sacred and dangerous figure (*deinos* as the Greeks might have said of Dionysus and his Maenads or 'beautiful and fierce' as Shelley described the Comet-figure in *Epipsychidion*).

If the notion of inspiration does no more than suggest a transcendence of individuality, Shelley is quite specific about it elsewhere. In 'To a Skylark' he finds himself once again struggling with the inadequacy of mere words and images, since 'the deep truth is imageless'. In an attempt not to define the skylark but to approximate to its essence through a series of similes, he makes a specific comparison between the unseen singer and the poet:

> Like a Poet hidden
> In the light of thought,
> Singing hymns unbidden
> Till the world is wrought
> To sympathy with hopes and fears it heeded not...
>   (lines 36–40)

The central image in this stanza as in the next three is of something beautiful but unperceived: the list continues with a maiden singing in a palace-tower, a glow-worm whose light is concealed in the flowers and grass, and a rose 'embowered in its own green leaves'. All of these similes offer analogies to the skylark, whose 'shrill delight' can be heard but who remains unseen by the listener.

The image of the poet is usually taken for granted as part of this series but it is worth examining for what it can tell us of Shelley's view of the poet, rather than of the skylark. We may note here the brief description of the social function of poetry, which operates *indirectly* to influence its public, and, once again, the involuntary nature of inspiration, this time with an eye to Milton's 'unpremeditated Verse' (*P.L.*, ix. 24). But the most significant detail concerns the position of the poet himself, who is 'hidden in the light of thought'. This seems to mean that the poet as man is rapt up into the radiance of inspiration and his individuality is absorbed in the intensity of that experience. A useful parallel can be found in Panthea's description of how she was visited by Prometheus in a dream:

> I saw not, heard not, moved not, only felt
> His presence flow and mingle through my blood
> Till it became his life, and his grew mine,
> And I was thus absorbed . . .
>
> (*P.U.*, ii, i. 79–82)

It might be argued that a description of love has nothing to do with the poetic process, but this is not how Shelley saw it. To him, poetry and love were, in some senses, interchangeable terms: both involved a going out of our own nature and an identification with the beautiful. Throughout the *Defence* love is used as a metaphor for poetry and the poetic process: for example, the onset and departure of inspiration is described in terms which might characterise with equal precision the sexual event.[24] Panthea's dream offers some intimations of those experiences in which we escape from the confines of self; yet the poetic experience is characterised by a locating detail which is specifically its own. It takes place in 'the light of *thought*' (my italics) or in that transcendental world associated with Intellectual Beauty. Thus, though poetry can not be dissociated from feeling, it is essentially an intellectual discipline, since 'it is at once the centre and circumference of knowledge; it is that which comprehends all science, and that to which all science must be referred'.

Shelley's meaning becomes clearer when we consider a passage from Plato's *Symposium* in which Diotima describes the supreme beauty. Here is Shelley's translation:

What then shall we imagine to be the aspect of the supreme beauty itself, simple, pure, uncontaminated with the intermixture of human flesh and colours and all other idle and unreal shapes attendant on mortality; the divine, the original, the supreme, the self-consistent, the monoeidic beauty itself? What must be the life of him who dwells with it and gazes on that which it becomes him to seek? Think you not that to him alone is accorded the prerogative of bringing forth not images and shadows of virtue [but reality], for he is in contact not with a shadow but with reality; with virtue itself, in the production and nourishment of which he becomes dear to the Gods, and, if such a privilege is conceded to any human being, himself immortal.[25]

Shelley must have had something like this in mind when he wrote of 'the light of thought'. However, although the poet is 'hidden' in this light, it is important to notice that he does not disappear. Shelley believed that the individuality of the poet was not dissolved in the creative process but subsumed : thus the greatest poetry was concerned not with the expression of a personality but with images of eternal truth, and yet in providing those images the poet would be expressing himself. All poetry bears the stamp of the creator's personality (Homer's style is not the same as Milton's, Keats differs from Byron) yet the poet's aim must be to transcend the limited objectives of self-expression.

Shelley is critical of poets who have not been able to achieve this liberation from self. There is a difficult passage in the unfinished *Triumph of Life* where Rousseau seems to be making this point :

> See the great bards of old, who inly quelled
>
> The passions which they sung, as by their strain
>   May well be known : their living melody
> Tempers its own contagion to the vein
>
>   Of those who are infected with it—I
> Have suffered what I wrote, or viler pain!—
>
>   And so my words were seeds of misery,
> Even as the deeds of others.
>   (lines 274–81)

In the generalised gesture which points to 'the great bards of old', Rousseau is referring to Homer, Lucretius, Virgil, Dante, Chaucer, Shakespeare, Calderón and Milton in particular, all of whom achieved the self-control which is necessary for great artistic achievement.[26] If their poetry has had unfortunate effects, that may be attributed not to any weakness which is inherent in the poetry but to the weakness of their readers, since 'of such truths / Each to itself must be the oracle' (*P.U.*, II, iv. 122–3). If the *Iliad* encourges the wrong kind of militaristic valour or *Paradise Lost* seems to sanction a vindictive dispensation of justice, it is not because Homer thirsted for blood or Milton for vengeance but because we impose our own selfishness and our own limitations on what they have written. Rousseau, on the other hand, did not succeed in mastering his own emotions: he was not able to repress 'the mutiny within' and did not transform to 'potable gold the poisonous waters which flow from death through life'.

This shortcoming becomes clearer when we set it in the context of Shelley's 'Sonnet to the Republic of Benevento', a poem which suggests that the significant revolutions are not the political ones, such as that which had taken place in Benevento, but the internal, psychological ones :

> Man, who man would be,
> Must rule the empire of himself; in it
> Must be supreme; establishing his throne
> On vanquished will; quelling the anarchy
> Of hopes and fears; being himself alone.

For all his greatness, Rousseau could not achieve this internal equilibrium as his *Confessions* publicly demonstrated; they were, said Shelley, 'either a disgrace to the confessor or a string of falsehoods'. To make such inadequacies public was a dangerous proceeding: though the structure of his feelings and his understanding closely resembled those of Christ, Rousseau gave licence by his writings to passions that only incapacitate and contract the human heart. In one sense, then, he was as much a tyrant as the French monarchs whom he despised, or as Napoleon for whom he paved the way: his words were 'seeds of misery' and 'he prepared the necks of his fellow-beings for that galling and dishonourable servitude which at this moment it bears'.[27] As *Prometheus Unbound* so forcefully asserts, man cannot be free until he dethrones the tyrants of his own soul, a process which involves self-knowledge, self-control and self-reliance. To concentrate, as Rousseau does, on one's own weaknesses, gloatingly as it seems, is to subject oneself to a despotic control as ruthless and as destructive as any which is exercised from the customary seats of power.

This helps to explain one puzzling detail in the dialogue between Julian and Maddalo, characters closely modelled on Shelley and Byron but distanced and fictionalised by a variety of artistic devices. Basically, Julian is an idealist, while Maddalo is a realist; however, the issue is not clear-cut otherwise Shelley would not have found it necessary to write the poem. Julian believes in human potentiality:

> We might be otherwise—we might be all
> We dream of happy, high, majestical.
> Where is the love, beauty, and truth we seek
> But in our mind? and if we were not weak
> Should we be less in deed than in desire?
> (lines 172–76)

These lines are closely related to Shelley's own view that 'Poetry is the record of the best and happiest moments of the happiest and best minds' and his belief that 'it strips the veil of familiarity from the world, and lays bare the naked and sleeping beauty, which is the spirit of its forms'. That is, poetry can apprehend the potential, the sleeping beauty which is concealed from us by the film of familiarity which restricts us to 'that inanimate cold world allowed / To the poor, loveless, ever anxious crowd' (Coleridge: *Dejection: An Ode*). Maddalo is not impressed. Such idealism ignores the facts of life, the grim realities which clip our wings. To prove his case he takes Julian to the madhouse where they visit a poet whose mind has been unhinged by calumny, misunderstanding and bad fortune. They overhear a long monologue in which it appears that the poet bears obvious similarities to Julian and to Shelley himself. Afterwards Julian and Maddalo discuss his sad position but the only specific comment we are given comes from Maddalo:

And I remember one remark which then
Maddalo made. He said: 'Most wretched men
Are cradled into poetry by wrong,
They learn in suffering what they teach in song.'
(lines 543–46)

Shelley would not have denied that poets were often motivated in this way but he would have claimed that the poet should learn to rise above such suffering, and transmute it from raw material into finished art. That Byron did not always succeed in doing this he lamented in a letter to Peacock where he alludes to the deficiencies of *Childe Harold*:

He is not yet an Italian [that is, not yet totally sunk in certain kinds of depravity] & is heartily & deeply discontented with himself, & contemplating in the distorted mirror of his own thoughts the nature & the destiny of man, what can he behold but objects of contempt & despair?[28]

In this kind of poetry, too deeply impregnated with self, the poet's own individuality acts as a kind of distorting mirror, whereas the best poetry 'is a mirror which makes beautiful that which is distorted'.

Julian and Maddalo itself is an excellent example of how this works. The monologue of the Ferrarese Maniac has given rise to much biographical speculation as to who he really is and what was Shelley's source for the story.[29] All of this speculation misses the point: *Julian and Maddalo* is not a document in biography or history but a poem. All that we need to know is contained in the poem itself. Admittedly, the poem is, in part at least, based on a real event—a visit which Shelley made to Venice in the autumn of 1818. Admittedly, it is tempting to equate the madman with Shelley (and there are obvious points of contact, such as the self-characterisation, '*Me*—who am as a nerve o'er which do creep / The else unfelt oppressions of this earth' or the madman's claim that he 'could see / The absent with the glance of phantasy'). Yet these facts make the achievement of the poem all the more spectacular and its avoidance of biographical specificity a more remarkable instance of tact and artistic control. There is no reason to believe that Shelley and Byron did visit the madhouse at Venice or that they ever encountered a character similar to the Ferrarese Maniac. On the other hand, there is every reason to believe that the career of the Maniac is closely based on that of Tasso, whose life Shelley had been studying in Sismondi, whose prison cell he had visited with deep emotion and who was the subject of a play he had started to write at this time.

If K. N. Cameron is right and if the Maniac's story does include details of an estrangement with Mary (the mysterious child, the hidden writings, the embittered love which leads to misery) the technical achievement is all the more notable. What Shelley is *not* doing is writing a *roman à clef* or addressing himself to Mary in an obscure form of public indiscretion. It may be possible to extract some biographical material from the poem, although this is a hazardous process, but the poem was not written with the intention that we should do so. Nor was it intended as a devious love letter mixed with complaint, whose ultimate function was to restore the breach between Mary and Shelley. It should be obvious that, if there are biographical materials in the maniac's story, these are combined with other materials some of which are historical, some fictional, and that all of these elements are deployed primarily for the purposes of the poem, not for the purposes of self-expression.

What the biographical reading fails to consider is how this lengthy and climactic section of the poem relates to the rest. Quite apart from his respect for reticence, Shelley's sense of structure would not have allowed him to insert a piece of autobiography in his poem simply because he wanted to get it off his chest. In fact, the tale of the Ferrarese Maniac is as much a moral fable and as carefully related to the central themes of *Julian and Maddalo* as the interpolated tales of Fielding are related to *his* larger purposes. The Ferrarese Maniac is to *Julian and Maddalo* what the Man of the Hill is to *Tom Jones* but more so, since the Maniac's story is such a central episode in Shelley's poem. Not only does Shelley impose form on his materials by using this story; he also concludes *Julian and Maddalo* with an episode which we know to be as imaginary in origin as the opening section is biographical. Finally, the whole poem is distanced even further by Shelley's Preface, where Julian and Maddalo are presented with great detachment. 'Julian,' says Shelley, 'is rather serious.'

The Preface ends with an explanation which every critic of Shelley should take to heart:

Of the Maniac I can give no information. He seems, by his own account, to have been disappointed in love. He was evidently a very cultivated and amiable person when in his right senses. His story, told at length, might be like many other stories of the same kind: the unconnected exclamations of his agony will perhaps be found a sufficient comment for the text of every heart.

Here, as always, Shelley is very clear about his intentions and his methods. He is aware of the disjointed structure of the Maniac's narrative: in fact, this is a deliberate tactic intended not only to convey the incoherencies of madness but to avoid the very specificity which his critics have attempted to impose on it. Quite consciously, he has avoided telling us the whole story, since we do not need to know the details. What matters is that the story should embody the 'elementary feelings of the human mind'[30] and that the reader should be able to project himself into these feelings so that he will finish the poem a wiser and a better man. To tell a story which is too specific, too limited to the particularities of its own time, place and circumstances, might be to distract the reader or even to hinder him.

It is essential, too, that the reader should be properly disposed, that he should approach the poem out of his own human experience. The relations between him and the poem as Shelley expresses them are unexpected and significant: 'the unconnected exclamations of his agony will perhaps be found a sufficient comment for the text of every heart.' According to this view, it is the poet himself who is the textual critic while human nature is the text on which he makes his commentary. This formulation suggests the central importance of elementary humanity and the peripheral significance, indeed the irrelevance, of the poet's own selfhood. He is a commentator, a critic, a scholar, a careful reader of the human heart, but not himself the subject of the investigation.

In its impersonal view of the poetic process, this concept might be placed alongside Eliot's statement that 'The business of the poet is not to find new emotions, but to use the ordinary ones and, in working them up into poetry, to express feelings which are not in actual emotions at all. And emotions which he has never experienced will serve his turn as well as those familiar to him.' For Eliot, the poetic process was not unlike 'the action which takes place when a bit of finely filiated platinum is introduced into a chamber containing oxygen and sulphur dioxide';[31] for Valéry the poet was a privileged mechanic and the poem a machine which he set into motion; for Auden the poet was a surgeon, dissecting words and emotions with clinical finesse and

c

lack of emotion. Shelley's image of the poet as textual critic and the poem as textual commentary is not perhaps so extreme as any of these three but there can be no doubt that it belongs to the same family. From this image it follows that the interpreter who reads the poem with his eye on its biographical significance is denying its relevance, placing it out there as part of Shelley's life or Byron's or even Tasso's, when he should be bringing it home to himself. This kind of reading is, in its way, a form of arrogance, a refusal to open the heart to the humanising influences of literature. Shelley's own poetry acknowledged a more compelling moral responsibility. He expressed his aims with great force and clarity in the Preface to *The Cenci*: 'The highest moral purpose aimed at in the highest species of the drama is the teaching the human heart, through its sympathies and antipathies, the knowledge of itself; in proportion to the possession of which knowledge, every human being is wise, just, sincere, tolerant and kind.'

(iv)

Julian and Maddalo conclusively demonstrates that, far from regarding poetry as a convenient means for projecting his ego, Shelley deliberately observed a strict, eighteenth-century decorum. *Epipsychidion* provides another instance of Shelley's concern that the man and the poet should not be confused in the mind of the reader. The passionate language and the romantic fervour of this poem are not suggestive of decorum and restraint and the life recounted bears certain obvious resemblances to Shelley's own; yet, in spite of these elements which seem to pull it towards autobiographical specificity, *Epipsychidion* is 'an *idealized* history of my life and feelings'.[32] In order to facilitate this effect, Shelley provided a fictional preface in which he described the deceased author of the poem, rather in the manner of certain eighteenth-century novelists. This allowed him to escape identification with the narrator, while it also gave him scope for some distancing ironies: the magnificently sensuous prospectus of life in the island paradise is, says the Preface, 'a scheme of life, suited perhaps to that happier and better world of which he is now an inhabitant, but hardly practicable in this'.

The avoidance of specificity was a carefully considered project. Shelley told his publisher that it 'should not be considered as my own' (that is, he wanted it to be published anonymously):

indeed, in a certain sense, it is a production of a portion of me already dead;

and in this sense the advertisement is no fiction. It is to be published simply for the esoteric few; and I make its author a secret, to avoid the malignity of those who turn sweet food into poison; transforming all they touch into the corruption of their own natures.[33]

It would be narrow-minded to suggest that Shelley's main concern was to avoid scandalous gossip, although there can be no doubt that he was particularly sensitive about the reviewers (and not without justification). His main motivation must have been that he did not wish matters that were merely personal ('chatter about Harriet') to interfere with what he considered the serious and central interest of his poem.

Two eminent precursors could be pointed to in his defence. First, there was Dante:

The present Poem, like the *Vita Nuova* of Dante, is sufficiently intelligible to a certain class of readers without a matter-of-fact history of circumstances to which it relates; and to a certain other class it must ever remain incomprehensible, from a defect of a common organ of perception for the ideas of which it treats.[34]

Secondly, there was Shakespeare, who is referred to in one of the unpublished drafts:

If any should be curious to discover
Whether to you I am a friend or lover,
Let them read Shakespeare's sonnets, taking thence
A whetstone for their dull intelligence
That tears and will not cut ...
                              (*P.W.*, p. 428)

Poetry is not biography and there are certain questions which we should not ask of it. Such facts as are necessary the poem will provide for us; beyond that, it is idle, impertinent and irrelevant to speculate. To the reader the true identity of Emilia should be a matter as indifferent as the true identity of the Dark Lady of Shakespeare's sonnets or the number of Lady Macbeth's children.

Poetry aspires to a condition in which the mere specificities of fact are transcended. Shelley's views on this subject run counter to current trends of concreteness, social realism and confessional revelation; they are also frequently misrepresented: for these reasons they need to be examined in some detail. First of all, Shelley believed that poetry had little to do with *facts* in Byron's sense of the word. In a letter of advice written in 1821 to a lady he explained some of the reasons:

The generous and inspiriting examples of philosophy and virtue, you desire intimately to know and feel; not as mere facts detailing names, and dates, and motions of the human body, but clothed in the very language of the actors,—that language dictated by and expressive of the passions and principles that governed their conduct. Facts are not what we want to know in poetry, in history, in the lives of individual men, in satire, or panegyric. They are the mere divisions, the arbitrary points on which we hang, and to which we refer those delicate and evanescent hues of mind, which language delights and instructs us in precise proportion as it expresses.[35]

Here Shelley, who is so often accused of insensitivity to the claims of language, unequivocally declares that it is a more integral part of poetry than raw fact. The quantitative approach to literature, focusing on names, dates, motions and other verifiable data, ignores one of the primary components of poetry—its rhythm or order—which 'springs from the nature itself of language, which is a more direct representation of the actions and passions of our internal being, and is susceptible of more various and delicate combinations, than colour, form, or motion' (that is, than the instruments and materials of painters, sculptors and musicians).[36] The meaning of poetry does not reside in the number of facts included but in the peculiar nature of its language and the relation between that language and the operations of mind:

Sounds as well as thoughts have relation both between each other and towards that which they represent. . . . Hence the language of poets has ever affected a certain uniform and harmonious recurrence of sound, without which it were not poetry, and which is scarcely less indispensable to the communication of its influence, than the words themselves, without reference to that peculiar order. Hence the vanity of translation; it were as wise to cast a violet into a crucible that you might discover the formal principle of its colour and odour, as seek to transfuse from one language into another the creations of a poet.[37]

It should be noticed that Shelley is not proposing that poetry is unfactual or that it is at odds with our experience of life or the world we live in. In these declarations Shelley is neither asserting that poetry is socially irresponsible nor that it practices a superior kind of lying. The letter to his female correspondent makes it clear that, when he is talking of facts, Shelley is thinking of certain limited data, essentially biographical or historical. Poetry may ignore these data or transcend them, but it remains true to its own sense of fact: primarily, it is responsive to the facts of mind, 'those delicate and evanescent hues of mind, which language delights and instructs us in precise proportion as it expresses'.

Behind all this there are two predominating influences which directed Shelley towards his special brand of idealism; one is derived from the history of literary theory, the other from philosophy. To begin with the philosophy—Shelley devoted much of his time to the problems of metaphysics; Mrs Shelley tells us that he planned to write prose metaphysical essays on the nature of man and that he 'considered these philosophical views of Mind and Nature to be instinct with the intensest spirit of poetry'.[38] Shelley did not live to complete this project but he did leave us a number of substantial fragments which give some idea of what he might have accomplished. As one might expect from someone so deeply read in eighteenth-century philosophy, much of his attention is devoted to the problems of knowledge and perception. Shelley's basic position as a philosopher (which must be carefully distinguished from his position as a poet) was a sceptical one. This led him to question the existence of individual minds. In the uncompleted *Essay on Life* he puts forward the following extreme proposition :

Nothing exists but as it is perceived. The difference is merely nominal between those two classes of thought which are vulgarly distinguished by the names of ideas and of external objects. Pursuing the same thread of reasoning, the existence of distinct individual minds, similar to that which is employed in now questioning its own nature, is likewise found to be a delusion. The words *I, you, they* are not signs of any actual difference subsisting between the assemblage of thoughts thus indicated, but are merely marks employed to denote the different modifications of the one mind.[39]

Having got so far, Shelley pulls himself up before his reader can assume that he is suggesting that *his* mind is sole creator of the universe it perceives:

Let it not be supposed that this doctrine conducts to the monstrous presumption that I, the person who now write and think, am that one mind. I am but a portion of it. The words *I* and *you* and *they* are grammatical devices invented simply for arrangement, and totally devoid of the intense and exclusive sense usually attached to them.[40]

These ideas could be traced more extensively but the two quotations reveal as thoroughly as is necessary the direction in which Shelley's mind was moving. There are times when this 'intellectual philosophy' seems to bring him to the verge of mysticism, yet the primary impetus was probably derived from his reading in Sir William Drummond, Berkeley, Hume, Locke, Reid and other eighteenth-century philosophers.

The second impetus was derived basically from literary theory, but it overlaps intriguingly with the more specifically philosophical. Here is Shelley in the *Defence of Poetry*:

A poet participates in the eternal, the infinite, and the one; as far as relates to his conceptions, time and place and number are not. The grammatical forms which express the moods of time, and the difference of persons, and the distinction of place, are convertible with respect to the highest poetry without injuring it as poetry; and the choruses of Aeschylus, and the book of Job, and Dante's Paradise, would afford, more than any other writings, examples of this fact.... The creations of sculpture, painting, and music, are illustrations still more decisive.[41]

There is here a strong tinge of neo-Platonism, particularly in the notion that the poet penetrates to the eternal realities beyond the shadowy images to which ordinary mortals are restricted. This view, with its almost mystical image of the poet enjoying a kind of beatific vision, carries obvious dangers for poetry. On the one hand, the poet is tempted to ecstatic contemplation; on the other, he is burdened with a sense of ineffability. On the one hand, we have poems like *The Witch of Atlas* which celebrate an elusive kind of divinity which Shelley detected in the world, or the final act of *Prometheus Unbound* which aspires to the condition of Dante's *Paradiso* in its attempt to evoke the Shelleyan equivalent to the state of the blessed. On the other hand, we have Demogorgon's statement that 'a voice / Is wanting, the deep truth is imageless', or the deliberate failure to sustain the flight of *Epipsychidion*, or the conscious inadequacies of the lists of similes in *Epipsychidion* and 'To a Skylark'. If Dante is struck dumb in the simplicity of fire at the end of the *Paradiso*, so, too, frequently and characteristically, is Shelley.

It is instructive that, in this discussion of universality, Shelley should link poetry with sculpture, painting and music, none of which is forced to employ the medium of language, with the result that they elude the distinctions of grammar which lie in wait for the poet. It would not be fair to Shelley to infer that he regrets the necessity of using language; his letter to the inquiring lady shows clearly enough that he rejoiced in its flexibility and the way in which it imaged forth the subtlest operations of mind. Yet, in the *Defence*, Shelley seems to be aspiring towards a transcendence of grammar, which he regards with suspicion because it codifies feelings which had once been fresh, personal and original. This belief that the inherited structures of grammar impose their patterns of preconception on all those who employ a language will not be surprising to modern students of linguistics. Shelley, who had a properly revolutionary attitude to systems of all kinds, whether religious, political or grammatical, seems to have believed that this inherited pattern blunted his atempts at pure poetic achievement, diverted him from his aim to 'mark the before unapprehended relations of things'. In these conditions he turned to Dante (not the whole of the *Divine Comedy* but specifically the *Paradiso*), to the Book of Job, and to the *choruses* of Aeschylus.

What all three, and particularly the last two, have in common is what might be described as a continuous lyrical intensity. Plot, development, narrative line are of minimal importance; the essential aim is the expression of a state of mind or of being, whether of suffering as in Job and Aeschylus or of blessedness as in Dante. Another example of Shelley's ideal might be found in Chinese or Japanese poetry, which characteristically dispenses with tense, person and gender. Certainly Shelley would have found many of his desiderata in, say, a *haiku* by Basho; but this would not have satisfied him since what he described was to prolong this effect not over seventeen syllables but throughout a number of stanzas, or a whole poem of several hundred lines, if that were possible. This kind of poetry might very properly be described as lyrical; that is, it aspires to an actionless condition of pure poetic intensity. Generally, *lyrical* is used to describe a poem which expresses the poet's own thoughts and sentiments; this is much the way in which it is employed by Cleanth Brooks when he asserts that the romantic movement was 'too much centered in the personal and the lyrical'.[42] But for Shelley the main attraction of this kind of poetry lay precisely in the fact that it transcended the personal and moved into a poetic world beyond these limitations.

Yet, if Shelley was intent on eluding the categories of grammar, he was equally determined to avoid the confinements of fact. He makes this very clear in a passage in the *Defence of Poetry* where he is offering his own version of a doctrine first stated by Aristotle in the *Poetics*:

A poem is the very image of life expressed in its eternal truth. There is this difference between a story and a poem, that a story is a catalogue of detached facts, which have no other connexion than time, place, circumstance, cause, and effect; the other is the creation of actions according to the unchangeable forms of human nature, as existing in the mind of the Creator, which is itself the image of all other minds. The one is partial, and applies only to a definite period of time, and a certain combination of events which can never again recur; the other is universal, and contains within itself the germ of a relation to whatever motives or actions have place in the possible varieties of human nature. Time, which destroys the beauty and the use of the story of particular facts, stripped of the poetry which should invest them, augments that of poetry, and for ever develops new and wonderful applications of the eternal truth which it contains. . . . A story of particular facts is as a mirror which obscures and distorts that which should be beautiful: poetry is a mirror which makes beautiful that which is distorted.[43]

This impassioned and highly imagistic piece of exposition bears some resemblance to Coleridge both in style and in some of its assertions but its primary debt is to Aristotle (and to Sidney who followed him quite closely on this point). Shelley would have agreed with Aristotle that poetry is more philosophical than history, since it expresses the universal rather than the particular. Far from offering an alluring but deceitful imitation or removing itself from life, poetry *is* 'the very image of life', but with the significant qualification that this image is 'expressed in its eternal truth'.

There is a famous description of the poetic process in *Prometheus Unbound* which develops the implications of this statement:

> On a Poet's lips I slept
> Dreaming like a love-adept
> In the sound his breathing kept;
> Nor seeks nor finds he mortal blisses,
> But feeds on the aërial kisses
> Of shapes that haunt thought's wildernesses.
> He will watch from dawn to gloom
> The lake-reflected sun illume
> The yellow bees i' the ivy-bloom,
> Nor heed nor see what things they be;
> But from these create he can
> Forms more real than living man,
> Nurslings of immortality!
>
> (I. 737–49)

Notoriously, it is widely believed that Shelley found the source of poetry in emotion rather than in thought but here, as in 'To a Skylark', he specifically connects the poetic process with thought. Though there is an aura of the phantasmal and the elusive in the 'shapes that haunt thought's wildernesses', these *shapes* are positive and should be identified with the 'benignant visitings', 'the vanishing apparitions which haunt the interlunations of life' in the *Defence of Poetry*. There is, too, a fostering relationship between these shapes and the poet, who is favoured by their 'aëreal kisses' rather as the lips of Homer were gently touched by bees as he slept in his cradle. The images of poetry are also watched over with parental solicitude: they too are the 'nurslings of immortality'.

Perhaps the most significant detail is the way in which the bees are illuminated by the sun as it glances off the waters of the lake. For Shelley reflections in water were often deceptive: as he put it in one of his prose fragments, they 'surpass and misrepresent truth.'[44] Before the revolution in *Prometheus Unbound* man is 'a many-sided mirror, / Which could distort to many a shape of error / This true fair world of things . . .', but after Jupiter has been overthrown and his perceptions are no longer distorted by fear and hate he becomes 'a sea reflecting love'. The reflection of the sun in water is particularly significant. In Shelley's symbolical world, heavily influenced as it was by Plato and the neo-Platonists, this symbol seems to have been connected with the beautiful appearances of the natural world, attractive but essentially illusory, 'the painted veil which those who live / Call Life'. The water reflects the sun but distorts it and disperses its concentrated force so that, for all its radiance, it only presents us with a shadowy representation of the real sun. Shelley makes use of this symbol in a number of his poems, most notably perhaps in *The Triumph of Life* where 'the Sun's image radiantly intense / Burned on the waters' (lines 345–6) with such seductive force that many critics have mistakenly believed that Shelley intended it for the real sun. So what is at issue in the passage about the poet in *Prometheus Unbound* is the limited nature of sense impressions (represented by the lake-reflected sun illumining the bees) as opposed to the creative force of imaginative perception (shapes that haunt thought's wildernesses). According to this theory, the poet does not keep his eye fixed firmly on the object; rather, he recreates the object according to the more perfect patterns of the imaginative world.

Shelley had a highly developed sense of genre and he was quite aware that this procedure would not be appropriate for satire, or political verse or more personal poetry (such as verse epistles). But in the poetry of beautiful idealisms, the highest kind of poetry, the poet had to transcend the limitations of particularity. Though the reflections in the water 'surpass' the truth they also 'misrepresent' it; in contrast, the poet achieves a higher kind of reality than that available to the common eye ('Forms more real than living man'). It is important to realise that although this approach specifically eschewed realism, the mere collection of particulars, it never disavowed reality which it hoped to approximate as closely as possible. Realism was a distortion or, at best, a limitation of reality. However, it was possible to go beyond the merely mimetic and to recreate nature through the plastic power of the imagination. Here Shelley was in accord with Plotinus, and with Philostratus, who said that great works of art are produced not by imitation (the

Aristotelian *mimesis*) but by imagination (*phantasia*), 'a wiser creator than imitation, for imitation copies what it has seen, imagination what it has not seen'.[45]

The resemblances to neo-Platonic theory are too close to be merely an accident, although it is quite possible that Shelley absorbed them indirectly through Coleridge and others. However, the insistence on avoiding particularity also has a ring about it which might remind one of such central theorists of the eighteenth century as Joshua Reynolds and Dr Johnson. It is worth recalling that Shelley's account of his training and qualifications to be a poet in the Preface to *The Revolt of Islam* bears some highly specific resemblances to Imlac's dissertation on poetry in chapter X of Johnson's *Rasselas*. Although Shelley was recounting his own experiences, the manner and the preconceptions of his *curriculum vitae* betray an obvious debt to Johnson. Indeed, Shelley's celebrated claim in the *Defence of Poetry* that poets are the unacknowledged legislators of the world may also derive from the same chapter, where Imlac declares that the poet 'must write as the interpreter of nature, and the legislator of mankind'. Again, in this same dissertation, Imlac puts forward the doctrine of generality:

The business of a poet, said Imlac, is to examine, not the individual, but the species; to remark general properties and large appearances: he does not number the streaks of the tulip, or describe the different shades in the verdure of the forest. He is to exhibit in his portraits of nature such prominent and striking features, as recal the original to every mind; and must neglect the minuter discriminations, which one may have remarked, and another have neglected, for those characteristicks, which are alike obvious to vigilance and carelessness.

For streaks of the tulip read yellow bees in the ivy bloom. Shelley's formulation is more transcendental and bases itself primarily on the creative power of the imagination; it is a more positive view which strikes a greater claim for poetry. And yet this almost religious response to the powers of the imagination is related, in part at least, to an eighteenth-century belief that the poet should concern himself with the whole rather than the parts, with the species rather than the individual. Here the neo-Platonists and Dr Johnson touch hands and here Shelley takes up his position.

Poetry is an ideal creation which gives us back an ideal world, a world transformed by imagination. Shelley wrote: 'It [poetry] creates anew the universe, after it has been annihilated in our minds by the recurrence of impressions blunted by reiteration. It justifies the bold and true word of Tasso: *Non merita nome di creatore, se non Iddio ed il Poeta*.'[46] If the poet is to live up to this high appellation of creator, if he is to deliver only a golden world in place of a brazen, it follows that he must rise above the limitations of his own character as a man: 'A poet, as he is the author to others of the highest wisdom, pleasure, virtue and glory, so he ought personally to be the happiest, the best, the wisest, and the most illustrious of men.' So he ought, and so he is, 'inasmuch as he is a poet' (that is, a true poet). Of course, Shelley was well aware of the usual imputations against the morality of poets: 'Let us assume that Homer was a drunkard, that Virgil was a flatterer, that Horace was a coward, that Tasso was a madman, that Lord Bacon was a peculator, that Raphael was a libertine, that Spenser was a poet laureate.' Even if these rumours were true, posterity has now done ample justice to these great creators:

Their errors have been weighed and found to have been dust in the balance; if their sins 'were as scarlet, they are now white as snow': they have been washed in the blood of the mediator and redeemer, time. Observe in what a ludicrous chaos the imputations of real or fictitious crime have been confused in the contemporary calumnies against poetry and poets; consider how little is, as it appears—or appears, as it is; look to your own motives, and judge not, lest ye be judged.[47]

Here, of course, Shelley is using the Bible against the hypocrites—the reviewers of the *Quarterly* and of *Blackwood's*, readers who were all too quick to cast the first stone. They are guilty, says Shelley, of a fundamental error; they confuse the man with the poet, or, perhaps one might say, they confuse the poet with the poem. Shelley proceeds to defend the moral character of poets, perhaps even beyond the call of duty when he claims that, whatever their weaknesses of character, they have never been accused of 'cruelty, envy, revenge, avarice, and the passions purely evil'. Yet his basic point is that there is a distinction between the poet when he is creating his poem under the influence of inspiration ('the interpenetration of a diviner nature through our own') and the poet when he is uninspired: in fact, 'The poet & the man are two different natures'.[48] Shelley would have accepted Yeats's statement that the poet is 'never the bundle of accident and incoherence that sits down to breakfast; he has been reborn as an idea, something intended, complete'.[94] Therefore, just as it is wrong for the critic to appraise the poem in the light of the private life of the poet, so it is wrong for the poet himself to introduce his personal idiosyncracies or his private griefs into his poetry, insofar as they remain merely personal or private.

On one of the very few occasions when he broke this rule and published something which seemed too closely related to a sorrow which was merely personal, he found it necessary to apologise:

If any one is inclined to condemn the insertion of the introductory lines, which image forth the sudden relief of a state of deep despondency by the radiant visions disclosed by the sudden burst of an Italian sunrise in autumn on the highest peak of those delighted mountains, I can only offer as my excuse that they were not erased at the request of a dear friend, with whom added years of intercourse only add to my apprehension of its value, and who would have had more right than anyone to complain, that she has not been able to extinguish in me the very power of delineating sadness.[50]

This apology has interested a recent critic who comments: 'On the face of it, this apology is needless, for a poet does not have to apologize for writing despondent lines',[51] from which he deduces that the true reason for the apology is that the lines are highly personal and concern Mary. Yet surely Shelley is apologising not so much for a personal indiscretion as for a breach of literary decorum. He is addressing himself not to Mary but to the reading public. Had he wished to apologise for being indiscreet, he would not have compounded the offence by doing so in public, thus drawing everybody's attention to the private nature of what he had written. The prefatory note seems to indicate that it was against his own better judgement that the offending lines were published and the defence which he offers is based not on literary grounds but on the claims of affection. In other words, Shelley can offer no defence which is acceptable in terms of literary principle.

The issue is slightly complicated by the fact that he is uneasy not only about the personal nature of these lines but also about their despondency. Near the end of the poem he evokes with great precision and yet with a kind of visionary insight an Italian afternoon in which both he and the landscape seem to be miraculously united, 'interpenetrated' by the glory of the sky; this brightness illuminates 'my spirit which so long / Darkened this swift stream of song' (lines 311–12). Here then Shelley admits that, up to this point, his mood of dejection has overshadowed his poem; yet this kind of dejection is essential to the progress of the poem and must be distinguished from the despondency for which he apologises in the prefatory advertisement. That is purely personal, merely domestic, whereas the despondency which predominates in 'Lines Written among the Euganean Hills' is generated by reflections on human misery, in particular by Shelley's glimpses of Italian history from his vantage point in the mountains. Yet even this kind of sadness must be resisted or transcended, if possible. For Shelley was perfectly in earnest when he said: 'Poetry is the record of the best and happiest moments of the happiest and best minds.'

(v)

The whole trend of Shelley's thinking about poetry drew him away from the particularities of individual experience, unless it was transmuted into the impersonality of art, alchemised into potable gold. This attitude was derived partly from his speculations on metaphysics and partly from his acquaintance with literary theory but, binding these together and providing the central force and impetus, was yet another area of concern—the realm of politics. Shelley seems to have been born with a strong sense of social responsibility, which conditioned his attitude towards poetry. As a later chapter will show, his views on the way in which the poet might interpret his social responsibilities underwent some subtle and interesting changes, but it still remains true that throughout his life Shelley regarded the writing of poetry as primarily a political function. What a poet wrote could potentially affect the way in which people lived their lives; it followed that poetry should not be written in an idle spirit, nor for amusement, but with a high and serious purpose. Of course, there was no reason why one should not write poetry for one's own purposes, provided one did not make it public; but the true poet had a duty to restrain himself, to issue his poems not in the interests of self-expression but with an eye towards the betterment of society. As Shelley told Godwin rather self-righteously, 'I therefore write, and I publish because I will publish nothing that shall not conduce to virtue . . .'[52]

Given these high ideals, Shelley recognised that his greatest adversaries both within and without, were self and selfishness. From the earliest days of his correspondence with Hogg, Godwin and Elizabeth Hitchener Shelley had identified his enemy: 'I am sick to death at the name of *self* . . . that *hateful* principle'.[53] In 1811 he tells Hogg: 'Solitude is most horrible; in despite of *aphilautia* [lack of self-love] which perhaps vanity has a great share in, but certainly not with my own good will I cannot endure the horror the evil which comes to *self* in solitude.' The Greek word *aphilautia* was apparently invented by Shelley after he had read and translated part of Aristotle's *Ethics* which discussed *philautia* or self-love. That Shelley felt the need to create this word is an interesting indication of the direction of his thoughts. Later in the same letter he comes back to the theme with an intensity which is almost melodramatic:

what [a] strange being I am, how inconsistent, in spite of all my bo[a]sted hatred of self—this moment thinking I could so far overcome Natures law as to exist in complete seclusion, the next shrinking from a moment of solitude, starting from my own company as it were that of a fiend, seeking any thing rather than a continued communion with *self*——[54]

Apparently, the enemy was within; Shelley concluded that 'the most exalted philosophy, the truest wisdom, consists in an habitual contempt of self',[55] and devoted much of his energy to a life-long attempt at exorcism. In August 1819 he complained to Leigh Hunt about '*self*, that burr that will stick to one. I can't get it off yet.'[56] And in July 1821, writing to Byron about *Adonais*, he was still rueful: 'And perhaps I have erred from the narrow view of considering Keats rather as he surpassed *me* in particular, than as he was inferior to others; so subtle is the principle of self!'[57] If he was to achieve those objectives to which he was so committed, it was necessary to counteract these insinuating pressures of self.

The battle-lines are clearly drawn in a letter of 1811 to Elizabeth Hitchener. In this he postulates two varieties of love: one is 'self-centred self-devoted self-interested' while the other is

Virtue Heaven disinterestedness, in a word friendship, which has as much to do with the senses as with yonder mountains—that which seeks the good of all; the good of its object first, not because that object is a minister to *its* pleasures, not merely because it even contributes to its happiness; but because it is really worthy, because it has power sensibilities is capable of abstracting self and loving virtue for Virtue's own loveliness, desiring the happiness of others *not* from the obligation of fearing Hell or desiring Heaven, but for pure simple unsophisticated Virtue.[58]

The consequence of this analysis was a direct antithesis in Shelley's philosophy between love and the principle of self. The implications extended far beyond the range of personal relations. The same necessity to escape from the bondage of self applied to those who hoped to make a significant contribution in politics. As Shelley wrote to Godwin from Dublin, where he had been engaged in a variety of political activities: 'Wholly to abstract our views from self undoubtedly requires unparalelled disinterestedness, there is not a completer abstraction than laboring for distant ages.'[59] A similar disinterestedness was required for the writing of poetry: the obvious lack of it caused Shelley to deplore the selfishness of some of his earlier poetry: 'As to the stuff which I sent you, I write all my poetry of that kind from the feelings of the moment—if therefore it neither has allusion to the sentiments which rationally might be supposed to possess me, or to those which my situation might awaken, it is another proof of that egotizing variability whilst I shudder when I reflect how much I am in its power.'[60]

Recognising the assaults of self from within, Shelley was sharply alerted to its existence in the outside world. The Roman empire, for example, had been founded on a system of selfishness, a system in which the master overvalued himself at the expense of his servants or his slaves, whom he undervalued. This was the basis of all tyrannical and unjust societies when considered from an ethical viewpoint: and to Shelley politics was primarily a matter of ethics, although he had an excellently intuitive understanding of economic and social factors. Even the failure of the Industrial Revolution to increase the sum of human happiness could be attributed, along with the other excesses and imbalances of a capitalist economy, to 'an excess of the selfish and calculating principle'.[61] In order to give full expression to the multifarious ways in which this selfish principle could operate, Shelley evolved a whole terminology, which included words such as *self-contempt*, *self-despising*, *self-flattering*, and *self-mistrust*. This special vocabulary enabled him to explore some of the more interesting forms of selfishness, notably *self-contempt*, an affliction which prevents man from realising his own true potential and which Shelley detected everywhere in the 'age of despair' which followed the failure of the French Revolution. *Self-contempt*, which is to be distinguished from *contempt of self*, was not merely a private matter, of interest only to those who suffer from it, for it could all too easily turn outwards into '... Hate— that shapeless fiendly thing / Of many names, all evil, some divine, / Whom self-contempt arms with a mortal sting ...' (*Revolt of Islam*, 3379–81).

This is the weakness to which Beatrice Cenci succumbs; it is one of the temptations which Prometheus is able to resist. In the *Revolt of Islam* Cythna prescribes a remedy in resonant terms:

> Reproach not thine own soul, but know thyself,
> Nor hate another's crime, nor loathe thine own.
> It is the dark idolatry of self,
>   Which, when our thoughts and actions once are gone,
>   Demands that man should weep, and bleed, and groan;
> O vacant expiation! Be at rest.—
>   The past is Death's, the future is thine own;
>   And love and joy can make the foulest breast
> A paradise of flowers, where peace might build her nest.
>   (lines 3388–96)

Self-contempt and its outward projection, hate, are both products of the dark idolatry of self. If that grim religion can once be overthrown and man can see himself for what potentially he might be, the idols can be broken, the fiend expelled from the garden and a paradise regained within.

Having identified *selfishness* as the corrupting principle both in private behaviour and in society at large, Shelley directed his energies towards negating its influence. This involved writing pamphlets, making speeches and directly concerning himself with a variety of political activities but it related even more centrally to his aims as a poet. Believing as he did that poetry could help to redeem the state of society, that it was potentially a messenger which could bring 'sweet news of kindred joy' to the hearts of its readers, Shelley allotted to the poet the all-important role of breaking down the monstrous régime of self, releasing the individual from the prison of his solitude and relating man to man as brother to brother.

The responsibility of the individual poet was a heavy burden, though a glorious one. It was essential that he should conquer his own weaknesses, trample down the insubordinate stirrings of self. As we have seen, Shelley himself acknowledged the constant temptations, the difficulty involved in detaching himself from the tenacious burr of self. He could see the process at work in his contemporaries, too. In the Preface to *Julian and Maddalo* he detects the symptoms in Maddalo, who bears obvious resemblances to Byron:

His ambition preys upon itself, for want of objects which it can consider worthy of exertion. I say that Maddalo is proud, because I can find no other word to express the concentered and impatient feelings which consume him; but it is on his own hopes and affections only that he seems to trample, for in social life no human being can be more gentle, patient, and unassuming than Maddalo.

Hence Maddalo's reluctance to accept Julian's belief in the possibilities of man's controlling his own fate; hence the periodic misanthropy of *Childe Harold*.[62] The key word in this analysis is *concentered*, a word which Shelley probably took from Byron himself who had declared that the human spirit is like that of Prometheus 'an equal to all woes', possessing 'a firm will, and a deep sense, / Which even in torture can descry / Its own concentred recompense'. For all its heroism, its tight-lipped self-sufficiency, Shelley was disappointed by this attitude, which perpetuated the isolation of man. 'Concentered' implies the very imprisonment in self which Shelley wished to eliminate.[63]

A somewhat different version of the problem could be seen in Wordsworth. In spite of its tone, Shelley's satire *Peter Bell the Third* is a poem which offers a serious critique of Wordsworth both as man and as poet. Shelley had always recognised the extraordinary virtues of Wordsworth's poetry and those he generously acknowledges, but he also suggests that they were intimately connected with a dangerous limitation:

> He had a mind which was somehow
>   At once circumference and centre
> Of all he might or feel or know;
> Nothing went ever out, although
>   Something did ever enter.
>
> He had as much imagination
>   As a pint-pot:—he never could
> Fancy another situation,
> From which to dart his contemplation,
>   Than that wherein he stood.
>
> Yet his was individual mind,
>   And new created all he saw
> In a new manner. and refined
> Those new creations, and combined
>   Them, by a master-spirit's law.
>
> Thus—though unimaginative—
>   An apprehension clear, intense,
> Of his mind's work, had made alive
> The things it wrought on; I believe,
>   Wakening a sort of thought in sense.

Here Shelley seems to be saying that Wordsworth is almost an exception to his rule, a poet devoid of imagination, incapable of projecting himself and yet undeniably responsive to the outward world. 'He had as much imagination / As a pint-pot' may, among other things, imply a kind of stolidity which is unable to yield itself to the true Bacchic intoxication of inspiration, a tough reserve which insists on holding on to itself. Clearly Shelley does not want to deny the greatness of the early poetry, yet he suggests that the very poetry contains the seeds both of Wordsworth's failure of inspiration and of his eventual conservatism. The Distributor of Stamps might nearly have been deduced from the *Lyrical Ballads*. So the poet has a difficult task if he is to elude the clutches of self. Not only must he try to escape from self-concentration, he must also open himself to the achievements of others. The cultivated imagination is the enemy of selfishness:

The only distinction between the selfish man and the virtuous man is that the imagination of the former is confined within a narrow limit, while that of the latter embraces a comprehensive circumference. In this sense wisdom and virtue may be said to be inseparable and criteria of each other. Selfishness is thus the offspring of ignorance and mistake . . . disinterested benevolence is the product of a cultivated imagination and has an intimate connection with all the arts which add ornament, or dignity, or power, or stability to the social state of man.[64]

Shelley's own intellectual history, which involved reading in and translation from no fewer than six languages, provides one excellent illustration. But the cultivated imagination is required in the reader of poetry as well as in the poet; without this collaboration poetry can have no influence on the state of society. If we are truly responsive, poetry disperses 'the dull vapours of the little world of self', opens our minds, expands our consciousness, 'enlarges the circumference of the imagination'. It will not permit us to remain concentered, bundled up in self: it 'distends, and then bursts the circumference of the reader's mind, and pours itself forth together with it into the universal element with which it has perpetual sympathy'. Again, more specifically, Shelley describes how 'The imagination is enlarged by a sympathy with pains and passions so mighty, that they distend in their conception the capacity of that by which they are conceived, the good affections are strengthened by pity, indignation, terror and sorrow; and an exalted calm is prolonged . . .' The little world is exchanged for the big one, microcosm for macrocosm and 'self appears as what it is, an atom to a universe'.

In fact, poetry operates on much the same principle as love:

The great secret of morals is love; or a going out of our own nature, and an identification of ourselves with the beautiful which exists in thought, action, or person, not our own. A man, to be greatly good, must imagine intensely and comprehensively; he must put himself in the place of another and of many others; the pains and pleasures of his species must become his own. The great instrument of moral good is the imagination; and poetry administers to the effect by acting upon the cause.[65]

That is why Shelley could not accept the advice which Keats offered him to 'curb his magnanimity and practise self-concentration'.[66] As Shelley saw it, the poet was engaged in the high endeavour of attempting to save human society from its enemies: 'Poetry, and the principle of Self, of which money is the visible incarnation, are the God and Mammon of the world.'[87] In such a momentous confrontation there could never be any doubt where his duty lay.

Notes to chapter two

1 *P.W.*, p. xi. See also *P. W.*, p. 825 for an explanation.

2 *Letters*, II. 310.

3 'Tradition and the Individual Talent', *Selected Essays*, Faber and Faber, 3rd ed., 1951, p. 21; *Modern Poetry and the Tradition*, University of North Carolina Press, Chapel Hill, 1967, p. 237.

4 *Shelley's Religion*, 1937, p. 280.

5 Jean Overton Fuller, *Shelley*, Cape, 1968, p. 266. There are also metaphorical possibilities (cf. *De Rerum Natura*, IV. 1133–4, which refers to the bitterness in the fountain of pleasures).

6 Cleanth Brooks and Robert Penn Warren, *Understanding Poetry*, rev. ed., Henry Holt, New York, 1958, pp. 174–6. Edward Bostetter detects in the poem Shelley's usual role of 'passivity and masochism' and draws the following conclusion: 'It was this sort of suggestion of the power of the woman and the weakness of the male that I suspect was responsible for much of the tremendous appeal that Shelley had for the Victorian woman' (*The Romantic Ventriloquists*, pp. 212, 215).

7 *Letters*, II. 50.

8 Clark, *Prose*, p. 201.

9 Leavis, *Letters in Criticism*, ed. John Tasker, Chatto and Windus, 1974, p. 143.

10 Frederick A. Pottle, 'The Case of Shelley' in *English Romantic Poets*, ed. M. H. Abrams, 1965, p. 292. Pottle goes on to quote Psalms 43:2, but his case is slightly weakened by the fact that he does not quote from the Authorised Version which is the version used by Shelley.

11 Cited by Harold Bloom, *Shelley's Mythmaking*, 1959, p. 86.

12 Bostetter, *The Romantic Ventriloquists*, p. 216.

13 *Paradiso*, I. 70–2. Compare Shelley's 'the deep truth is imageless'.

14 Bod. MS. Shelley adds. e. 8, pp. 131–2, e. 6, p. 143v and *The Shelley Notebooks*, ed. H. B. Forman, II. 119–22.

15 *Nemean*, 3, 80–2, cited from *The Odes of Pindar*, tr. by Richmond Lattimore, University of Chicago Press, 1960, p. 103.

16 *The Revolt of Islam*, lines 544–5.

17 *Letters*, II. 384, 437; cited in Matthews, 'Shelley's Lyrics', p. 198. The statistics are also largely derived from Matthews.

18 *Letters*, II. 306, 246.

19 *Defence*, p. 27.

20 *Revelation*, 16: 17.

21 *Defence*, p. 59.

22 *Defence*, p. 27. See 'The Science of Metaphysics', *Prose*, pp. 182 ff.

23 Bod. MS. Shelley adds. e. 12, pp. 159–60. There is a version of this in *P.W.*, pp. 428–9. Two possible sources for Shelley are Pindar, fr. 137 (Bowra) and Lucretius, *De Rerum Natura*, I. 736–9 ('in making many excellent and inspired discoveries they have given responses as it were from the holy place of the heart, with more sanctity and far more certainty than the Pythia who speaks forth from Apollo's tripod and laurel').

24 *Defence*, p. 53.
25 Cited from Notopoulos, *Platonism*, p. 450.
26 The MS. draft refers to 'Homer & his bretheren' (Reiman, *The Triumph of Life*, p. 173).
27 *Shelley and his Circle*, II. 785; Clark, *Prose*, pp. 209, 67.
28 *Letters*, II. 58.
29 For a detailed list, see Cameron, *Shelley: The Golden Years*, p. 614.
30 Clark, *Prose*, p. 307.
31 'Tradition and the Individual Talent', *Selected Essays*, pp. 21, 18.
32 *Letters*, II. 434.
33 *Letters*, II. 262–3.
34 Preface to *Epipsychidion*, *P. W.*, p. 411.
35 *Letters*, II. 277.
36 *Defence*, pp. 27–8.
37 *Defence*, pp. 28–9.
38 *P.W.*, p. 272.
39 Clark, *Prose*, p. 174.
40 Clark, *Prose*, p. 174. Cf. *Hellas*, lines 766–85.
41 *Defence*, p. 27.
42 *Modern Poetry and the Tradition*, p. 217.
43 *Defence*, pp. 30–1.
44 Clark, *Prose*, p. 337.
45 W. R. Inge quoted by Notopoulos, *Platonism*, p. 349.
46 *Defence*, p. 56. ('No one merits the name of creator but God and the Poet.')
47 *Defence*, p. 57.
48 *Letters*, II. 310.
49 'A General Introduction for my Work', *Essays and Introductions*, Macmillan, 1961, p. 509.
50 Clark, *Prose*, p. 320.
51 Cameron, *Shelley: The Golden Years*, p. 267.
52 *Letters*, I. 259.
53 *Letters*, I. 34.
54 *Letters*, I. 77–8.
55 Cf. Shelley on Claire Clairmont: '. . . she is not entirely insensible to concessions; new proofs that the most exalted philosophy, the truest virtue, consists in an habitual contempt of self; a subduing of all angry feelings; a sacrifice of pride and selfishness' (*Journal*, p. 20).
56 *Letters*, II. 109.
57 *Letters*, II. 309.
58 *Letters*, I. 173.
59 *Letters*, I. 277.
60 *Letters*, I. 43–4.
61 *Defence*, p. 53. For an explication of these matters, see Cameron, *Shelley: The Golden Years*.
62 Shelley regarded the Fourth Canto as the product of Byronic self-contempt rather than misanthropy: 'The spirit in which it is written is, if insane, the most wicked & mischievous insanity that ever was given forth. It is a kind of obstinate & selfwilled folly in which he hardens himself. I remonstrated with him in vain on the tone of mind from which such a view of things alone arises. For its real root is very different from its apparent one, & nothing can be less sublime than the true source of these expressions of contempt & desperation' (*Letters*, II. 58).
63 Byron saw it differently: 'To withdraw *myself* from *myself* (oh that cursed

selfishness!) has ever been my sole, my entire, my sincere motive in scribbling at all; and publishing is also the continuance of the same object, by the action it affords to the mind, which else recoils upon itself' (*Letters and Journals*, ed. R. E. Prothero, 1898–1901, II. 351).

64 Clark, *Prose*, p. 189.
65 *Defence*, p. 33.
66 *The Letters of John Keats, 1813–1821*, ed. H. E. Rollins, Harvard University Press, Cambridge (Mass.), 1958, II. 322.
67 *Defence*, p. 52.

CHAPTER THREE

RESPONSIBILITIES

(i)

Politics were probably the dominating concern in Shelley's intellectual life. Though he sometimes longed to escape from 'the great sandy desert of Politics' into 'the odorous gardens of literature',[1] he was always responsive to the exigencies of the political element. This fact has never been widely acknowledged, and when the political dimension has been recognised it has generally been dismissed as insignificant. Even so perceptive a critic as Walter Bagehot was quite firm about this: 'Shelley's political opinions were ... the effervescence of his peculiar nature. The love of liberty is peculiarly natural to the simple impulsive mind. It feels irritated at the idea of a law; it fancies it does not need it: it really needs it less than other men.'[2]

That Shelley's political opinions could be taken so lightly by so sympathetic an interpreter indicates the persuasive strength of the biographical/critical tradition which has been traced in the first chapter. Our own century has discovered new significances in the poetry yet the prevailing image of Shelley is still politically castrated. Those who dismiss him tend to concentrate on his lyrics and occasional verses, conveniently ignoring his central preoccupations and his main achievements, while many of those who claim to be sympathetic effectively deny his political commitment by concentrating exclusively on the philosophical or metaphysical elements in his poetry. For some he is a kind of spiritual Houdini forever trying to find a quick way of escaping from the inconvenient box of the flesh, for others he is the great oscillator forever rolling the philosophical dice, sceptically aloof from permanent belief or commitment. For yet others his political interests are genuine but superficial. As F. W. Bateson puts it: 'The retreat from politics ... had been implicit in Shelley's poetry almost from the beginning. ... The political façade that Shelley's poems retain was a form of unconscious hypocrisy—the tribute of the escapist to the social conscience. They are pretending to be more serious than they really are.'[3]

Shelley would have been much surprised, and disappointed, by all of these responses. He once told Leigh Hunt that he had confidence in his moral sense alone;[4] and that sense was keenly attuned to the realities of nineteenth-century politics, politics being 'the morals of the nations'. In the Preface to *Prometheus Unbound* he publicly admitted to 'a passion for reforming the world' and most of his published works were written and printed with that end in view. *Queen Mab, The Revolt of Islam, Prometheus Unbound, The Mask of Anarchy, Peter Bell the Third, Swellfoot the Tyrant, Hellas, Charles the First* and *The Triumph of Life* are all concerned, directly or indirectly, with the world of politics. Other long poems such as *Julian and Maddalo, The Witch of Atlas, Adonais* and even *Alastor* have political implications which are readily demonstrable. To this one can add a wide range of shorter poems including, most notably perhaps, 'Lines Written among the Euganean Hills', 'England in 1819', 'Ode to the West Wind', 'Ode to Liberty', 'Ode to Naples' and 'Lines Written on Hearing the News of the Death of Napoleon'. Shelley also produced a number of pamphlets and essays on political matters, the most important being *A Philosophical View of Reform*, for which he was seeking a publisher in the summer of 1820. If this catalogue of Shelley's writings were not sufficient to show that his interest in politics was more than a mere façade, the evidence of his letters and of his reading lists would amply prove the point. From his Oxford days to the end of his life, Shelley was acutely aware of the political dimension. The *Posthumous Fragments of Margaret Nicholson* (1810) and the poems in the *Esdaile Notebook* include a number of youthfully indignant pieces on war, revolutionary politics and grim social realities (one poem is entitled 'A Tale of Society as it is: from facts'); while Shelley's last major poem, left unfinished at his death, was *The Triumph of Life*, which presented among other things a bleak survey of European political history.

In his correspondence, too, politics were a constant topic; only nine days before his death he analysed the state of contemporary England feelingly and with insight:

It seems to me that things have now arrived at such a crisis as requires every man plainly to utter his sentiments on the inefficacy of the existing religions no less than political systems for restraining & guiding mankind. Let us see the truth whatever that may be ... England appears to be in a desperate condition, Ireland still worse, & no class of those who subsist on the public labour will be persuaded that *their claims* on it must be diminished. But the government must content itself with less in taxes, the landholder must submit to receive less rent, & the fundholder a diminished interest,—or they will all get nothing, or something worse [than] nothing.—I once thought to study these affairs & write or act in them—I am glad that my good genius said *refrain*. I see little public virtue, & I foresee that the contest will be one of blood & gold two elements, which however much to my taste in my pockets & my veins, I have an objection to out of them.[5]

In spite of the declared relief that he had not been directly involved with political action, these are clearly the words of a man who thought deeply about politics and to whom they were an inescapable and personal concern.

In fact, Shelley concerned himself with politics even in the most unlikely circumstances. An anecdote in Leigh Hunt's *Autobiography* illustrates this very well:

It was a moot point when he entered your room, whether he would begin with some half-pleasant, half-pensive joke, or quote something Greek, or ask some question about public affairs. He once came upon me at Hampstead, when I had not seen him for some time, and after grasping my hands with both his, in his usual fervent manner, he sat down, and looked at me very earnestly, with a deep, though not melancholy, interest in his face. We were sitting with our knees to the fire, to which he had been getting nearer and nearer, in the comfort of finding ourselves together. The pleasure of seeing him was my only feeling at the moment; and the air of domesticity about us was so complete, that I thought he was going to speak of some family matter, either his or my own, when he asked me, at the close of an intensity of pause, what was 'the amount of the national debt'.[6]

This, of course, was the young Shelley, recognisably the same man who had launched his message to the world in bottles and air-balloons, engaged in an earnest correspondence with William Godwin, actively assisted in land reclamation at Tremadoc, and taken a courageous and public part in the Irish struggle for independence. This Shelley had walked a hospital so that he might be able to offer practical assistance to the impoverished lace-workers of Marlow; he even considered becoming a doctor because this might afford 'greater opportunities for alleviating the sufferings of humanity'.[7] This concern never deserted him. Several years later he found that his delight in the natural beauty and the artistic heritage of Italy was undermined by the sight of chained convicts hoeing out the weeds in St Peter's Square.[8] He was profoundly affected by the sight of people's faces in the street, by the 'marks of weakness, marks of woe' as Blake called them while, according to

Trelawny, the sound of the wind in the pine tops reminded him of 'the eternal wailing of wretched men'.[9]

His imagination was highly politicised. Characteristically he translated actions, events, sometimes even objects, into political terms. The family, for example, could be classified as a political organisation: in *The Cenci* the Count plays the role of a tyrant, and parental authority and tyrannical power are seen to depend on each other. It is essential to the Pope and to authority outside the family that the father should have absolute control over his daughter, since any weakening of his power is a weakening of the whole system. Again, the educational system could be interpreted as a miniature model of the larger political system: the schoolroom was an area for 'The harsh and grating strife of tyrants and of foes'.[10] It is easy to laugh at this and to feel superior to the ingenuous young poet as he rescues Harriet Westbrook from the bondage of her boarding school in Clapham; but, stripped of its rhetoric, Shelley's insight was exceptionally acute, as contemporary educationists might agree.

If the school repeated the pattern of the political system and inculcated the peculiar morality by which it subsisted, so too did the Bible. As Shelley saw it, the orthodox view of the Devil presented him as an *agent provocateur* working on the side of the government.[11] Even a garden could prompt political thoughts, as it might have done in the Renaissance: in one of the drafts of *The Sensitive Plant* Shelley describes the garden as 'a Republic of odours and hues'.[12] That Shelley could think so habitually and so naturally in political terms was not merely the result of sensibility or of youthful impetuosity: his view of politics was intelligent and well-informed, as a reading of *A Philosophical View of Reform* would immediately demonstrate. He watched carefully and anxiously the turbulent events which were taking place around him in Italy while, through the periodicals, he kept in touch with the latest developments in England. At the same time he also read extensively in political theory and in world history. Thus, his reflections on 'the war of the oppressed against the oppressors' were the product not only of personal experience and observation but of reading in a number of languages, spanning several thousand years of history.

More important, Shelley's political concern is at the back of most of his significant poetry. Even when he might seem to have escaped temporarily into a world which was less threatening, politics would surface alarmingly. In the summer of 1820 he produced his *Letter to Maria Gisborne*, a charming, urbane and witty verse epistle, in which

he sets out to delight and amuse his correspondent with charming word
pictures and exuberant flights of imagistic invention. Here, if any-
where, one might expect him to take a holiday from the pressing
realities of politics. Indeed, the poem has no difficulty in recreating the
Italian scene in precise and loving detail :

> I recall
> My thoughts, and bid you look upon the night.
> As water does a sponge, so the moonlight
> Fills the void, hollow, universal air—
> What see you? unpavilioned heaven is fair,
> Whether the moon, into her chamber gone,
> Leaves midnight to the golden stars, or wan
> Climbs with diminished beams the azure steep,
> Or whether clouds sail o'er the inverse deep
> Piloted by the many-wandering blast,
> And the rare stars rush through them dim and fast—
> All this is beautiful in every land . . .
>
> (lines 253–64)

There is a characteristic fluency about this and an easy panache (as
for example in the strikingly original yet apt image for the moonlight).
Gently, almost imperceptibly, Shelley has begun to make the transition
from Leghorn to London; but the night sky, the stars and the moon,
present a picture which still is lullingly calm and beautiful. Then,
suddenly and brutally, the dream is broken :

> But what see you beside?—a shabby stand
> Of hackney coaches, a brick house or wall
> Fencing some lordly court, white with the scrawl
> Of our unhappy politics; or worse—
> A wretched woman reeling by, whose curse
> Mixed with the watchman's, partner of her trade,
> You must accept in place of serenade . . .
>
> (lines 265–71)

This is sharp, graphic, unsentimentally observed; the style is as
direct as the subject-matter is grimly realistic. What makes it more
effective is a double contrast with what has gone before : a contrast
with the natural beauty of the nocturnal setting and with the gentle,
colourful and 'poetic' style in which it is evoked. The mythological,
fanciful world of the first—the moon gone into her chamber, the sailing
clouds, the animated stars—is replaced by the dark actualities of 'our
unhappy politics'—a drunken prostitute and a representative of the

system, which, in Hunt's words, 'seems to despise it, and which, in more opinions than his, is a main cause of it'.[13] The beauties of the natural scene are followed by the harsher features of urban life—hackney stands, brick houses, lonely squares, graffiti emblematic of discontent. The *Letter to Maria Gisborne* soon returns to the charm of the Italian scene:

> Beyond, the surface of the unsickled corn
> Trembles not in the slumbering air—and borne
> In circles quaint, and ever-changing dance,
> Like wingèd stars the fire-flies flash and glance
> Pale in the open moonshine, but each one
> Under the dark trees seems a little sun,
> A meteor tamed, a fixed star gone astray . . .
>   (lines 278–84)

Yet the image of London is a potent one, the most impressive example of that ballast of discontent which consistently prevents Shelley from escaping into more Elysian realms. He was one of 'those to whom the miseries of the world / Are misery, and will not let them rest' (*The Fall of Hyperion*, ll. 148–9).

An even better illustration than the verse epistle is *The Witch of Atlas*. This poem offended Shelley's wife, who felt that it was too ethereal and lacked 'human interest'; he even included six introductory stanzas in which he defended himself against her criticism. But he did not defend himself on the grounds that he was being realistic, nor did he make any grandiose claims for his poem, confining himself to a plea for indulgence: 'Prithee, for this one time, / Content thee with a visionary rhyme'. Obviously *The Witch of Atlas* was intended as a form of light relief, a temporary escape from cares and responsibility: like Mercury's music it was to be 'A strain of unpremeditated wit, / Joyous and wild and wanton,—such you may / Hear among revellers on a holiday' (*Hymn to Mercury*, lines 69–71). The poem does achieve a remarkable festivity, but much of the time it hovers close to a subject which lies 'too deep for tears', the contrast between the joyous freedom of the semi-divine Witch and the turbulent lives of mortal men and women:

> But other troubled forms of sleep she saw,
>   Not to be mirrored in a holy song—
> Distortions foul of supernatural awe,
>   And pale imaginings of visioned wrong;
> And all the code of Custom's lawless law

Written upon the brows of old and young :
'This,' said the wizard maiden, 'is the strife
Which stirs the liquid surface of man's life.'

(lines 536–44)

Because of her divinity she is little disturbed by this; but in the closing
stanzas of the poem she performs a series of mischievous tricks which
have the effect of undoing the ruling systems in religion and politics
and uniting man to man in equality and fraternity and man to woman
in equal and guiltless love. So behind the 'holiday' high spirits and the
seeming inconsequence there is a serious concern for human welfare.
The tone of the poem is unusual for Shelley but it ends where almost
all his best poems end, imagining man's release from his bondage and
the coming of a new heaven and a new earth. The significance of this
was perfectly understood by Leigh Hunt :

Is the quitting the real world for the ideal in search of consolation, the
same thing as thrusting one's foot against it in contempt, and flying off on
the wings of antipathy? And what did Mr Shelley carry thither when he
went? A perpetual consciousness of his humanity; a clinging load of the
miseries of his fellow-creatures. The *Witch of Atlas*, for example, is but a
personification of the imaginative faculty in its most airy abstractions; and
yet the author cannot indulge himself long in that faery region, without
dreaming of mortal strife. If he is not in this world, he must have visions
of it. If fiction is his reality by day, reality will be his fiction during his
slumbers.[14]

For a final example consider the beginning of 'Ode to the West Wind' :

O wild West Wind, thou breath of Autumn's being,
Thou, from whose unseen presence the leaves dead
Are driven, like ghosts from an enchanter fleeing,

Yellow, and black, and pale, and hectic red,
Pestilence-stricken multitudes . . .

This energetic fanfare is so familiar that it is all too easy for us not to
notice what Shelley is doing. The preliminary address to the wind is
vivid, impassioned, and colourful. It presents a world which is conceived
more in terms of literary tradition than in terms of a direct and living
relationship with the landscape itself. The ghosts and the enchanter
seem to suggest the world of Spenser and the realm of romance. Behind
this image, too, is Milton's description of the fallen angels : 'Angel forms,
who lay entranced / Thick as autumnal leaves that strew the brooks /

In Vallombrosa . . .' (*P.L.*, I. 301–3). But the significant feature in Shelley's stanza is the way in which he shifts the focus of interest from the world of romance and of literary tradition to the harsher realities of contemporary politics. At first, the colourings of the leaves may appear to add a glamorously adjectival note but *black* suggests decay and *pale* introduces a note which is unmistakeably human. Finally *hectic red* completes the transference of the whole spectrum into images of wasting disease and human suffering. So, in the course of this line, the ghosts are transformed into human beings and translated from the unreal if frightening world of spells and enchanters to the sickbeds and the crowded and unhealthy streets of great cities. 'Pestilence-stricken multudes' may have a Biblical ring about it but there can be no doubt that Shelley was referring to one of the greatest social evils of his time—epidemic disease. For Shelley and his contemporaries pestilence was not a rhetorical trope but a threatening reality. Anyone who doubts this should consult the abstract of statistics printed in *Blackwood's Magazine* at the end of each year.

What is striking about Shelley's imagination here is the way in which it sends him back from the woods by the Arno to the huddled and disease-ridden population of the cities. It is the same process which we saw at work in *Letter to Maria Gisborne* and in *The Witch of Atlas*, a process which springs from Shelley's essential *humanitas*, his inescapable need to associate himself with human concerns and to project himself sympathetically into human suffering. Shelley's language here is certainly not colloquial, since an ode demands the stilts of the high style which alone is commensurate with the greatness of the subject: but even if 'Pestilence-stricken multitudes' is more resonant than colloquial, even if it does suggest that the epidemics of nineteenth-century Europe are the successors of a long line of Biblical plagues, there is no denying the realism of the phrase. If the typically Romantic poem points away from contemporary realities, then 'Ode to the West Wind' is not typically Romantic. Shelley, like Keats, actually employs dark realities to undermine those seductive romantic visions into which he might like to escape. The odorous gardens of literature are cultivated out of the sandy desert of politics; and the desert is all around.

(ii)

Politics, then, was the element which Shelley inhabited. Consequently it should be no surprise that his theory of poetry attaches great significance to the social function of literature. Over the years, Shelley's theory underwent some subtle changes but his strong sense of social responsibility never deserted him. It is worth remembering that Shelley was born into a political family, his father being an M.P. (however unworthily) and attached to the liberal faction of the Duke of Norfolk. Shelley must often have heard politics discussed at home, and it was generally understood that when he came of age he would succeed to his father's seat in the House. Thus, though the radical extremism of his views and his conduct far exceeded what was expected from him, the serious concern with contemporary affairs was entirely what his family would have wished. Shelley displayed a kind of upper-class self-confidence and belief in his own rightness which allowed him, for example, to intervene in the tangled world of Irish politics without any sense of embarrassment. It was this impetus which caused him to become 'self-constituted steward of universal happiness'. Tillyard perceived this very shrewdly when he said :

... he retained the masterful, energetic, and forthright disposition of an English squire of the eighteenth century; and in most of his poetry he has no more doubt of what he is after than Sir Timothy Shelley and his like riding to hounds. . . . If, as the French habitually do, we should use the words classical and romantic in the sense of social and individual respectively, we shall see that Shelley is not a romantic at all but, for all his rebellion, the faithful heir of the social conscience of the eighteenth century.[15]

This minimises certain important aspects of Shelley but, for all that, it does lay its finger on the central pulse of his mind and work. Though his political ideals were essentially radical, though his style was often revolutionary, Shelley was always impelled by a strong social conscience which allied him with some unlikely companions. He would have concurred wholeheartedly with Dr Johnson's view that it was a writer's duty 'to make the world better'. He would also have approved of Addison's statement in The Spectator : '. . . I have endeavoured to make nothing ridiculous, that is not in some measure criminal. I have set up the immoral man as the Object of Derision': it was largely because it did not attain these objectives that he was revolted by Restoration comedy.[16]

Where Shelley differed from his eighteenth-century predecessors was in his view of didacticism. He started out with an attitude to poetry which was crudely didactic. At the end of 1810 he wrote to his publisher: 'I have in preparation a Novel; it is principally constructed to convey metaphysical & political opinions by way of conversation; it shall be sent to you as soon as completed, but it shall receive more correction than I trouble myself to give to wild Romance & Poetry.'[17] The novel was probably *Hubert Cauvin*, which was to explore some of the central issues raised by the French Revolution. It is interesting to see that, at this stage, Shelley actually regards philosophical prose as a medium superior to 'wild Romance & Poetry'. Six months later his view of poetry is perhaps more generous but still strictly functional: '... my opinion is that all poetical beauty ought to be subordinate to the inculcated moral—that metaphorical language ought to be a pleasing vehicle for useful & momentous instruction.'[18] In 1812, though he could tell Godwin that an attachment to poetry 'has characterised all my wanderings and changes', he was also convinced that 'the science of things is superior to the science of words'.[19] Being a public service, poetry had nothing to do with self-expression. And he himself was a public servant: 'I therefore write, and I publish because I will publish nothing that shall not conduce to virtue, and therefore my publications so far as they do influence shall influence to good.'[20] This strenuous moral line in theory was borne out in practice. Few poets can have felt impelled to use bottles and air-balloons to 'scatter' their 'words among mankind'. Years later in Italy, at the very time when he was working on *Prometheus Unbound*, Shelley could still say:

I consider Poetry very subordinate to moral & political science, & if I were well, certainly I should aspire to the latter; for I can conceive a great work, embodying the discoveries of all ages, & harmonizing the contending creeds by which mankind have been ruled. Far from me is such an attempt & I shall be content by exercising my fancy to amuse myself & perhaps some others, & cast what weight I can into the right scale of that balance which the Giant (of Arthegall) holds.[21]

Yet, after he had completed *Prometheus Unbound*, Shelley made a rather surprising declaration in the Preface: 'Didactic poetry is my abhorrence; nothing can be equally well expressed in prose that is not tedious and supererogatory in verse.' Two years later he proposed an image of the poet's function which developed the implications of this statement: 'A Poet is a nightingale, who sits in darkness and sings to cheer its own solitude with sweet sounds; his auditors are as men entranced by the melody of an unseen musician, who feel that they are moved and softened, yet know not whence or why.'[22] These last two statements seem to run counter to all that has gone before. Was Shelley contradicting himself? Or had he changed his mind?

   These questions are not easy to answer since Shelley's view of poetry was subtle and flexible and since it does seem to have changed its emphases from time to time. Basically, it would appear that Shelley never lost his conviction that poetry should not be offered as a mere entertainment but should have the power to affect the quality of human lives. In 1813 he told his publisher Hookham, 'One fault they [some poems recently written] are indisputably exempt from, that of being a volume of *fashionable literature*'.[23] Like his friend Peacock, Shelley recognised the limitations of what was merely fashionable and it was never his intention to delectate ladies in drawing-rooms or to make himself agreeable to those who presided over the whims of mode. In his earlier days he underestimated the potential effects of poetry but this was because he took the function of literature too seriously rather than too lightly. With the passage of time he began to realise the limits of didacticism. The savage criticism of the reviews, the difficulties involved in getting his more outspoken poems into print, the apparent failure of those to whom he was addressing himself to rise up and take action—all of these factors must have helped to shift the focus away from direct didacticism towards the more sophisticated aim of 'teaching the human heart, through its sympathies and antipathies, the knowledge of itself'[24] which characterises most of the later poetry. There was, too, a gradual maturing, a drawing away from youthful impatience and impetuosity, a richer and wiser distillation of experience. Finally, there was a growing delight in the 'brilliance and magnificence of sound', in the harmony of language itself and in the vitally metaphoric mode of poetry, all of which melted away the puritanical reserve of the younger Shelley. Yet, right up to the time of his death, Shelley could never conceive of a poem as autotelic, a creation which was self-referring and self-delighting. He could not accept Keats's advice to retire to the monastery of his imagination, curb his magnanimity and be more of an artist. For him the poetry which really mattered projected itself outwards. It was possible, desirable and cathartic even, to compose verses which were personal and which relieved one's own feelings, but the essential aim of poetry was grander and higher. Poetry was the record of the best and happiest moments of the happiest and best minds. The poet was a legislator and a prophet. Poetry could recreate the world.

One instructive way of examining this shift in attitude is provided by the history of Shelley's views on *Queen Mab*. This, of course, was the most violent, the most outspoken and the most nakedly didactic of all his poems. Because it was so unmistakeably revolutionary, Shelley was unable to have it published in the normal fashion; instead, he was forced to bring out a private edition of which he distributed about seventy copies. Later he rewrote some of the sections and published

D

revised versions of sections 1 and 2 in the *Alastor* volume (1816) under the title *The Daemon of the World*. In 1817, four years after the poem had made it first appearance, Shelley sent a copy to a Mr Waller accompanied by the following note:

The Author sends 'Queen Mab' to Mr Waller, as Cardinal Wolsey was sent to Heaven, 'with all his imperfections on his head'. It was composed in early youth, & is full of those errors which belong to youth, as far as arrangement of imagery & language & a connected plan, is concerned.—But it was a sincere overflowing of the heart & mind, & that at a period when they are most uncorrupted & pure. It is the Author's boast and it constitutes no small portion of his happiness that, after six years of added experience & reflection, the doctrines of equality & liberty & disinterestedness, & entire unbelief in religion of any sort, to which this Poem is devoted, have gained rather than lost that beauty & that grandeur which first determined him to devote his life to the investigation & inculcation of them—[25]

Thus the man of twenty-five passing judgement on the youth of twenty-one (or nineteen, as he seems to be claiming in this letter). The terms of his criticism are very interesting. The faults which he detects are aesthetic blemishes in language, imagery and structure. At no point does Shelley suggest that he disapproves of *Queen Mab* because it is didactic: on the contrary, he endorses its views of life and society enthusiastically and with no little dignity. We may also presume that he would not have presented the poem to Mr Waller had he seriously disapproved of its fundamental approach to the subject.

The next significant letter on this matter was written four years later in the summer of 1821. It was provoked by the appearance of a pirated edition of *Queen Mab*. Shelley wrote to his publisher Ollier: 'I have not seen it for some years, but inasmuch as I recollect [it] it is villainous trash; & I dare say much better fitted to injure than to serve the cause which it advocates.'[26] Consequently, he called on Ollier to protest against the publication 'in the name of poetry'. To his friend Gisborne he was more outspoken:

A droll circumstance has occurred. Queen Mab, a poem written by me when very young, in the most furious style, with long notes against Jesus Christ, & God the Father and the King & the Bishops & marriage & the Devil knows what, is just published by one of the low booksellers in the Strand, against my wish & consent, and all the people are at loggerheads about it.... You may imagine how much I am amused.—For the sake of a dignified appearance however, & really because I wish to protest against all the bad poetry in it, I have given orders to say that it is all done against my desire.[27]

He also wrote a public letter which Hunt printed in *The Examiner*, in the course of which he stated:

I am a devoted enemy to religious, political, and domestic oppression; and I regret this publication, not so much from literary vanity, as because I fear it is better fitted to injure than to serve the cause of freedom.[28]

One has to be cautious in interpreting these statements, particularly this last one which was intended as a public disclaimer, because Shelley may have been trying to cover himself against possible prosecution. However, it seems fairly clear that, although he had modified his views, he was still basically in sympathy with the general thrust of *Queen Mab*. What he seems to object to in these last letters is the 'bad poetry'. *Queen Mab*, he tells the readers of *The Examiner*, is 'perfectly worthless in point of literary composition'. This dismissal is probably based on an increasing dislike for poetry which is crudely didactic—observe, for example, his satirical description of the 'long notes'. It is probably fair to conclude that though Shelley retained strong views on Jesus Christ, God the Father, the king, the bishops, marriage etc. etc., he became more and more concerned with the way in which these views were presented.[29] It is sometimes said that his departure for Italy early in 1818 marked the beginning of a new dedication to poetry and philosophy, even to selfish complacency, rather than to politics. This is quite untrue. It is a distorted reading of *Prometheus Unbound* or *Adonais* or *The Triumph of Life* which fails to recognise its political relevance. Naturally Shelley was further from the centre of British politics but he was, of course, a close, though not a closely involved, spectator of the revolutionary movement in Italy. This geographical distancing may have helped to develop a tendency which was already evident before he left England—the tendency to write of politics at one remove, as in *The Revolt of Islam*, rather than bluntly and didactically as in *Queen Mab*. This tendency increased between the years 1818 and 1822. None the less, a shift in emphasis should not be confused with a change of view.

We seem to have here a nicely graduated course of development in which Shelley progresses towards a subtler view of the function of poetry. At one end of this intellectual and moral progress stands *Queen Mab*, baldly didactic; at the other end stands the *Defence of Poetry*, which images the poet as a nightingale who works upon the emotions of his audience without their knowing 'whence or why'. The poet becomes less obviously calculating, less a manipulator. The old medicine of wormwood sweetened by drops of honey is replaced by a drink which is more unequivocally itself.[30] Such a pattern would be easy to accept and it would bear a tolerably close resemblance to the facts. There is, however, one difficulty. While Shelley is undoubtedly on record as an enemy of didactic poetry and while most of his own work does display an obvious movement away from brute didacticism, he did produce a number of poems which seem to belie this growing antipathy towards poetry which 'has a deliberate design on us'.

The poems in question are *The Mask of Anarchy*, 'Lines Written during the Castlereagh Administration', 'Song to the Men of England', 'To Sidmouth and Castlereagh', 'A New National Anthem' and 'An Ode to the Assertors of Liberty'. To these one might add *Peter Bell the Third* and *Swellfoot the Tyrant*, which are similarly outspoken, though *Peter Bell* is essentially a satire and *Swellfoot* is a burlesque. Two important factors link virtually all of these poems. First, as far as we know, they were all written in 1819. Secondly, six of the eight were not published in Shelley's lifetime. *Swellfoot* was published anonymously in 1820 only for the whole impression to be withdrawn on threat of prosecution after seven copies had been sold, and 'An Ode to the Assertors of Liberty' appeared with *Prometheus Unbound* discreetly camouflaged as 'An Ode written October, 1819, before the SPANIARDS had recovered their Liberty'. That the other six poems did not appear in print was not due to caution on Shelley's part. *The Mask of Anarchy* was sent to Hunt, who considered it too inflammatory and did not publish it until after its main purpose had been achieved with the passing of the Reform Bill in 1832. *Peter Bell* was sent to Ollier in 1819 but remained unpublished till 1839. The shorter poems were intended to compose a separate volume. In May 1820 Shelley inquired of Hunt: 'I wish to ask you if you know of any bookseller who would like to publish a little volume of *popular songs* wholly political, & destined to awaken & direct the imagination of the reformers.' These poems exist in fair copies as if ready for the printer but apparently Hunt was unable to propose a likely candidate and the project was left in abeyance.

This flurry of interest in poetry which was directly political is highly significant. It seems to indicate that, some time in 1819, Shelley was so depressed by the political situation in England that he decided to do everything within his means as a writer to bring about the desired changes. The catalyst was almost certainly the news of the Peterloo Massacre which reached Shelley in early September. In all probability he then decided that to confine himself to 'beautiful idealisms' like

Prometheus Unbound was not an adequate response to the needs of the situation. In the 'terrible and important news of Manchester' could be heard 'as it were, the distant thunders of the terrible storm which is approaching'.[31] In such evil times a writer could not be idle. So Shelley produced *The Mask of Anarchy*, a political fable with a message directed at the people of England; the 'Ode to the West Wind', a complex address to the powers of nature, symbolic of those forces which might help to bring about a change in society and make the poet–prophet the instrument of that change; and the long letter to *The Examiner* which unravelled the philosophical and legal basis for the imprisonment of Richard Carlile, publisher of Paine's *Age of Reason*, on a charge of blasphemous libel.[32] There was the brutally uncompromising sonnet 'England in 1819', which Shelley despatched to Hunt with the comment, 'I do not expect you to publish it, but you may show it to whom you please';[33] and there were the shorter political poems, poems of exhortation, of vituperation and of fundamental political analysis, designed for the popular reader. The pride of the artist was abandoned to the urgency of the hour. Shelley's letter of May 1820 reveals very forcefully what had been in his mind, the feelings of despair and the certainty that, like Prometheus, one must learn 'To defy Power, which seems omnipotent':

The system of society as it exists at present must be overthrown from the foundations with all its superstructure of maxims & of forms before we shall find anything but disappointment in our intercourse with any but a few select spirits. This remedy does not seem to be one of the easiest. But the generous few are not the less held to tend with all their efforts towards it. If faith is a virtue in any case it is so in politics rather than religion; as having a power of producing that a belief in which is at once a prophesy & a cause——[34]

In such circumstances, as Shelley had told Hunt in the letter which accompanied 'England in 1819', 'Every word a man has to say is valuable to the public . . .'[35]

(iii)

Thus, though Shelley did not lack a sophisticated appreciation of the highest possibilities inherent in poetry, he was quite ready to produce a different kind of poetry at the prompting of his social conscience. Keats would have said that Shelley's 'passion for reforming the world' was a hindrance to the perfecting of his art; Shelley would have replied that he had elected to serve God rather than Mammon and that his primary duty was to assist and promote the regeneration of man. Shelley was perfectly conscious of what he was trying to do. His letters and his prefaces show an acute self-awareness and a shrewd appreciation of what he might hope for from different genres or different styles.

He was always particularly sensitive to the needs of a given reading public and whatever he wrote, whether in prose or in verse, was approached in a properly rhetorical spirit. His *Essay on Christianity* throws an interesting light on this. Shelley approaches the words of Christ as the product, in part at least, of rhetorical necessities: 'It cannot be precisely ascertained [in] what degree Jesus Christ accomodated his doctrines to the opinions of his auditors...' Quoting a passage from the Sermon on the Mount he comments, 'Thus like a skilful orator (see Cicero's *De Oratore*), he secures the prejudices of his auditors and induces them by his professions of sympathy with their feelings to enter with a willing mind into the exposition of his own.' He goes on to examine the compromises with truth which all reformers are often forced to make, the 'misrepresentation of their own true feelings and opinions'. He admits that any kind of deception is a falling away from the highest ideals: 'It is deeply to be lamented that a word should ever issue from human lips which contains the minutest alloy of dissimulation, or simulation, or hypocrisy, or exaggeration, or anything but the precise and rigid image which is present to the mind and which ought to dictate the expression.' But circumstance is a hard master: 'In fact, truth cannot be communicated until it is perceived. The interests, therefore, of truth required that an orator should so far as possible produce in his hearers that state of mind in which alone his exhortations could fairly be contemplated and examined.'[36] There is no evidence that Shelley himself ever made such a compromise but his elaborate explanation of the conditions under which Christ attempted to spread his message shows that he had reflected deeply on the relations between the teacher, the public he addresses and the society which he means to regenerate.

This acute sensitivity to the ambient circumstances had its effect on Shelley's literary tactics. For example, he distinguished at least two potential reading publics and he recognised that each demanded an appropriate and different literary style. Hence his instructions to Leigh Hunt concerning his 'lines on the Manchester affair': 'They are of the exoteric species, and are meant not for the *Indicator*, but the *Examiner*. I would send for the former if you like some letters on such subjects of art as suggest themselves in Italy.'[37] *The Indicator* was more or less devoted to literature and the fine arts, a journal whose focus was primarily aesthetic, while *The Examiner* was directly political. It was in *The Examiner* that the Hunts had published the attack on the Prince Regent that had led to their imprisonment in 1812. Shelley preferred *The Examiner* because he intended that *The Mask of Anarchy* should not be dismissed as mere poetry, puzzled over perhaps by a few dilettanti, but that it should make a positive contribution to the political life of the country. To that end the style and the imagery had been simplified and a basic and memorable verse form had been selected.

Likewise *The Cenci*, which was intended for Covent Garden and 'partly to please those whom my other writings displeased', was 'studiously written in a style very different from any other compositions'.[38] In the preface, Shelley explained his intentions with great care. He had set out to avoid 'the introduction of what is commonly called mere poetry' and he claimed that there was scarcely 'a detached simile or a single isolated description' in the whole play. After a rather Wordsworthian passage on the way in which strong feeling energises and elevates the most familiar imagery and levels to the apprehension that which is lofty and remote, he introduces the subject of style, again with obvious debts to the Preface to *Lyrical Ballads*:

In other respects, I have written more carelessly; that is, without an over-fastidious and learned choice of words. In this respect I entirely agree with those modern critics who assert that in order to move men to true sympathy we must use the familiar language of men, and that our great ancestors the ancient English poets are the writers, a study of whom might incite us to do that for our own age which they have done for theirs. But it must be the real language of men in general and not that of any particular class to whose society the writer happens to belong.

Having made all these adjustments and directed himself, as he thought, towards a popular audience, Shelley was all the more galled when the play was not accepted by Covent Garden and suffered the customary mammocking from the critics: '. . . nothing is so difficult and unwelcome as to write without a confidence of finding readers; and if my play of 'the Cenci' found none or few, I despair of ever producing anything that shall merit them.'[39] (In fact, *The Cenci* went into a second edition, the only one of Shelley's works to achieve that distinction during his lifetime, with the exception of a Gothic novel published while he was still at school.)

The day after this outburst of despair, Shelley wrote to his publisher Ollier and enclosed the manuscript of *Epipsychidion*. This poem was quite different from *The Cenci*:

It is to be published simply for the esoteric few; and I make its author a
secret, to avoid the malignity of those who turn sweet food into poison;
transforming all they touch into the corruption of their own natures. My
wish with respect to it is, that it should be printed immediately in the
simplest form, and merely one hundred copies: those who are capable of
judging and feeling rightly with respect to a composition of so abstruse a
nature, certainly do not arrive at that number . . .[40]

Later in the year he told a friend that he had asked Ollier not to
circulate the poem except to the *sunetoi*. This was obviously intended
as a reference to the highly complex and aristocratic Pindar who had
proudly described his poems as *belē phōnanta sunetoisin* (arrows which
speak to the initiated). In much the same spirit Shelley stated, 'Prometheus was never intended for more than 5 or 6 persons', while *Adonais*,
which was 'perhaps the least imperfect of my compositions' was 'little
adapted to popularity'.[41] One is irresistibly reminded of Peacock's
portrait of Scythrop Glowry. Some months after the publication of his
treatise which was intended to regenerate the world,

He received a letter from his bookseller, informing him that only seven
copies had been sold, and concluding with a polite request for the balance.
    Scythrop did not despair. 'Seven copies,' he thought, 'have been sold.
Seven is a mystical number and the omen is good. Let me find the seven
purchasers of my seven copies, and they shall be the seven golden candle-
sticks with which I will illuminate the world.'[42]

Much like Scythrop, Shelley may have been smoothing his ruffled ego
when he said that *Prometheus Unbound* had only been intended for
five or six readers; yet, though he must have been exaggerating or
rather minimising for rhetorical effect, there can be no doubt that he
was sincere in his protestations. All the evidence goes to show that he
distinguished between the needs of the common reader and those of
'the more select classes of poetical readers'.

    In making this distinction, Shelley may have been guilty of under-
estimating the ordinary man. In his earlier days, his doctrines of equality
did not succeed in eradicating a certain degree of inherited snobbery.
'Perhaps you will say that my Republicanism is proud', he told Hogg;
'it certainly is far removed from pot-house democracy, and knows with
what smile to hear the servile applauses of an inconstant mob.' In
another letter he admitted 'certain habitudes' which he could not shake

off; thus, he could not image two persons of opposite sexes 'unconnected by certain ties' sleeping in the same apartment without offence to 'invincible ideas of delicacy'.[43] The necessities of working class existence were hard for him to accept or understand. The record which he and Mary kept of their first visit to Europe betrays a kind of snobbery which one would not have expected from the generous-hearted Shelley and the daughter of William Godwin and Mary Wollstonecraft. Mary describes their fellow-travellers as 'creepers'; 'our only wish', she records 'was to absolutely annihilate such uncleanly animals.' If these unfortunate creepers attempted to speak English, they were frightened away 'with talk of cutting off kings' heads'.[44] This was Mary more than Shelley, but he probably shared in these reactions to a degree. Years later he was to tell Medwin how he was revolted by the carnival crowds in Pisa. Yet, even if Shelley had a sense of delicacy, he was essentially no snob. In the notes to *Queen Mab* he does speak of 'The vulgar, ever in extremes' but he also makes the following statement: 'The vulgar *of all ranks* are invariably sensual and indocile.'[45] Shelley feared the mob but he also lamented the existence of those systems which depended on unthinking multitudes for their survival. Besides, if Shelley feared 'the Great Beast', he was no respecter of persons, as the second sentence makes clear. In a letter of 1819 he states bluntly: 'the vulgarity of rank and fashion is as gross in its way as that of Poverty.'[46] Leigh Hunt, who knew him well, admitted that, although he might have retained some residual snobbery as a result of his up-bringing, he did not recognise distinctions of rank: 'I have seen him indeed draw himself up with a sort of irrepressible air of dignified objection, when moral vulgarity was betrayed in his presence, whatever might have been the rank of the betrayer; but nobody could hail with greater joy and simplicity, or meet upon more equal grounds, the instinct of a real delicacy and good intention, come in what shape it might.'[47]

Hunt goes on to say that 'if an aristocracy of intellect and morals were required, he was the man for one of their leaders'. This is suggestive: Shelley was not a snob but he wrote his popular songs *de haut en bas*, assuming responsibility for the fate of the working classes and altering his manner of speech in order that he might be understood. One cannot but admire the generous concern and the passionate involvement of these poems; yet, for the most part, they do not bring out the best in Shelley as a poet. The need to simplify sometimes leads to crudeness which Shelley would not have allowed in another context.

A good test case is provided by *The Mask of Anarchy*. Everybody seems to be agreed that the opening pageant is highly effective:

I met Murder on the way—
He had a mask like Castlereagh,
Very smooth he looked, yet grim;
Seven blood-hounds followed him:

All were fat; and well they might
Be in admirable plight,
For one by one, and two by two,
He tossed them human hearts to chew
Which from his wide cloak he drew.

Next came Fraud, and he had on,
Like Eldon, an ermined gown;
His big tears, for he wept well,
Turned to millstones as they fell.

And the little children who
Round his feet play to and fro,
Thinking every tear a gem,
Had their brains knocked out by them.

Clothed with the Bible, as with light,
And the shadows of the night,
Like Sidmouth, next Hypocrisy
On a crocodile rode by.

And many more Destructions played
In this ghastly masquerade,
All disguised, even to the eyes
Like Bishops, lawyers, peers and spies.

This is magnificently simple, direct and uncomplicated; it has the same
graphic clarity of outline as the cartoons of Shelley's contemporary,
Gillray. The details are exaggerated, grotesque, yet inescapably true
to the facts. The basic quatrains with their emphatic rhymes are sometimes reminiscent of those popular ballads, songs and broadsheets from
which Blake also drew; sometimes the poignantly awkward rhythms
might even remind one of folksong. What binds all this together is the
clarity of Shelley's vision and the directness of his response. An anger
and an animus which might have remained merely personal (Eldon
was responsible for removing Shelley's children by Harriet from his
custody) have been translated into the flaming line of art.

Shelley's success here is remarkable, all the more so because he has
managed to capture a tone of voice not normally associated with his
poetry. The general trend of Romanticism was directed away from

the *saeva indignatio* which characterised so much of the best eighteenth-century literature; already the movement had begun which was to reach its climax with Arnold's statement that Dryden and Pope were classics of our prose, largely because of the inadmissibility of the more savage emotions in poetry. Shelley's theory of poetry must have contributed to that shift of taste. Yet Shelley himself had a strong satirical streak, a kind of downrightness which sometimes reminds one that he was not only the contemporary of Byron but the product of much the same social class. Like Byron, Shelley enjoyed the cathartic pleasures of cursing: 'To the Lord Chancellor' is a remarkably fluent example of the flyting. Here again the subject is Lord Eldon:

> Thy country's curse is on thee, darkest crest
>   Of that foul, knotted, many-headed worm
> Which rends our Mother's bosom—Priestly Pest!
> Masked Resurrection of a buried Form!
>
> Thy country's curse is on thee! Justice sold,
> Truth trampled, Nature's landmarks overthrown . . .

For all its use of political catch-cries and for all its abstractions, this opening is irresistibly energetic. Shelley soon modulates into a ritual curse which he invokes directly on the Lord Chancellor and which he sustains with great verve and rhetorical momentum for the space of twelve whole stanzas. Eight lines will suffice to convey the characteristic flavour:

> By thy most impious Hell, and all its terror;
>   By all the grief, the madness, and the guilt
> Of thine impostures, which must be their error—
>   That sand on which thy crumbling Power is built;
>
> By thy complicity with lust and hate,—
>   Thy thirst for tears,—thy hunger after gold,—
> The ready frauds which ever on thee wait,—
>   The servile arts in which thou hast grown old . . .

The indictment is none the less specific for all the fluency of the invective. Almost all the accounts of Shelley's earlier life make it clear that he was a man of violent temper, prone to explosive outbursts of rage under provocation. In his poetry this rage sometimes manifests itself in his reaction to political events, or to kings and priests in the abstract, or to specific figures in the dark political landscape. The early poetry is full of the slogans of political protest, and is densely populated by hyenas, vultures and other beasts of prey. At this stage, Shelley's view of the political world as expressed in his poetry is not far removed from the melodramatics of the Gothic novel. Strangely, his prose works and letters written during the same period show much greater sophistication and subtlety. His problem was that he had not yet discovered how to channel his anger productively, so that the naive violence of the poetry usually belies the authenticity of the involvement and the genuine political intelligence behind it. Shelley never completely solved this problem. Even in his later poems his voice has a tendency to become shrill when he approaches the accustomed targets. But this happened less and less as he learnt from experience that the worst response to anger was anger and that he must discover how to ride victoriously over his own instinct to lash back vindictively. This did not mean that all passion was then spent: the most important lesson which Shelley taught himself was how to canalise his anger into the controlled artistic aggression of passages such as the opening of *The Mask of Anarchy*.

This new power is evident in some of the other poems written in 1819. For example, here are two stanzas from the description of Hell in *Peter Bell the Third*:

> Hell is a city much like London—
>   A populous and a smoky city;
> There are all sorts of people undone,
> And there is little or no fun done;
>   Small justice shown, and still less pity ...
>   ...
> There is a Chancery Court; a King;
>   A manufacturing mob; a set
> Of thieves who by themselves are sent
> Similar thieves to represent;
>   An army; and a public debt ...
>   lines 147–51, 162–6)

Here again the control of tone is exemplary. The mixture of colloquial ease ('manufacturing mob', 'set of thieves'), intense conviction and clarity of vision is highly effective.

This particular style might perhaps remind one of Byron but 'Lines written during the Castlereagh Administration', though equally striking, is characteristically Shelleyan. It begins with a grim panache, driving home a series of epigrams with hammer-like blows:

Corpses are cold in the tomb;
Stones on the pavement are dumb;
Abortions are dead in the womb,
And their mothers look pale—like the death-white shore
Of Albion, free no more.

Shelley develops the implications of these horrible images, leaving no room for misunderstanding:

Her sons are as stones in the way—
They are masses of senseless clay—
They are trodden, and move not away,—
The abortion with which *she* travaileth
Is Liberty, smitten to death.

Here Shelley seems to have crossed the borderline between conventional literature and the broadsheet or popular song. In so doing he displays an effective touch but the greater part of this poem is crudely emphatic compared to the lines quoted from *Peter Bell* and *The Mask of Anarchy*. Shelley, of course, was not here concerned with artistic niceties but with conveying a message to a popular audience. These verses teeter on the edge of Gothic sensationalism but the intellectual control of the argument and the vigorous rhythms just succeed in turning the Gothic elements to good account. Indeed, the first stanza achieves a memorable effect which is more surrealistic than melodramatic.

So the writing of popular verse had a double effect on Shelley: it sometimes brought him close to the Gothic excesses of his earlier poetry but it also helped him to develop a vigorous, direct and satirical vein which previously had not achieved adequate expression. Though most of his best work was written in another style (or styles), Shelley is recognisably the contemporary of Blake and Byron as well as of Cruikshank and Gillray. And the edged force of his best popular verse helped to shape the uncompromising voice of sophisticated poems like *The Triumph of Life*.

Notes to chapter three

1 *Letters*, II. 150.
2 *Literary Studies*, vol. I. Dent/Dutton, 1951, p. 89.
3 *English Poetry: A Critical Introduction*, 2nd corrected ed., Longmans, 1971, pp. 151–2.
4 *Letters*, II. 153.
5 *Letters*, II. 442.
6 *Autobiography*, p. 271. See also *Letters*, II. 207.

7 Medwin, *Life*, p. 136.
8 *Letters*, II. 93–4.
9 Trelawny, *Records*, p. 114. Cf. 'A Dirge', *P.W.*, p. 673.
10 Dedication to *The Revolt of Islam*, p. 27.
11 See pp. 133–5.
12 Bod. MS. Shelley adds. e. 12, pp. 145–6.
13 Redpath, *The Young Romantics*, p. 413.
14 Redpath, *The Young Romantics*, p. 409.
15 *The Metaphysicals and Milton*, Chatto and Windus, 1956, pp. 39, 42.
16 *Defence*, p. 38.
17 *Letters*, I. 25.
18 *Letters*, I. 98.
19 *Letters*, I. 303, 318.
20 *Letters*, I. 259.
21 *Letters*, II. 71. Shelley is referring to *The Faerie Queene*, v. iii. Peacock comments: 'The Giant has scales, in which he professes to weigh right and wrong, and rectify the physical and moral evils which result from inequality of condition. Shelley once pointed out this passage to me, observing: "Artegall argues with the Giant; the Giant has the best of the argument; Artegall's iron man knocks him over into the sea and drowns him. This is the usual way in which power deals with opinion." I said: 'That was not the lesson which Spenser intended to convey." "Perhaps not," he said; "it is the lesson which he conveys to me. I am of the Giant's faction." ' (*Works*, VIII. 501.)
22 *Defence*, p. 31.
23 *Letters*, I. 348.
24 *P.W.*, p. 276.
25 *Letters*, I. 566–7.
26 *Letters*, II. 298.
27 *Letters*, II. 300–1.
28 *Letters*, II. 305.
29 In this respect it is worth noting that as late as 1821 he considered producing a second edition of *The Revolt of Islam*, noting that 'I could materially improve that poem on revision' (*Letters*, II. 263, 354.)
30 The image is from Lucretius, *De Rerum Natura*, I. 936 ff.
31 *Letters*, II. 119.
32 See *Letters*, II. 136–48.
33 *Letters*, II. 167.
34 *Letters*, II. 191.
35 *Letters*, II. 166.
36 Clark, *Prose*, pp. 198–200.
37 *Letters*, II. 152.
38 *Letters*, II. 186.
39 *Letters*, II. 262.
40 *Letters*, II. 263.
41 *Letters*, II. 363, 388, 299.
42 *Nightmare Abbey*, Penguin ed., p. 48.
43 *Letters*, I. 352, 314.
44 *Journal*, pp. 12–14.
45 *P.W.*, pp. 820, 831.
46 *Letters*, II. 108.
47 Brimley Johnson, *Shelley–Leigh Hunt*, pp. 81–2.

CHAPTER FOUR

PATTERNS OF HOPE

(i)

If the political situation sometimes prompted Shelley to despair, it often roused him to anger. That anger, combined with a sense of social responsibility, gave rise to popular poems such as *The Mask of Anarchy* in which the targets of his indignation are picked off with scornful precision. As we have seen, that precision was not easily achieved; Shelley had to subdue the temptation to indulge in abuse which was merely hysterical. The struggle for stylistic control was also a struggle for moral equilibrium. This is well illustrated by *The Mask of Anarchy* where it is the controlled indignation of the opening pageant which makes possible the crucial transition from anger to hope. However, this victory could not be won by style alone; Shelley also faced the problem of finding a moral structure which would embody the transition convincingly. After presenting the grim pageant with which the poem begins, Shelley introduces 'A maniac maid' called Hope who interrupts the triumphal progress of Anarchy:

> Then she lay down in the street
> Right before the horses' feet,
> Expecting with a patient eye
> Murder, Fraud and Anarchy ...

This act of defiance and clear-sighted courage (committed 'with a patient eye') is immediately rewarded by the appearance of a bright shape, which is not defined but which presumably represents Liberty; she passes over the heads of men, public opinion is transformed,

> And the prostrate multitude
> Looked—and ankle-deep in blood
> Hope, that maiden most serene,
> Was walking with a quiet mien,

And Anarchy, the ghastly birth,
Lay dead earth upon the earth . . .

The remainder of the poem (266 lines out of 372) is devoted to an address by Mother England to her children. It is as if, through the voice of England, Shelley is completing for Henry Hunt the speech which was so tragically interrupted at Peterloo. This address is notable for two points—its definition of Freedom and its proposal of a course of action for the next Peterloo. The essence of the definition of Freedom is economic:

For the labourer thou art bread
And a comely table spread,
From his daily labour come,
In a neat and happy home;

Thou are clothes and fire and food
For the trampled multitude—
No—in countries that are free
Such starvation cannot be
As in England now we see.

Specifically Shelley was thinking of the Corn Laws and of the disastrous effects of the economic slump resulting from the Napoleonic Wars.

Yet, being a direct response to the events at Peterloo, *The Mask of Anarchy* is ultimately less concerned with the economic problem than with the means of political expression. It recommends that there should be a great Assembly 'of the fearless and free', obviously another attempt to meet as at Peterloo and discuss the question of political reform. This assembly is to declare that 'ye / Are, as God has made ye, free'. Should this bring down the wrath of the government, as it did at Peterloo and as it probably will again, the military must be met with passive resistance:

And if then the tyrants dare,
Let them ride among you there,
Slash and stab and maim and hew—
What they like, that let them do.

With folded arms, and steady eyes,
And little fear, and less surprise,
Look upon them as they slay
Till their rage has died away.

Chastened and alerted to the reality of their situation, the soldiers will make alliance with people. If blood is shed, it will portend the birth of a new society. The poem ends with the marching song of freedom:

> Rise like lions after slumber
> In unvanquishable number,
> Shake your chains to earth like dew
> Which in sleep had fallen on you—
> Ye are many—they are few——

These final stanzas have given rise to two critical objections. First, there is the stylistic objection trenchantly expressed by Humphry House:

As one reads Bamford's autobiography, the evidence of John Jones and his wife, the account by Prentice in his *Historical Sketches and Personal Recollections of Manchester*, and so on, all these Lancashire people do not appear much like lions, and not at all as if they had been slumbering; the old image of the chains is stale and feeble compared with their vigorous descriptions of their lives and troubles and sufferings.[2]

House compares Shelley's poem with eyewitness accounts of Peterloo and finds that Shelley's lions shaking their chains to earth like dew are lacking in immediacy when compared to the words of this man of seventy-four who was knocked down by the Yeomanry and permanently disabled when the horses rode over him: 'And what is wur than aw, mesters, they'n broken my spectacles, and aw've ne'er yet been able to get a pair that suits me.' This, says House, 'is a speech, and a kind of speech, that Shelley never heard, and all his poetry suffers for it. But Shakespeare knew about this sort of thing, and in his history plays we have just the multiform variety of idiom and rhythm and vocabulary that the documents for Peterloo provide.'[3]

Much of this is undeniably true but it is also irrelevant. Shelley's concern was not to give a realistic account of what had actually taken place at Peterloo but to offer to the sorely tried people of England an image of hope and perhaps a practical course of political action. Broken spectacles were as foreign to his purpose as they would have been to *A Proposal for Putting Reform to the Vote* or the *Social Contract* or Plato's *Republic* or the *Communist Manifesto*. Had he wished, Shelley could have provided the poignant and symptomatic detail:

> My Father Time is weak and grey
> With waiting for a better day;—
> See how idiot-like he stands,
> Fumbling with his palsied hands.

This is sufficiently precise, unsentimental and uncompromising to show what he could have done had it been to his purpose. As for the objection that the people of Lancashire were not very much like lions, this again is true or would constitute truth for a George Orwell or a Zola; but Shelley's intention is to make these people *feel* like lions. The traditional connection with the strength of England and the Biblical flavour of the whole stanza is not an accident but is calculated to appeal to a popular audience.

The second criticism must be considered more seriously. Shelley's intention is to advocate passive resistance on a gigantic scale but the prevailing tone of the final stanzas seems to imply a resistance which is revolutionary rather than passive. The volcano's voice which features in many of Shelley's political poems inevitably suggests a violent shift in the balance of power. His most acute and most sympathetic political interpreter sets out the problem very lucidly:

... Shelley is torn between his love for the people, his hatred of the ruling class, and his fear that insurrectionary violence, should it fail, would lead to a military dictatorship. He (rather naively) urges the people not to fight the military, but he advocates a massive action that would clearly have had revolutionary consequences.[4]

In such circumstances it is not perhaps given to mortals to offer advice which is perfect. It may be that, if Shelley's poems had been published and if his advice had been taken literally, a bloody confrontation would have followed. Yet to believe this is also, perhaps, rather naive; Shelley was offering 'a succession of pictures' 'in the view of kindling within the bosoms of my readers a virtuous enthusiasm for those doctrines of liberty and justice, that faith and hope in something good, which neither violence nor misrepresentation nor prejudice can ever totally extinguish among mankind' (*P.W.*, p. 23). And the grounds for hope could not very well exclude an emphasis on the strength of the people and the weakness of their enemies. Inevitably there is a note of triumph but careful reading shows that this triumph is as closely allied to passive and pacific resistance as the political situation would allow. The slaughter which is to steam up like inspiration from the mephitic vapours of the volcanic chasm is the slaughter of the people by the military, *passively endured*. Shelley is not portraying a climactic battle in which blood is gloriously shed in a just cause. What he offers instead is a battle in which blood is gloriously allowed to be shed by those who raise no weapons in their defence: 'such strength is in meekness' that death itself can be a victory. Just as in the Homeric world the shedding of blood enables the dead to speak from beyond the grave, so in Shelley's image the shedding of innocent blood in a consciously elected martyrdom can give a voice to Liberty.

The Mask of Anarchy comes near to endorsing violence but for all the exultation of the closing stanzas Shelley's message is one of self-control rather than of violent resistance. Much the same point is made in the 'Ode to the Assertors of Liberty'. This begins with great vigour:

> Arise, arise, arise!
> There is blood on the earth that denies ye bread;
> Be your wounds like eyes
> To weep for the dead, the dead, the dead.
> What other grief were it just to pay?
> Your sons, your wives, your brethren, were they;
> Who said they were slain on the battle day?

In spite of its original title, which referred to the Spanish revolutionary movement, Shelley was obviously referring to Peterloo, which should be indicated by the close similarity between these lines and The Mask of Anarchy. The poem continues to exhort the people to rise, shake off their chains and wave high the banner of Freedom. This exultant series of injunctions leads Shelley close to the militaristic ethos so, quite specifically, he makes the distinction:

> And ye who attend her imperial car [the triumphal chariot of Freedom],
> Lift not your hands in the banded war,
> But in her defence whose children ye are.

In the next stanza he goes even further:

> Conquerors have conquered their foes alone,
> Whose revenge, pride, and power they have overthrown:
> Ride ye, more victorious, over your own.

Thus, the truest victory is that which has to be won over the vindictive forces in one's own nature.

Nobody has understood better or given more delicate expression to the nature of these political views than Leigh Hunt. Of The Mask of Anarchy he wrote:

It has the usual ardour of his tone, the unbounded sensibility by which he combines the most domestic with the most remote and fanciful images, and the patience, so beautifully checking, and in fact produced by the extreme impatience of his moral feeling. His patience is the deposit of many impatiences, acting upon an equal measure of understanding and moral taste. His wisdom is the wisdom of a heart overcharged with sensibility, acquiring the profoundest notions of justice from the completest sympathy, and at once taking refuge from its pain, and working out its extremest purposes, in the adoption of a stubborn and loving fortitude which neutralizes resistance.[5]

This catches exactly the quandary in which Shelley found himself and the complicated and admirable way in which he reacted. Finally, Shelley himself offers an enlightening commentary in the very letter to Hunt which accompanied the manuscript of *The Mask of Anarchy* :

I fear that in England things will be carried violently by the rulers, and that they will not have learned to yield in time to the spirit of the age. The great thing to do is to hold the balance between popular impatience and tyrannical obstinacy; to inculcate with fervour both the right of resistance and the duty of forbearance. You know my principles incite me to take all the good I can get in politics, for ever aspiring to something more. I am one of those whom nothing will fully satisfy, but who am ready to be partially satisfied by all that is practicable. We shall see.[6]

As Shelley was well aware, this balance was difficult to hold. From an ethical point of view, his sentiments here and in *The Mask of Anarchy* are entirely admirable. In the politics of psychology this posture of passive resistance and self-control, this refusal to meet force with force, may well be valid, but in terms of practical politics it is rather questionable. The real problem in *The Mask* is the way in which Shelley bridges the gap between his grim presentation of the current political scene and his final attempt to present a formula for rendering it harmless. Shelley felt it his solemn duty to inculcate the virtue of hope and to deprecate revenge and retribution, yet the authenticity of the intention does not make up for the weakness of the proposed solution. After the apocalyptic presences of Eldon, Sidmouth and Castlereagh, the intervention of Liberty seems insubstantial and merely wished for. Her message is a stirring one but it can never compensate entirely for the inevitable feeling that she is only a god in a flying machine. Compare, for example, Castlereagh. He is followed by seven bloodhounds whom he keeps well fed : 'He tossed them human hearts to chew / Which from his wide cloak he drew.' This is memorably graphic. *Seven* is not the result of poetic licence like the kisses of Keats's *Belle dame sans merci* : it refers specifically to Austria, France, Portugal, Prussia, Russia, Spain and Sweden, who together with England had agreed not to abolish the slave trade.[7] So, in addition to a precise and clearly outlined picture, there is a highly specific frame of reference.

Here, in contrast, is the manifestation of Liberty:

> ... between her and her foes
> A mist, a light, an image rose,
> Small at first, and weak and frail
> Like the vapour of a vale ...
>
> It grew—a Shape arrayed in mail
> Brighter than the Viper's scale,
> And upborne on wings whose grain
> Was as the light of sunny rain.
>
> On its helm seen far away
> A Planet, like the Morning's, lay;
> And those plumes its light rained through
> Like a shower of crimson dew ...

Shelley is doing his best but it is hard to materialise the merely potential. Liberty is primarily a state of mind and Shelley goes on to describe its effects on the hearts of men with charm and grace but with none of the gripping intensity with which he portrays Castlereagh. Above all, the failure to present Liberty directly as a tangible presence renders her powerless beside the dark potency of the rogues' gallery. The acid of the etching bites more deeply than the pale wash of the watercolour.

The difficulty becomes more obvious if we consider another poem which was written late in the same year, the sonnet 'England in 1819'. The impulse behind it is much the same as the impulse behind the longer poem: indeed, the sonnet could almost be described as *The Mask* in miniature.

> An old, mad, blind, despised and dying King;
> Princes, the dregs of their dull race, who flow
> Through public scorn,—mud from a muddy spring;
> Rulers who neither see nor feel nor know,
> But leechlike to their fainting Country cling
> Till they drop, blind in blood, without a blow;
> A people starved and stabbed on the untilled field;
> An army whom liberticide and prey
> Makes as a two-edged sword to all who wield;
> Golden and sanguine laws which tempt and slay;
> Religion Christless, Godless, a book sealed;
> A senate, Time's worst statute, unrepealed,—
> Are graves from which a glorious Phantom may
> Burst, to illumine our tempestuous day.

This is a remarkable achievement—a vivid and comprehensive analysis of the nation's ills compressed into fourteen lines. Many of the targets will be familiar: the depravity of the Royal family, the use of the army against the people, the employment of *agents provocateurs* ('laws which tempt and slay'), the neglect of the true spirit of religion and the unreformed state of Parliament. In line 12 Shelley orginally wrote *A cloak of lies worn on Power's holiday*, then *A senate full of lies* and finally, *A senate, Time's worst statute, unrepealed*.[8] The first version might have been intended to refer back to the indictment of religion in the previous line; certainly it bears a resemblance to the description of Fraud (Eldon) in *The Mask of Anarchy*, 'Clothed with the Bible, as with light'. It also suggests the heartless masquerade on which is based the whole structure of government, the system operated with such duplicity by the 'Men in the Brazen Masks of power' (as *The Examiner* once described them).[9] Peterloo is in the catalogue also, linked this time to the failure to cultivate land ('the untilled field') which might have helped to relieve the distress of the poor. All the details are precise and quite specific in their reference, yet the poem gains in power because Shelley does not press home the specificity. Though 'Princes', 'Rulers', 'An army' and 'A Senate' can all be readily identified by his readers, each seems to suggest that the particular instance with which we are dealing is only another example in the endless process of history, the never-ceasing 'war of the oppressed against the oppressors', the struggle in which 'power and will / In opposition rule our mortal day'. Thus, the grim scene of 'England in 1819' is both general and particular at once.

The tone of this sonnet bears an obvious relation to the terms of political debate employed by the radicals. In particular there is a close similarity between Shelley's poem and Sir Francis Burdett's Election Address as published in *The Examiner* on 11 October 1812: Burdett speaks of 'an army of spies and informers . . . a Phantom for a king; a degraded aristocracy; an oppressed people . . . vague and sanguinary Laws . . .'. Further parallels could be found with Burdett's *Address to the Prince Regent* delivered when he interrupted the Speaker, who was about to pay the customary flattering tribute, and proceeded to lay bare the appalling condition in which the country found itself. Shelley is remarkably successful in managing this kind of attack; Hazlitt shrewdly acknowledged this when he said, 'Indignation makes him pointed and intelligible enough, and breathes into his verse a spirit very different from his own boasted spirit of Love.'[10] Everyone would agree that the first twelve lines are powerful and impressive. The problem for Shelley is how to bring the poem to an end or, perhaps one might say, how to find a way out of this political impasse. The main body of the sonnet implies the possibility of change. The king is dying, the rulers will drop 'blind in blood, without a blow', the army is a two-edged sword and therefore will destroy those who wield it as much as those against whom it is employed. Here there are intimations of a doctrine which Shelley makes explicit elsewhere: the doctrine that the tyrant will eventually destroy himself.[11]

However, this will not serve as a resolution in 'England in 1819'. For one thing, the prevailing sense of evil is too strong and, for another, that very generality which has been remarked earlier underlines the impression that, even if the *dramatis personae* change, the evil play of power will go on for ever. Since the possibility of evil crumbling from within as a result of its own corruption seems so remote, Shelley has recourse to a god in a machine, exactly as in *The Mask of Anarchy*. He allotted two-thirds of that poem to the influence of the redeeming Shape (even more if one counts the patient Hope as a precursor); here the glorious Phantom is given one and a half lines out of fourteen. The indefiniteness of this glorious Phantom as opposed to the tangibility of the evils she will come to redress is as damaging as it is in the longer poem. Furthermore, Shelley's intellectual honesty prevents him from even believing wholeheartedly in such an incarnation: the rhyme scheme insists that we underline the improbability of this redemption by stressing the word *may*.

The Phantom had made a previous appearance in Shelley's work in his *Address to the People on the Death of the Princess Charlotte* (1817). In this he had drawn a contrast between the public mourning for the death of the young Princess and the lack of public recognition for the death of British Liberty, symbolised by the execution of Brandreth, Ludlam and Turner, who had been led on to insurrection by a government agent. In his peroration he called on the people of England to go into mourning:

Let us follow the corpse of British Liberty slowly and reverentially to its tomb; and if some glorious Phantom should appear and make its throne of broken swords and sceptres and royal crowns trampled in the dust, let us say that the Spirit of Liberty has arisen from its grave and left all that was gross and mortal there, and kneel down and worship it as our Queen.[12]

This is better managed than the conclusion of the sonnet, not least because the apparition is more carefully particularised ('broken swords and sceptres and royal crowns trampled in the dust'); but it also evidences the same kind of wishful thinking.

At this point it is worth considering the comments of Dr Leavis, who also notices the strength of the main body of the sonnet and the 'pathetic weakness' of the final couplet:

Contemplation of the actual world being unendurable, Shelley devotes himself to the glorious Phantom that may . . . work a sudden miraculous change but is in any case as vague as Demogorgon and as unrelated to actuality—to which Shelley's Evil is correspondingly unrelated.[13]

About the weakness of the Phantom Leavis is surely right. But his conclusion seems oddly twisted. 'England in 1819' is not an index of Shelley's ethereality or his inability to portray a tangible evil. In fact, it is precisely the opposite. Shelley would like to imagine a happy deliverance for his ailing country but his strong sense of reality makes it impossible for him to do so convincingly. A mere escapist would not have allowed that ironical and limiting stress on *may*. Surely the point is that Shelley's sense of evil is too strong rather than too weak? Here is an excellent example of how even an attentive and supposedly 'close' reading can be damaged by preconceptions. In passing one might also note that Leavis has also misread *Prometheus Unbound* and is using his misreading against Shelley: it is not Demogorgon who brings down Jupiter but Prometheus who achieves this result by collaborating positively with the forces of historical necessity and causation embodied in Demogorgon.

However, *as a poem* 'England in 1819' is ultimately a failure as is *The Mask of Anarchy*. Both are noble in their failure and both are poems of remarkable power, yet neither is completely satisfying as a poem in its own right. Shelley has not been able to bridge successfully the gap between reality and desire. We might remember the exchange between Julian and Maddalo: *Julian*: '. . . if we were not weak / Should we be less in deed than in desire?' *Maddalo*: 'Ay, if we were not weak—and we aspire / How vainly to be strong! You talk Utopia.' In order to achieve that Utopia convincingly, to wed deed indissolubly to desire, it was necessary for Shelley to write another kind of poem.

(ii)

In such an age it was natural to ask whether a poet had any right to devote his attention to poetry. Shelley told Medwin early in 1820: 'These are not times in which one has much spirit for writing Poetry;

although there is a keen air in them that sharpens the wits of men and makes them imagine vividly even in the midst of despondence.'[14] He had never been averse to political involvement and would not have agreed with Coleridge that there was 'something inherently mean in the idea of action'. His launching into the Bristol Channel of bottles bearing political pamphlets may seem laughable from the security of our own age but it was a real political gesture which might have had disastrous personal consequences. The Inspecting Commander of Revenue Cruisers, Western District, sent a warning to the Home Secretary that seditious agitators by 'this novel mode of disseminating their pernicious opinions' might do 'incalculable mischief' among 'the seafaring part of the People'.[15] For some time Shelley was under surveillance both in Ireland and in England and reports on his behaviour were despatched to Lord Sidmouth in the Home Office.

His later involvement in politics was less direct, though a letter of July 1818 seems to indicate that the bad health which was one of the primary causes for his emigrating to Italy may have hindered his activities.[16] His final cry of relief that his good genius had restrained him from political involvement[17] should be taken in context: it may be no more than an expression of the prevailing mood, the atmosphere which permeates the unfinished *Triumph of Life*. It also contradicts the facts, since Shelley did compose his popular songs and did try to have them published and since he also produced political pamphlets such as *A Philosophical View of Reform*. Shelley's contribution to the political life of his country would certainly have been greater had his publishers been less cautious (though they had every reason for caution as Eaton, the Hunts, Carlile and many others could testify: in 1819 alone there were seventy-five prosecutions for seditious or blasphemous libel).[18] So, with some very notable exceptions particularly in 1819, the main drift of Shelley's later years was away from direct political involvement or from poetry which was plainly didactic towards a more idealised kind of poetry which would ultimately help to change the climate of opinion.

It seems that Shelley never regarded poetry as a private activity. His most serious poems were intended to be read; as he put it in the Preface to *The Revolt of Islam*: 'It is the business of the Poet to communicate to others the pleasure and the enthusiasm arising out of those images and feelings in the vivid presence of which within his own mind consists at once his inspiration and his reward.' Again, though certain experiences and feelings might be considered necessary qualifications for writing poetry, a 'more essential attribute' is 'the power of awakening in others sensations like those which animate my own bosom'. Therefore, poets must not write 'with the fear of Reviews before their eyes'. Where would Homer, Lucretius, Shakespeare and Milton be, if they had not produced their poetry 'with an utter disregard of anonymous censure'?[19] For all this magniloquence, Shelley had his own problems with the critics. He could declare, 'The man must be enviably happy whom Reviews can make miserable' but the reviews often did make him miserable. They were 'nothing but a series of wet blankets'; he was in the purgatory or poetry; writing poetry without a public was a disease; poetry was downgraded to 'this jingling food for the hunger of oblivion, called *verse*'.[20] If chameleons live on light and air, poets' food is love and fame; finding nothing but criticism, Shelley was finally goaded into responding. In two short poems, 'Lines to a Critic' and 'Lines to a Reviewer', both of which were probably intended for Southey and neither of which appeared during Shelley's lifetime, he turned the other cheek and refused to greet hatred with hatred.[21]

For all the assumed calm, his letters show that he was often tempted to give up:

I am, speaking literarily, infirm of purpose. I have great designs, and feeble hopes of ever accomplishing them. (November 1820)

As to me, I am, perhaps, morbidly indifferent to this sort of praise or blame [as handed out to Keats]; and this, perhaps, deprives me of an incitement to do what now I never shall do, i.e., write anything worth calling a poem. (May 1821)

I write nothing, and probably shall write no more. It offends me to see my name classed among those who have no name. If I cannot be something better, I had rather be nothing, and the accursed cause to the downfall of which I dedicated what powers I may have had—flourishes like a cedar and covers England with its boughs. My motive was never the infirm desire of fame; and if I should continue an author, I feel that I should desire it. (August 1821)

I am employed in nothing—I read—but I have no spirits for serious composition—I have no confidence & to write [in] solitude or put forth thoughts without sympathy is unprofitable vanity. (December 1821)[22]

In spite of these doubts and despairs Shelley remained resilient. The bulk and range of the *Poetical Works* is sufficient indication of that. This is a matter of great importance since what is involved takes us far beyond the merely personal difficulties of Shelley to the problems of the age. Fearing that he was a candidate for the Academy of Disappointed Authors,[23] lamenting the lack of a sympathetic reading public, Shelley went on writing and preparing his works for publication. In the sacred war in which he was engaged on behalf of the party 'of liberty & of the oppressed'[24] there could be no turning back. If faith was ever a virtue, it was so in politics rather than in religion. And hope 'as Coleridge says is a solemn duty which we owe alike to ourselves & to the world'.[25] Shelley's refusal to give in to personal despair is intimately related to the high ideals which he conceived for poetry and to the way in which he pursued them in a dark and 'tempestuous day'.

The great temptation to despair was the failure of the French Revolution and the transformation of Napoleon from liberator into tyrant (the young Shelley began a poem on the fall of Napoleon with characteristic vehemence, 'I hated thee, fallen tyrant!'). Shelley recognised that the Revolution was the 'master theme of the epoch' and he devoted a novel (*Hubert Cauvin*) and an epic poem (*The Revolt of Islam*) to exploring its implications. He advised Byron that it would make a suitable subject 'involving pictures of all that is best qualified to interest and to instruct mankind'.[26] Coleridge had offered similar advice to Wordsworth :

... I wish you would write a poem ... addressed to those, who, in consequence of the complete failure of the French Revolution, have thrown up all hopes of the amelioration of mankind, and are sinking into an almost epicurean selfishness, disguising the same under the soft titles of domestic attachment and contempt for visionary *philosophes*. It would do great good ...[27]

The Revolt of Islam might have been written to Coleridge's specifications, so closely does it address itself to these purposes.

Shelley's Preface explains that 'It is an experiment on the temper of the public mind, as to how far a thirst for a happier condition of moral and political society survives, among the enlightened and refined, the tempests which have shaken the age in which we live'. This experiment is of great significance because up to now 'gloom and misanthropy have become the characteristics of the age in which we live, the solace of a disappointment that unconsciously finds relief only in the wilful exaggeration of its own despair'. Literature has been infected. 'Metaphysics, and inquiries into moral and political science have become little else than vain attempts to revive exploded superstitions, or sophisms like those of Mr Malthus, calculated to lull the oppressors of mankind into a security of everlasting triumph.' Such a situation is quite understandable but, says Shelley, it is foolish to expect that those who have been fettered for many years can behave with reason and self-control as soon as they are released:

Could they listen to the plea of reason who had groaned under the calamities of a social state according to the provisions of which one man riots in luxury whilst another famishes for want of bread? Can he who the day before was a trampled slave suddenly become liberal-minded, forbearing, and independent? This is the consequence of the habits of a state of society to be produced by resolute perseverance and indefatigable hope, and long-suffering and long-believing courage, and the systematic efforts of generations of men of intellect and virtue.[28]

So one might conclude, now in 1817; such was the lesson of experience. But it had taken time for people to recognise these hard political facts, so roughly at odds with starry-eyed idealism. Shelley realised that 'those who now live have survived an age of despair'. The emphasis here is on *survived* because Shelley also says, 'mankind appear to me to be emerging from their trance. I am aware ... of a slow, gradual, silent change.' Yet, even if there was a slow birth of optimism, it was only too easy to sink back into the rut of despair. Byron was an example, and Shelley devoted much energy to trying to persuade him that man was marked out for something better than the 'funereal destiny' and the 'sad, unallied existence' acknowledged in his *Prometheus*.

The Revolt of Islam was written in order to consolidate that slow, gradual, silent change; it was intended to embody man's hopes of something better and to foster his belief in his own capabilities. Shelley intended to influence his readers but the poem was only didactic in the widest sense.

... I have chosen a story of human passion in its most universal character, diversified with moving and romantic adventures, and appealing, in contempt of all artificial opinions or institutions, to the common sympathies of every human breast. I have made no attempt to recommend the motives which I would substitute for those at present governing mankind, by methodical and systematic argument. I would only awaken the feelings, so that the reader should see the beauty of true virtue, and be incited to those inquiries which have led to my moral and political creed, and that of some of the sublimest intellects in the world. The Poem therefore ... is narrative, not didactic.

Thus, through presenting a 'succession of pictures' Shelley would take his reader through a series of events bearing an obvious similarity to the pattern of the French Revolution. He himself would take care not to intrude his own ideas directly into the narrative, though his must remain the guiding intelligence. Indeed, some of the ideas expressed might be contrary to his own convictions:

I trust that the reader will carefully distinguish between those opinions which have a dramatic propriety in reference to the characters which they are designed to elucidate, and such as are properly my own. The erroneous and degrading idea which many have conceived of a Supreme Being, for instance, is spoken against, but not the Supreme Being itself.

What gives this long, and at times rather awkward, narrative its focus and direction is the conception of the two central characters, Laon and Cythna, and of their relation to each other. They achieve their eminence as revolutionary leaders not only because of their love of their fellow-man but because of their love for each other. But for all that, Shelley does not suggest that love alone will make the world go round. It must be leagued with the tougher virtues, fortitude, persever-ance, patience, faith and hope. His narrative line does not exclude the journey through despair which marked the later days of the French Revolution and the rise of Napoleon. It concludes with the following sequence of events:

... the confederacy of the Rulers of the World, and the restoration of the expelled Dynasty by foreign arms; the massacre and extermination of the Patriots, and the victory of established power; the consequences of legitimate despotism,—civil war, famine, plague, superstition, and an utter extinction of the domestic affections; the judicial murder of the advocates of Liberty; the temporary triumph of oppression, that secure earnest of its final and inevitable fall; the transient nature of ignorance and error, and the eternity of genius and virtue.

In the worldly sense, Laon and Cythna are failures, since they are captured by their enemies and executed and the success of their revolu-tion is short-lived. In the final canto they are gathered into eternity, being received into a kind of gentle Valhalla presided over by a star-shining spirit, 'The better Genius of this world's estate'. Adonais and some other late poems may come to mind here. Shelley is claiming two things: first, that 'virtue, though obscured on Earth, not less / Survives all mortal change in lasting loveliness' (compare the Conclusion to The Sensitive Plant); second, that virtue such as this is not only self-delighting but has an invaluable social function since it can raise 'That lamp of hope on high, which time nor chance / Nor change may not extinguish' (lines 1555–6). The poem constantly acknowledges the grounds for despair only to rise triumphantly above them. In the highly allegorical first canto the narrator is searching for love when 'black despair, / The shadow of a starless night, was thrown / Over the world in which I moved alone'; obviously, this refers to that 'melancholy desolation' caused by the Revolution, which Shelley had analysed in the Preface. Later, we meet a kindly old man who rescues Laon, but for all his solicitude turns out to be another Man of the Hill, a recluse who has given up hope of the world:

> But custom maketh blind and obdurate
>   The loftiest hearts:—he had beheld the woe
> In which mankind was bound, but deemed that fate
> Which made them abject, would preserve them so . . .
>   (lines 1486–9)

He is also rather similar to Maddalo, bearing within him those 'dim labyrinths, where / Hope, near imagined chasms, is struggling with despair' (lines 4205–6). By their example, Laon and Cythna (and Shelley as author) try to swing the balance in favour of hope or, in a memorable phrase, to 'cast the vote of love in hope's abandoned urn' (line 1611). This involves a long and unremitting effort in which we must devote ourselves to the selfless service of the cause. As Shelley told Godwin in one of his letters from Dublin: 'Wholly to abstract our views from self undoubtedly requires unparalelled disinterestedness, there is not a completer abstraction than labouring for distant ages.'[29] Or, as Cythna told Laon:

> This is the winter of the world:—and here
>   We die, even as the winds of Autumn fade,
> Expiring in the frore and foggy air.—
>   Behold! Spring comes, though we must pass, who made
>   The promise of its birth,—even as the shade
> Which from our death, as from a mountain, flings
>   The future, a broad sunrise; thus arrayed
>   As with the plumes of overshadowing wings,
> From its dark gulf of chains, Earth like an eagle springs.
>   (lines 3685–93)

Cythna does not expect personal immortality: Heroes, Poets and Sages

>   . . . perish, but they leave
>   All hope, or love, or truth, or liberty,
>   Whose forms their mighty spirits could conceive,
> To be a rule and law to ages that survive.

The whole passage is delicately balanced between Cythna's regret that she and Laon must part from each other in 'senseless death' and her joyful hope in a better future for succeeding generations. Thus, the final canto with its Senate of the departed great must not be interpreted as a sentimental picture of the afterlife. It is Shelley's attempt to convey his belief in the high dignity of man and in the ultimate relevance of all actions which are designed to improve his condition. A vote in hope's abandoned urn is never wasted.

(iii)

Prometheus Unbound is a much greater poem than The Revolt of Islam; indeed it is one of Shelley's finest sustained achievements and one of the major poetic successes of the nineteenth century. Yet its basic concerns are fairly similar to the Revolt; it, too, is an attempt to deliver Shelley's contemporaries from despair and it, too, directs itself to the French Revolution and its meaning. One of the temptations which Prometheus has to resist is the temptation to apathy or despair induced by two historical panoramas unveiled by the Furies: one represents the history of Christianity, notably the wars of religion, while the other illustrates how high hopes of freedom and equality in France soon led to 'the vintage-time for Death and Sin' and what might appear to be the ultimate victory of Despair. After he has been subjected to this orientation process, Prometheus is faced by the most insinuating temptation:

> In each human heart terror survives
> The ravin it has gorged: the loftiest fear
> All that they would disdain to think were true:
> Hypocrisy and custom make their minds
> The fanes of many a worship, now outworn.
> They dare not devise good for man's estate,
> And yet they know not that they do not dare.
> The good want power, but to weep barren tears.
> The powerful goodness want: worse need for them.
> The wise want love; and those who love want wisdom;
> And all best things are thus confused to ill.
> Many are strong and rich,—and would be just,—
> But live among their suffering fellow men
> As if none felt: they know not what they do.
>   (I. 618–31)

This is a magnificent example of Shelley's ability to feel into the moral implications of a situation and to gauge the temperature of his own times. It shows a characteristic virtuosity in its combination of abstract theme with direct and forcible expression. The point of this vividly realised temptation is that the analysis it presents is undeniably true; and Prometheus knows this. His response is that the words the Fury has spoken to him are terrible, 'And yet I pity those they torture not'. Thus he escapes the temptation because he is still capable of feeling an agonising pity, which means that he is still free from the taints of apathy or despair.

Having survived this last and greatest temptation, Prometheus receives support and consolation. His mother, the Earth, has organised a visitation to counteract the assault of the Furies:

> To cheer thy state
> I bid ascend those subtle and fair spirits,
> Whose homes are the dim caves of human thought,
> And who inhabit, as birds wing the wind,
> Its world-surrounding aether; they behold
> Beyond that twilight realm, as in a glass,
> The future: may they speak comfort to thee!
>
> (I. 657–63)

The Spirits ascend from within, that is, from the depths of human consciousness; but since they inhabit the 'world-surrounding aether' they also seem to represent something like the spirit of the age or the general climate of opinion. Yet they transcend the limitations of the *Zeitgeist* or, as Shelley puts it later, 'we breathe, and sicken not, / The atmosphere of human thought'; this seems to mean that they represent man's best thoughts, those benignant visitings and intimations of better things which he experiences from time to time. These Spirits offer Prometheus six visions as an antidote to the visions produced by the Furies. The first four present a battle victoriously fought under the banner of love, a man giving up his life to save a drowning enemy, a philosopher dreaming of a regenerated society and a poet creating from the mortal world 'Forms more real than living man'. The last two visions are quite unexpected, a fine example of Shelley's subtle invention. The fifth begins with an image of love's electrical powers: 'Scattering the liquid joy of life from his ambrosial tresses: / His footsteps paved the world with light.' Suddenly the image turns sour and we find ourselves once again on the treadmill of history: as the light fades, 'hollow Ruin yawned behind' and we catch a glimpse of 'headless patriots, and pale youths who perished, unupbraiding'. The Sixth Spirit develops the implications:

Ah, sister! Desolation is a delicate thing:
  It walks not on the earth, it floats not on the air,
But treads with lulling footstep, and fans with silent wing
  The tender hopes which in their hearts the best and gentlest bear;
Who soothed to false repose by the fanning plumes above,
  And the music-stirring motion of its soft and busy feet,
Dream visions of aërial joy, and call the monster Love,
  And wake, and find the shadow Pain—as he whom now we greet.
                                                      (I. 772–9)

This is one of the most remarkable examples of the direct influence of Shelley's reading and translation of Plato. In the *Symposium*, which Shelley translated in 1818, there is a celebration of the operation and influence of Love, which in its turn is based on a passage of Homer:

For Homer says, that the Goddess Calamity is delicate, and that her feet are tender. 'Her feet are soft,' he says, 'for she treads not upon the ground, but makes her path upon the heads of men.'... Love walks not upon the earth, nor over the heads of men, which are not indeed very soft, but he dwells within, and treads on the softest of existing things, having established his habitation within the souls and inmost nature of Gods and men; not indeed in all souls—for wherever he chances to find a hard and rugged disposition, there he will not inhabit, but only where it is most soft and tender. (Shelley's version).[30]

Where the poet Agathon (the speaker in the *Symposium*) turns Homer's Ate or Calamity into Love, Shelley reverses the process and identifies Love with Ate. He recognises the vulnerability of the good and the tender-hearted and how easy it is for the generous impulse of love and pity to turn into the hand-wringing of despair. The process is enacted before our eyes (and those of Prometheus) as the Fifth Spirit's song turns from joy to sorrow. For reformers and idealists, such as Prometheus, this is an occupational hazard; for those who can hear the Fury's message of how all best things are confused to ill, without any stirrings of pity or concern, desolation is an unknown experience. Yet there is the consoling fact that because desolation with its soft and busy feet arises within the heart of man it is ultimately subject to his own control. It can be expelled, or more appropriately perhaps, it can be transformed back into Love and the dangerous process reversed by an act of hope and faith. So Agathon's linking of Love and Calamity had proved highly suggestive for Shelley: it helped him to see how closely the two were connected and how easily desolation could make its mark on 'a nerve o'er which do creep / The else unfelt oppressions of this earth'.[31] This melancholy experience was partly what he had

E

in mind in the Preface to *Alastor* when he distinguished between those who are 'deluded by no generous error', who neither rejoice in human joy nor mourn with human grief, and the pure and tender-hearted. The former are morally dead but they live on till their hearts burn to the socket, while the good die first when 'the vacancy of their spirit suddenly makes itself felt'.

Eventually, Prometheus is able to conquer these dark murmurings from his own heart but only with the help of Asia, who is not only the equivalent of Cythna, the beloved female comrade in arms, but who also represents the capacity for love within Prometheus himself. Two acts out of four are devoted to a detailed analysis of the patient and difficult process by which a victory is achieved; the last two acts are mostly given over to a celebration of the new order and an examination of what it implies. Yet even at the high points of this celebration, Shelley admits significant qualifications:

> The loathsome mask has fallen, the man remains
> Sceptreless, free, uncircumscribed—but man:
> Equal, unclassed, tribeless and nationless;
> Exempt from awe, worship, degree,—the king
> Over himself; just, gentle, wise—but man:
> Passionless? no—yet free from guilt or pain,
> Which were, for his will made, or suffered them;
> Nor yet exempt, though ruling them like slaves,
> From chance, and death, and mutability,
> The clogs of that which else might oversoar
> The loftiest star of unascended Heaven,
> Pinnacled dim in the intense inane.
>
> (III, iv. 193–204)

This, as Leigh Hunt says, is 'the consummation of a state of things for which all the preceding part of the poem has been yearning':[32] at last man is his own master, free to be himself, delivered from the bondage for which he was responsible by his acquiescence in or his active support of a system which prevented him from recognising his own best self. Yet he is still only man and therefore remains subject to the limitations of mortality. Chance, death and mutability he may turn 'to the best and most philosophical account', in that sense ruling them like slaves; yet he remains subject to their influence. Certain goals must remain beyond his grasp: heaven must remain 'unascended'. This sobering note may have been intended as a riposte to Godwin, Condorcet and others whose view of man's perfectibility was too simple-minded for Shelley.

Another qualification can be found in this brief exchange between Asia and the Spirit of the Hour, which is one of the vehicles of revolution:

Asia: Thou breathest on their nostrils, but my breath
        Would give them swifter speed.
Spirit: Alas! it could not.

(II,V. 6–7)

This comes in a passage which is usually taken to be beautiful but meaningless; polite conversation to pass the time until the revolution has been prepared.[33] But, as Kenneth Cameron has brilliantly pointed out, Shelley's meaning here is very precise. There are, in fact, two chariots, one bearing Demogorgon and the other bearing Asia and Panthea. Both are the chariots of the 'immortal hours', that is, both are associated with a particular point in the unfolding process of history. Demogorgon's chariot is the chariot of revolution driven by 'A spirit with a dreadful countenance', the violent destiny which awaits Jupiter. Asia's chariot is driven by a spirit who, the imagery suggests, may be identified with love, energy and regeneration. The point of the dialogue between Asia and the Spirit seems to be: 'If love arrives close after the revolutionary hour, the new order will be born; if it does not, the hour will be aborted and fade; but love can neither hasten nor retard its arrival, since this is determined by necessity alone.'[34] The shape of history depends on the way in which man can learn to manage for his own benefit the laws of consequence, which in themselves are blind and inexorable.

One further example of the way in which Shelley thwarts any likelihood of complacency can be seen in the description of the temple of Prometheus at the end of Act Three Scene Three:

It is deserted now, but once it bore
Thy name, Prometheus; there the emulous youths
Bore to thy honour through the divine gloom
The lamp which was thine emblem—even as those
Who bear the untransmitted torch of hope
Into the grave, across the night of life,
As thou hast borne it most triumphantly
To this far goal of time.

The basic image is derived from the Athenian festival in honour of the fire-gods during which a race was run with lighted torches from the altar of Prometheus to the city. The first to arrive without letting the torch out was the winner.[35] Thomas Taylor the Platonist commented in his translation of Pausanias: 'This custom . . . was intended to signify that he is the true conqueror in the race of life, whose rational part is not extinguished . . .'.[36] This is not how Shelley interprets it, though he may have found Taylor's interpretation suggestive. The strikingly Pindaric image was well calculated to appeal to him since it is memorably graphic while its implications are richly metaphysical. Life is seen as a torch-race through darkened streets to a goal or finishing-line beyond the grave. Though the example and prowess of others may be inspiring and though we may encourage each other to greater efforts (the youths are 'emulous'), this is a race which each man must run for himself. The most significant word in the whole description is *untransmitted*, yet another of Shelley's negatives limiting the scope of optimism, a clog on the free flight of revolutionary man. The torch is untransmitted because, in the simplest sense, this is not a relay race. Each man has to carry the torch on his own account.

As some interpreters have noted with disapproval, Prometheus ultimately withdraws from the scene of human struggle and retires to a temple. One may attribute this to Shelley's intermittent desire utterly to desert all human society, to retire with his wife and child to a solitary island and to 'shut upon my retreat the floodgates of the world'.[37] Undoubtedly the retirement of Prometheus *is* informed by this personal sense of world-weariness but Shelley's grasp of his mythological scheme was sufficiently firm not to be deflected by emotions which were merely private. Prometheus has blazed his trail, and pioneered the regeneration of society. If we regard him as a *character* in his own right, his retreat might be seen as a weakness, a failure to remain meaningfully involved. Yet, to react in this way is to miss Shelley's point. In the first place, Prometheus is 'the type of the highest perfection of moral and intellectual nature', that is, he represents what man should aspire to rather than what is tangibly within his grasp. That Prometheus is more than human is not due to Shelley's incompetence in harmonising the original myth with his own intentions but might suggest that Prometheus represents man's highest self, the potentiality within him for becoming his own divinity.

Secondly, and perhaps even more important, since Prometheus is not a character, his retreat suggests not a sudden loss of interest on his part but the necessity that the revolution which he has brought about should be perpetually renewed by the human race. The revolution will only be real and effective in so far as we in our own lives are able to recreate it. The end of the play suggests clearly enough that it is possible for us to slide back as, for example, the French had done during the Terror and under the tyranny of Napoleon. Should this danger threaten, we have before us the example of Prometheus and the cardinal virtues whose value he taught us: observing this code, we should be able to 'reassume / An empire o'er the disentangled Doom' (reassert our authority over the destructive forces which are potential within us). Thus, what Prometheus has achieved for us is a notable enhancement of human possibility (Shelley would have said the same of Christ or Socrates); but the torch remains *untransmitted*, since whether we continue to possess that freedom or not is entirely our responsibility.

(iv)

Responsibility is, in fact, the keynote of much of Shelley's political poetry. Here again we find an emphasis which seems to link Shelley more closely with his eighteenth-century predecessors than with the generally acknowledged goals of Romanticism. As we have seen, Shelley's political views were undoubtedly radical, but he generally qualified his radical ardour with an insistence on restraint. Like other prophetic poets, such as Blake and Lawrence, he recognised the importance of the inner revolution: it was no use regenerating the institutions of society until man had regenerated himself. Indeed, since political metaphors were so often employed, one might say that what man required was a new *state of mind*. In the *Essay on Christianity* Shelley interpreted a passage from the Sermon on the Mount to mean that every man possesses the power to legislate for himself: 'It is in the power of each individual to level the inequality which is the . . . complaint of mankind. . . . Let him be well aware of his own worth and moral dignity.'[38] Thus, though Shelley can be seen as an anarchist in the sense that he did not approve of government (more particularly of Governments), he believed strongly in the need for internal order. Tyrants were incapable of achieving this self control: hence, they were dominated by their own worst feelings and those who served them were 'the slaves of slaves'.[39] So the ghost of Mahomet the Second tells his successor of the ironical kingdom which awaits him in the afterlife:

> The Anarchs of the world of darkness keep
> A throne for thee, round which thine empire lies
> Boundless and mute; and for thy subjects thou,
> Like us, shalt rule the ghosts of murdered life,
> The phantoms of the powers who rule thee now—

Mutinous passions, and conflicting fears,
And hopes that sate themselves on dust, and die!—
Stripped of their mortal strength, as thou of thine.
(*Hellas*, lines 879–86)

So, in *The Triumph of Life* Rousseau explains the fall of the famous, who pass by chained to the triumphal chariot of life, their conqueror:

'The wise,

The great, the unforgotten: they who wore
    Mitres and helms and crowns, or wreaths of light,
Signs of thought's empire over thought; their lore

    Taught them not this—to know themselves; their might
Could not repress the mutiny within,
    And for the morn of truth they feigned, deep night

Caught them ere evening.'[40]

It should be noticed that Shelley includes here the leaders of both the political and intellectual realm; all are victims of an interior insurrection which they are unable to control.

Shelley applied the same principles to the revolutionary politics of his own time. The impassioned 'Ode to Liberty' celebrates the march of freedom and looks hopefully from France and Spain towards England which may be next to receive this glorious contagion; yet it also stresses the need for restraint:

He who taught man to vanquish whatsoever
    Can be between the cradle and the grave
Crowned him the King of Life: O vain endeavour!
    If on his own high will, a willing slave,
He has enthroned the oppression and the oppressor.
(lines 241–5)

Most explicit of all is the sonnet normally known as 'Political Greatness', Mary Shelley's tactful substitution for Shelley's own title 'Sonnet to the Republic of Benevento'. This poem, which refers to the rising of the Carbonari against Ferdinand of Naples in July 1820, deserves to be given in full:

Nor happiness, nor majesty, nor fame,
Nor peace nor strength, nor skill in arms or arts,
Shepherd those herds whom Tyranny makes tame:
Verse echoes not one beating of their hearts;

History is but the shadow of their shame;
Art veils her glass, or from its pageant starts
As to Oblivion their blind millions fleet,
Staining that Heaven with obscene imagery
Of their own likeness.—What are numbers, knit
By force or custom? Man, who man would be,
Must rule the empire of himself, in it
Must be supreme; establishing his throne
On vanquished will; quelling the anarchy
Of hopes and fears; being himself alone.

Shelley never came closer to expressing despair of active politics. Yet his letters indicate that he was excited by the revolution at Naples and supported it emotionally and intellectually. When the Austrian armies advanced to win back the city, Shelley was led to prophesy that even their military capabilities

...if the spirit of Regeneration is abroad are chaff before the storm, the very elements & events will fight against them, indignation & shameful repulse will burn after them to the vallies of the Alps ... If the Austrians meet with any serious check—they may as well at once retire, for the good spirit of the World is out against them.—If they march to Naples at once— let us hide our heads in sorrow, for our hopes of political good are in vain.[41]

Yet, for all his enthusiasm, Shelley was perfectly aware of the realities of the situation; not least he recognised the limitations of the people of Naples themselves. The King had signed a new constitution ('as Bankers sign their Bills', said Claire Clairmont) but a new constitution meant very little unless the people could achieve inner freedom, as it were reconstitute themselves from within. Otherwise they would fail to realise the perfection latent in themselves and in their city, appearing as obscene distortions of what they might have been. This emphasis on the need for an interior revolution and the futility of constitutional reforms which are not endorsed and validated by a corresponding change of heart does not mean that Shelley had abandoned hope in active politics. Though there were times when he came close to doing this, he could never consent to such passivity in the face of difficulties. It has been suggested that, like Wordsworth, he deserted direct political involvement for the poetic world in which the revolution could be enacted through myth and ritual.[42] This is true but only if one makes three qualifications: Shelley never *deserted* politics in the widest sense; he sought for the paradise within but he also yearned for a new society which would be more acceptable as a political structure; he did not regard poetry, mythological, ritualistic or whatever, as an end in itself. Poetry itself was a social factor which could make a significant contribution to the world in which we all live. Shelley was by no means a political naif and yet he would never have agreed with Auden's blunt assertion that 'Poetry makes nothing happen'.

Shelley believed that a poet was inevitably influenced by the spirit of the age: in a limited sense, the Furies and the Spirits of the First Act of *Prometheus Unbound* might be interpreted as the contemporary influences which could lead Prometheus either to the paradise of hope or to the hell of despair. It was the poet's responsibility not to give in to the insinuating message of those darker spirits but to attune himself to the 'wandering voices and the shadows . . . / Of all that man becomes, the mediators / Of that best worship, love'.[43] Poetry was 'the record of the best and happiest moments of the happiest and best minds': it was 'the faculty which contains within itself the seeds at once of its own and of social renovation'. Indeed poetry could redeem the time: 'it is ever still the light of life; the source of whatever of beautiful or generous or true can have place in an evil time.'[44]

Notes to chapter four

1   Compare the 'dazzling form' in Coleridge's *The Destiny of Nations*, l. 433.
2   *All in Due Time*, p. 56.
3   *All in Due Time*, p. 57.
4   Cameron, *Shelley:The Golden Years*, p. 350.
5   Brimley Johnson, *Shelley–Leigh Hunt*, pp. 77–8.
6   *Letters*, II. 153.
7   I owe this identification to Geoffrey Matthews, *Shelley: Selected Poems and Prose*, Oxford University Press, 1964, p. 197.
8   Bod. MS. Shelley adds. e. 12, p. 182.
9   Cameron, *Shelley: The Golden Years*, p. 346.
10 Redpath, *The Young Romantics*, p. 394.
11 e.g. 'Falsehood is a scorpion that will sting itself to death' (*Prose*, p. 71) and *Queen Mab*, VI. 32–8, which employs the same image.
12 Clark, *Prose*, p. 169.
13 *Revaluation*, p. 228.
14 *Letters*, II. 169.
15 A. M. D. Hughes, *The Nascent Mind of Shelley*, 1947, p. 156.
16 *Letters*, II. 22.
17 *Letters*, II. 442.
18 Richard Holmes, *Shelley:The Pursuit*, p. 540.
19 *P.W.*, pp. 33–6.
20 *Letters*, II. 382–3, 245, 258, 213, 374.
21 See 'A Satire on Satire', which is also concerned with his reactions to Southey.
22 *Letters*, II. 244, 289, 331, 368.
23 *Letters*, II. 290.

24   *Letters*, II. 148.
25   *Letters*, II. 125.
26   *Letters*, I. 508.
27   *Collected Letters*, ed. E. L. Griggs, Oxford, 1956, I. 527.
28   *P.W.*, pp. 32–4.
29   *Letters*, I. 277.
30   Cited from Notopoulos, *Platonism*, p. 435.
31   *Julian and Maddalo*, ll. 449–50.
32   Brimley Johnson, *Shelley–Leigh Hunt*, p. 71.
33   e.g. by Matthew Arnold in *The Study of Poetry* (1880).
34   Cameron, *Shelley: The Golden Years*, p. 524.
35   A note on Bod. MS Shelley adds. e. 3, 28r reads 'The beginning of Plato's
     Republic——' This passage describes the torch-race which Shelley refers to.
36   Cited in Peter Butter, *Alastor, Prometheus Unbound, Adonais and other
     Poems*, Collins, 1970, p. 299.
37   *Letters*, II. 339.
38   Clark, *Prose*, p. 208.
39   *Revolt of Islam*, l. 987.
40   Lines 208–15. The MS shows that Shelley wrote *the rebels in their heart*
     before settling on *the mutiny within* (Reiman, *The Triumph of Life*, p. 165).
41   *Letters*, II. 267.
42   See Gerald MacNiece, *Shelley and the Revolutionary Idea*.
43   *Prometheus Unbound*, III, iii. 57–9.
44   *Defence*, pp. 54, 40.

CHAPTER FIVE

THE POLITICS OF RELIGION

(i)

Less than twenty years after Shelley's death, his wife noted in one of her letters: '... so many of the religious particularly like Shelley'.[1] This must have been rather shocking to those Tory and High Church reviewers who had thundered against his impieties only so recently. The *Quarterly*, for example, had responded to the audacities of *The Revolt of Islam*[2] by noting that Shelley was too young to be a reformer and too little acquainted with the Bible, which was 'a sealed book to a proud spirit'. The anonymous reviewer (who has since been identified as J. T. Coleridge) went on to corroborate his own rightness by suggesting that 'infidelity and immorality' were having an adverse effect on Shelley's *literary* achievements; his latest book was a clear proof that the impious are quickly deprived of their abilities by a self-induced process of deterioration:

Scarcely any man ever set himself in array against the cause of social order and religion, but from a proud and rebel mind, or a corrupt and undisciplined heart: where these are, true knowledge cannot grow ... Like the Egyptian of old, the wheels of his chariot are broken, the path of 'mighty waters' closes in upon him behind, and a still deepening ocean is before him ... finally, he sinks 'like lead' to the bottom and is forgotten.[3]

One can only assume that the readers of the *Quarterly* were not particularly surprised when they heard only three years later that Shelley had been drowned.

Shelley himself reacted in jocular terms in a letter to his publishers:

I was amused, too, with the finale; it is like the end of the first act of an opera, when that tremendous concordant discord sets up from the orchestra, and everybody talks and sings at once. It describes the result of my battle with their Omnipotent God; his pulling me under the sea by the hair of my head, like Pharaoh; my calling out like the devil who was *game* to the last; swearing and cursing in all comic and horrid oaths, like a French postillion on Mount Cenis; entreating everybody to drown themselves; pretending not to be drowned myself when I *am* drowned; and, lastly, *being* drowned.[4]

However, for all the insouciance of this, Shelley did care and he was hurt by the insinuations against his personal morality. Believing Robert Southey to be the author, he entered into a correspondence which showed that, even though Southey was less violent than J. T. Coleridge, he was just as censorious and just as patronising. All of this confirmed Shelley's suspicions of those who professed to be practising Christians: he told Southey that this sort of charity, this violation of what was due from man to man, was all too common ('Christ would have taught them better').[5]

Although Shelley began a reply to the editor of the *Quarterly* he never completed it and he offered no public defence. Leigh Hunt did, and the precise terms of his apologia are very instructive:

We will undertake to say that Mr Shelley knows more of the Bible, than all the priests who have anything to do with the Review or its writers. He does not abjure 'the pomps and vanities of this wicked world', only to put them on with the greater relish. To them, undoubtedly, the Bible is not a sealed book, in one sense. They open it to good profit enough. But in the sense which the Reviewer means, they contrive to have it sealed wherever the doctrines are inconvenient.[6]

He then goes on to quote Shelley's prescription for good behaviour which the *Quarterly* had printed in horrified italics:

Nor hate another's crime, nor loathe thine own . . .
And love and joy can make the foulest breast
A paradise of flowers, where peace might build her nest.

The *Quarterly* had interpreted this to mean that we should hate no crime and abstain from no gratification. But Hunt points out that Shelley's doctrine is 'infinitely nearer to that Christian benevolence so much preached and so little practised, than any the most orthodox dogmas ever published'. He also defends Shelley's private life which, he knows from experience, was in perfect conformity with his beliefs. Far from being 'shamefully dissolute in his conduct', he lived abstemiously, spent most of his time in writing and reading and visited when necessary 'the sick and the fatherless, whom others gave Bibles to and no help'.[7]

This exchange of views is highly significant for an understanding of Shelley, not because we need to know the true facts about his private life but because of what it reveals about the climate of opinion in which he was working. It is no accident that the *Quarterly* and Leigh Hunt's *Examiner* represented opposing political points of view, no accident that politics and religion should be so closely involved in their expositions. The *Quarterly* recognised that Shelley's view of religion was a challenge not only to the Established Church but to all kinds of establishment, especially the political. Though it was not incapable of recognising literary merit even in an infidel, it appreciated, quite correctly, that what was at stake was a matter of concern not merely to the arbiters of literary taste but to the whole community. Shelley's challenge was an intellectual challenge. What he was attempting to subvert was nothing less than the whole fabric of received ideas. These ideas had to be defended, the *status quo* had to be maintained, at whatever cost; therefore, the *Quarterly* did not scruple to employ libellous attacks on Shelley's personal morality in the hope that these would effectively silence him and expose his ideas to ridicule. Shelley recognised the method: it was a modified version of what he once called 'the most conclusive of syllogisms—persecution'.[8]

Hunt's reply amply demonstrates, if demonstration is needed, the selfishness and the injustice of this attack. His description of Shelley's life at Marlow is corroborated by an array of evidence and a variety of witnesses. Yet it must be admitted that, for all its wilful misrepresentation of the facts and the doctrines, the *Quarterly* was not entirely wrong. It recognised the seriousness of the issues involved. Shelley's contemporaries did not make the mistake of approaching him as a pallid writer of lyrics: they acknowledged him for what what he was, a poet of ideas, a reformer who wanted to challenge the prevailing orthodoxies and substitute for them his own revolutionary principles. They understood that Shelley was a dangerous force and they acted accordingly. As Leigh Hunt suggested, and as 'the religious' apparently discovered for themselves, there was a certain religious quality in Shelley's poetry—but it was a highly personal and challenging kind of religion, little suited to the complacencies of orthodox belief. Hunt was speaking the truth when he said that Shelley often had the Bible in his hands but, as a comparison between Hunt's own review and J. T. Coleridge's in the *Quarterly* will quickly show, the Bible could be interpreted in more ways than one. As another opponent of orthodoxy put it: 'Both read the Bible day & night, / But thou read'st black where I read white.'[9]

(ii)

Shelley read the Bible regularly and critically throughout his life. In her note to the *Revolt of Islam* Mary records his 'constant perusal of portions of the Old Testament—the Psalms, the Book of Job, the Prophet Isaiah, and others, the sublime poetry of which filled him with delight'.[10] From her *Journal* we know that in 1820 he read the New Testament, the Apocrypha and the Old Testament until the end of Ezekiel. Talking to Medwin about his perfect library he specified fifteen authors and 'last, yet first, the Bible'.[11] In 1812 he planned an anthology of biblical extracts: 'I have often thought that the moral sayings of Jesus Christ might be very useful if selected from the mystery and immorality which surrounds them—it is a little work I have in contemplation.'[12] This little work was promised to his publisher at the end of 1812 but it never appeared in print, though it may have contributed to what is now known as the *Essay on Christianity*. One of his later notebooks includes a carefully written out series of quotations from The Wisdom of Solomon which Shelley was reading in 1820. Another notebook (which includes *Letter to Maria Gisborne* and *Adonais*) has extensive and careful notes based on the first twenty chapters of St Luke. Yet another contains the beginnings of a tabular comparison of the four Gospels.[13] The evidence of the letters, the prose works and the poetry also goes to show that the Bible was regularly in Shelley's thoughts and that its ideas and images haunted not only the rationalising side of his nature but also his creative imagination. In one way or another, the Bible is at the root of much of his work.

One reason for this continuing interest was that Shelley was genuinely attracted to the literary qualities of the Bible or, more precisely, to the literary qualities of certain books such as Job and the Psalms and some of the prophets. In one of his essays he wonders why God tolerated the expostulations of Job which 'are of the most daring character' and remarks with slight acidity: 'If God were a refined critic, which from his inspiration of Ezechiel would never have been suspected, one might imagine that the profuse and sublime strain of poetry, not to be surpassed by anything in ancient literature, had found favour with him.'[14] Temperamentally, too, Shelley was well attuned to the patterns of elevation and despair which are so common in the prophets and in the Psalms. Whatever his beliefs, Shelley had a deeply religious sensibility, a readiness to open himself to the invisible energies, which must have attracted him to the poetry of the Bible and which gives to much of his work a visionary or prophetic quality.

However, this in itself would not be enough to explain the intensity and duration of Shelley's interest. The Bible also provided the traditional answers to many of the metaphysical problems which had obsessed him from an early age—was there a God? was there an existence after death? were our lives truly meaningful? Shelley showed a quite exceptional hunger for certainty in these matters and it was this which led, indirectly, to his being sent down from Oxford after publishing *The Necessity of Atheism*. In spite of its title, this little pamphlet did not proclaim that god was dead. It examined the reasons normally put forward for believing in his existence, found these inadequate and asked if anyone could answer the objections. It was a cry for help addressed to the heads of the Oxford colleges and the Bishops of England, each of whom received a copy in the post and not one of whom cared to reply. Shelley had had his first experience of the closed mind; but he persevered in his investigations. *A Refutation of Deism* which was privately printed in 1814 was a dialogue in the manner of Hume in which Shelley dispassionately explored the reasons for and against a belief in the existence of God. The discussion was buttressed by carefully selected quotations from the Bible, mostly from the Old Testament which Shelley regarded as a disgraceful record of crime and cruelty. In particular, through the mouth of Theosophus, he objected to the degraded notion of a God presented by the Old Testament: 'An unnatural monster, who sawed his fellow beings in sunder, harrowed them to fragments under harrows of iron, chopped them to pieces with axes, and burned them in brick-kilns, because they bowed before a different and less bloody idol than his own.'[15]

The political conscience of Shelley is at work here translating Biblical history into terms which were all too intelligible to a man of his generation. Though he never abandoned his concern for metaphysics, Shelley's interest in Christianity gradually shifted its focus away from the metaphysical implications of theology towards the political realities which they embodied. He came to believe that religion was 'intimately connected with politics'[16] and could not be dissociated from a variety of repressive systems which had prevented the vast majority of Europeans from reaching their full human potential. He was thinking specifically of institutionalised Christianity as interpreted by the Church, not of the genuine Christianity of those few individuals who had responded from their hearts to the true message of Christ.

The sanguinary God which Christianity has inherited from Judaism is a projection of man's own imperfections and his selfishness:

> What is that Power? Some moon-struck sophist stood
> Watching the shade from his own soul upthrown
> Fill Heaven and darken Earth, and in such mood
> The Form he saw and worshipped was his own,
> His likeness in the word's vast mirror shown;
> And 'twere an innocent dream, but that a faith
> Nursed by fear's dew of poison, grows thereon,
> And that men say, that Power has chosen Death
> On all who scorn its laws, to wreak immortal wrath.
>
> (*Revolt of Islam*, 3244–52)

If there was a God it was logically impossible that, being all-good, he could have devised the system of retaliation and revenge accepted by Christian orthodoxy. This repugnant system of an eye for an eye and a tooth for a tooth had outlived even the Greek love of liberty and destroyed Greek civilisation in a series of futile and retaliatory wars. Following in the footsteps of Aeschylus, but offering a final solution which did not involve compromising with power, Shelley devoted *Prometheus Unbound* to showing how man could and should escape from this seemingly endless cycle of retributive 'justice'. Man must be released from fear and guilt and the evil personifications of his heart must be demythologised and destroyed. The action of *Prometheus Unbound* deals largely with this—the dethronement of Jupiter, a false god who reigned simply because man's will 'made or suffered' him and who has chained Prometheus, the potential saviour, to his rock and thwarted humanity from achieving its true potential. Here Shelley is following not only the philosophers of the eighteenth century, Hume, Gibbon, Voltaire and others, but he is particularly indebted to the example of Lucretius, whose *De Rerum Natura* was designed to rid his contemporaries of the crippling fears induced by superstitious religion. *Queen Mab*, though it exhibits some youthful deficiencies, is a fair index of Shelley's approach to these matters: it bears an epigraph from Lucretius which concludes: *magnis doceo de rebus; et arctis / Religionum animos nodis exsolvere pergo* ('I tell of great matters, and I shall go on to free men's minds from the crippling bonds of superstitions').[17] For much of his career, that remained one of Shelley's main objectives.

In particular, he was much exercised by the Christian doctrine of eternal punishment. In the essay *On the Devil and Devils* he objects to the licence given to the Devils to tempt mankind into offences for which they will be punished in eternity. Such behaviour could be understood in the case of an earthly tyrant who is afraid of losing power:

But to tempt mankind to incur everlasting damnation must, on the part of

God and even on the part of the Devil, arise from that very disinterested love of tormenting and annoying which is seldom observed on earth except from the very old ... The thing that comes nearest to it is a troop of idle dirty boys baiting a cat; cooking, skinning eels, and boiling lobsters alive, and bleeding calves, and whipping pigs to death. ... It is pretended that God dislikes it, but this is mere shamefacedness and coquetting, for he has everything his own way and he need not damn unless he likes. The Devil has a better excuse ...[18]

In this passage Shelley is characteristically downright; the brutal physicality of his images is the index of his disgust. Furthermore, although he is examining a theological problem, it is clear that he is transferring it into terms which are recognisably political. Since God is a projection of the darker powers within man himself, it is not surprising if he appears to behave himself in a fashion which we might expect from 'earthly tyrants'.

As soon as we have recognised this, we can see that the whole of God's behaviour with regard to the human race is consistent and explicable. God is not the spirit of God who rules over the universe; he is a peculiarly odious distortion of a human tyrant. Consider for example the collaboration between God and the Devil:

These two considerable personages are supposed to have entered into a sort of partnership in which the weaker has consented to bear all the odium of their common actions and to allow the stronger to talk of himself as a very honourable person, on condition of having a participation in what is the especial delight of both of them—burning men to all eternity. The dirty work is done by the Devil in the same manner as some starving wretch will hire himself out to a King or Minister with a stipulation that he shall have some portion of the public spoil as an instrument to betray a certain number of other starving wretches into circumstances of capital punishment, when they may think it convenient to edify the rest by hanging up a few of those whose murmurs are too loud.[19]

Once again Shelley displays an unusual ability to project himself feelingly into the abstractions of theological dispute. Specifically, what he has in mind is the use by the British Government of informers and *agents provocateurs* to discredit radical movements. A notorious example was the Pentridge rising of 1817 in which the government spy Oliver ('the archetype of the radical Judas')[20] had played an important part. Shelley was not in agreement with the leaders of this rising and he criticised 'those thoughtless men who imagine they can find in violence a remedy for violence'; none the less, the government's behaviour was inexcusable. Of the spies he wrote:

It was their business, if they found no discontent, to create it. . . . It was their business to produce upon the public an impression that, if any attempt to attain national freedom, or to diminish the burdens of debt and taxation under which we groan, were successful the starving multitude would rush in and confound all orders and distinctions, and institutions and laws in common ruin. The inference with which they were required to arm the ministers was that despotic power ought to be eternal.[21]

What was buried with Brandreth, Ludlam and Turner was the corpse of British Liberty, murdered by a conspiracy of government in which the people had silently acquiesced. Three years later a similar pattern was disclosed in the Cato Street Conspiracy, causing Shelley to lament that 'Every thing seems to conspire against Reform'.[22] It was this kind of tyrannical repression of liberties he had in mind when he wrote in 'England in 1819' of 'Golden and sanguine laws which tempt and slay'. This political system was based on money and on violent oppression, and it provoked revolutions in order that they might be put down *pour encourager les autres*.

The legal system itself was intimately part of the repressive process. For example, Oliver's exposure as an *agent provocateur* might have been expected to undermine the practice of informing. The immediate result was that a number of conspiracy trials did end in acquittal. However the Government took good care that this did not happen in the case of the Derby rioters: the jury was hand-picked; the Prosecution was allowed ten lawyers, the Defence only two; and throughout the course of the trial Oliver's name was never mentioned, although he had been the prime instigator. Finally, even on the scaffold, the condemned men were denied their right to the traditional last words, the chaplain interposing himself between them and the crowd.[23] Here is Shelley on the legal system of Heaven as presented by Christian orthodoxy:

In this view he [the Devil] is at once the informer, the attorney general, and the jailor of the celestial tribunal. It is not good policy, or at least cannot be considered as constitutional practice, to unite these characters. The Devil must have a great interest to exert himself to procure a sentence of guilty from the judge; for I suppose there will be no jury at the resurrection—at least if there is it will be so overawed by the bench and the counsel for the Crown as to ensure whatever verdict the Court shall please to recommend. No doubt that as an incentive to his exertions, half goes to the informer. (What an army of spies and informers all Hell must afford, under the direction of that active magistrate, the Devil! How many plots and conspiracies . . .)[24]

Trials, it would seem can always be rigged. For God, read George the

Third; for the Devil, read Lord Sidmouth and Lord Eldon; for the plaintiffs, read the poor, the wretched and the oppressed. As it is on earth so shall it be in Heaven.

All of this is precisely relevant to Shelley's interpretation of orthodox theology since, on the one hand, the theology was a projection of those repressive instincts which were so obviously evidenced in politics and since, on the other, the political system was reinforced with deterrent sanctions by the theology.[25] Orthodox theology directed man's attentions towards life after death, threatening punishment for those who did not believe in it or for those who did believe but were wicked enough to ignore it. This approach had the advantage that it diverted and frustrated attempts to alter the *status quo*. The essential message of Christianity implied a redistribution of property or, more precisely, not a strictly communistic system but a system of moral responsibility according to which every man 'considers himself with respect to the great community of mankind as the steward and guardian of their interests in the property which he chances to possess'.[26] Christ had been quite unequivocal about this: 'Sell all that thou hast, give it to the poor, and follow me.' Likewise, his injunction that we should take no thought for the morrow was directed against the materialistic view of life: 'He simply exposes with the passionate rhetoric of enthusiastic love towards all human beings the miseries and mischiefs of that system which makes all things subservient to the subsistence of the material frame of man'.[27] You cannot serve God and Mammon: 'it is impossible at once to be high-minded and just and wise, and comply with the accustomed forms of human society, seek honour, wealth, or empire either from the idolatry of habit or as the direct instruments of sensual gratification.' This part of Christ's message was inconvenient and therefore it was neglected since, after all, the kingdom of Heaven is not of this world.

Shelley gives us an illustration of how this system works in *The Cenci*, where he examines specifically the mind of Italian Catholicism. The action of the play exhibits a close connection between power, wealth and authority, a nexus of self-interest which binds together Count Cenci, the Pope, and God. Beatrice prays to God 'Whose image upon earth a father is' hoping that she will not be abandoned to her father's will. But it soon appears that the will of the father is the will of the Father. Cenci assumes this with great certainty:

With what but with a father's curse doth God
Panic-strike armèd victory, and make pale

Cities in their prosperity? The world's Father
Must grant a parent's prayer against his child,
Be he who asks even what men call me.
                                                    (IV, i. 104–8)

This belief seems to be confirmed by the way in which his rebellious
sons have been eliminated in one night, apparently by divine intervention. This league of force is strengthened and confirmed by God's
representative on earth, the Holy Father, who refuses to intervene
against the Count except for the purpose of lining his own purse. He
knows that it is not in his interest to stand in the way of Cenci:

He holds it of most dangerous example
In aught to weaken the paternal power,
Being, as 'twere, the shadow of his own.
                                                    (II, ii. 54–6)

The connection between sanctions and self-interest could hardly be
made clearer. As Shelley put it in the *Essay on Christianity*:

[The doctrines of Christ] are the very doctrines which, in another shape, the
most violent assertors of Christianity denounce as impious and seditious;
who are such earnest champions for social and political disqualification as
they? This alone would be a demonstration of the falsehood of Christianity,
that the religion so called is the strongest ally and bulwark of that system
of successful force and fraud and of the selfish passions from which it has
derived its origin and permanence, against which Jesus Christ declared the
most uncompromising war, and the extinction of which appears to have been
the great motive of his life.[29]

(iii)

The first poem to handle these matters with true sophistication is
'Mont Blanc' which was written in Switzerland in the summer of 1816.
This is a highly complex poem in which Shelley explores the relation
between mind and the universe, between subject and object, taking as
the metaphorical base for his explorations the ravine through which
flows the river Arve. He then turns his gaze upwards towards the
mountain 'Far, far above, piercing the infinite sky' and towards the
desolate and barren world beneath, with its shapes hideously 'heaped
around! rude, bare, and high, / Ghastly, and scarred, and riven.' If

one asks the cause—was it earthquake perhaps or a flood of volcanic lava—there is no reply:

> None can reply—all seems eternal now,
> The wilderness has a mysterious tongue
> Which teaches awful doubt, or faith so mild,
> So solemn, so serene, that man may be
> In such a faith with nature reconciled;
> Thou hast a voice, great Mountain, to repeal
> Large codes of fraud and woe; not understood
> By all, but which the wise, and great, and good
> Interpret, or make felt, or deeply feel.
>
> (lines 75–83)

The text of line 79 is much disputed; even the manuscript draft can not settle the matter with certainty, since Shelley seems to have considered two versions of the fourth line and there is no way of being sure that what was actually printed does not represent his final intention. However, the standard reading (*But for such faith*) can only be justified by the most tortuous explanations; some critics have even been forced to interpret it as meaning exactly the opposite of what it appears to say. If we accept the manuscript reading *In such a faith*, the passage can be interpreted as follows.[30] Man can respond to the intimations in nature with awful doubt or with mild faith; the choice and the responsibility rest with him. The precise implications of 'awful doubt' are not defined (perhaps deliberately) but this doubt would appear to take one of two forms: the terrifying traces of chaos indicate *either* that there is no god and no rational plan in the universe *or* that the natural world is ruled over by an evil deity. This evil deity might be the Christian God, who finds room in his permissive scheme for violence, fear and disorder; or he might be the dark divinity of the Zoroastrian scheme, the Ahrimanes whose reign and influence Peacock had attempted to explore in his unfinished poem of that name.[31] In either case, the natural world is the violent manifestation of a callous divinity who kills us for his sport. If there is no god and no plan, the situation is equally depressing.

However, it is possible to interpret the same evidence in a more positive sense; this faith 'so mild, / So solemn, so serene' is probably the recognition that the processes of nature are governed by laws of their own, not by the capricious will of a god. This substitution of 'faith' for fear is very similar to Lucretius' policy of dispelling the darkness of terror by the light of reason. In the first book of *De Rerum*

Natura he outlines a situation which corresponds fairly exactly with Shelley's state of 'awful doubt':

> quippe ita formido mortalis continet omnis,
> quod multa in terris fieri caeloque tuentur
> quorum operum causas nulla ratione videre
> possunt, ac fieri divino numine rentur.[32]

This fear can be eliminated through the application of reason:

> quas ob res ubi viderimus nil posse creari
> de nilo, tum quod sequimur iam rectius inde
> perspiciemus, et unde queat res quaeque creari
> et quo quaeque modo fiant opera sine divom.[33]

Although 'faith' is a more enthusiastic word than Lucretius would have allowed himself, the basic pattern is very similar to that of 'Mont Blanc'.

Shelley's poem suggests that nature is oracular and speaks in a 'mysterious tongue' which is not understood by all; yet, if one is properly attuned to the messages sent out by the wilderness and the Mountain, if one can listen in to their voices, the shape of society may be altered: 'Large codes of fraud and woe' obviously refers to the reigning systems of politics and religion. Thus, Shelley seems to be saying that the encounter with the mountain presents man with a problem whose consequences are social and political as much as metaphysical. But what is the 'mysterious tongue' and what is the voice of the mountain? and how do they communicate? This is difficult; but the meaning appears to be that nature has a message for those who are able to listen. The centre of power is located in man himself; only the specially gifted can unriddle the meaning of the oracle and their understanding is intimately linked to their ability to feel. Thus, if the secret of nature is to be properly interpreted, man must apply to the task the full range of his imaginative gifts. In the next section of the poem Shelley clarifies the implications:

> Power dwells apart in its tranquillity,
> Remote, serene, and inaccessible:
> And *this*, the naked countenance of earth,
> On which I gaze, even these primaeval mountains
> Teach the adverting mind.
>
> (lines 96–100)

The first two lines present an image of divinity which closely resembles the Lucretian version (*remote* and *serene* are both used by Lucretius to describe the demesne of the gods where they enjoy complete freedom from responsibility).[34] This is the voice which can be heard by the wise, the great and good; this is the message for the adverting mind. If there is a God, he is not here in the mountain. The 'city of death, distinct with many a tower / And wall impregnable of beaming ice', the traces of earthquake and ruin, are not the handiwork of the Lord. To believe so is to impose our own fantasies on the patterns of nature which are without volition. To free oneself from that belief, to be liberated from the fear of a destructive creator, is to take a step towards repealing 'large codes of fraud and woe'. Thus, the investigation of perception with which the poem began, is crucial to its whole meaning.

In the final section Shelley reverts to it explicitly:

Mont Blanc yet gleams on high :—the power is there,
The still and solemn power of many sights,
And many sounds and much of life and death.
In the calm darkness of the moonless nights,
In the lone glare of day, the snows descend
Upon that Mountain; none beholds them there,
Nor when the flakes burn in the sinking sun,
Or the star-beams dart through them. Winds contend
Silently there, and heap the snow with breath
Rapid and strong, but silently! Its home
The voiceless lightning in these solitudes
Keeps innocently, and like vapour broods
Over the snow. The secret strength of things
Which governs thought, and to the infinite dome
Of Heaven is as a law, inhabits thee!
And what were thou, and earth, and stars, and sea,
If to the human mind's imaginings
Silence and solitude were vacancy?

Although this powerful passage acknowledges the impressiveness of nature, it suggests clearly that it is man who has imposed his own meaning on nature by imagining it as the work of a personalised deity. It is important that the poem should end with an insistence on the creative powers of the human mind: ultimately, Shelley suggests, man is the master of his universe.

Shelley's meaning is illuminated by a lengthy descriptive letter written to Peacock at the time when he was composing the poem. In it Shelley sums up his impressions in terms which are very similar to the conclusion of 'Mont Blanc': 'All was as much our own as if we had been the creators of such impressions in the minds of others, as now occupied our own.'[35] His letter also includes this mythopoeic passage, which refers to Ahrimanes, the principle of darkness and evil in the Zoroastrian scheme, which Peacock had used as the framework for a long poem:

Do you who assert the supremacy of Ahriman imagine him throned among these desolating snows, among these palaces of death & frost, sculptured in this their terrible magnificence by the unsparing hand of necessity, & that he casts around him as the first essays of his final usurpation avalances, torrents, rocks & thunders—and above all, these deadly glaciers at once the proofs & the symbols of his reign.—Add to this the degradation of the human species, who in these regions are half deformed or idiotic & all of whom are deprived of anything that can excite interest & admiration. This is a part of the subject more mournful & less sublime;—but such as neither the poet nor the philosopher should disdain.[36]

When one relates this passage to the poem, it emerges that 'Mont Blanc' is in part at least an answer to Peacock's gloomy philosophy; even more significantly it is an answer to Shelley's own gloomy forebodings before the mountain. To accept such dark idolatries is to degrade the destiny of man, as Julian was later to tell Maddalo. And to acquiesce in these grim religious thoughts is to open the way for other kinds of tyranny. It is not entirely an accident that the setting of the opening scene of *Prometheus Unbound* is based on this experience of the Alps: that play, like 'Mont Blanc', tries to restore to man his own 'divine control'.

So far we have explored the meaning of the poem and seen how Shelley proposed in it an answer to his own more pessimistic specula- tions. But the power of 'Mont Blanc' cannot be appreciated fully until it is placed in a contemporary context. During the same expedition which took him to Chamonix, Shelley publicly identified himself as democrat, lover of mankind and atheist: the self-descriptions appear in no fewer than three visitors' books. One of them was made on the very day when he wrote 'Mont Blanc' and may be a response to another entry which reads, 'Such scenes as these, then, inspire most forcibly the love of God'.[37] Under the heading of destination he entered with eloquent simplicity *L'Enfer*, fully aware that according to the credit- sheet of public morality he and Lord Byron had long since booked their passages to the burning lake. This youthful flourish should not blind us to the fact that Shelley was seriously committed in this flouting of convention and that his self-description was a deliberate act of defiance with significant moral and political implications. In Shelley's mind the three characters—lover of mankind, democrat and atheist—were logic- ally connected, each one implying the other two. These three words were written in Greek, not because Shelley wanted to baffle the authorities, but because Greek was the language of intellectual liberty, the language of those courageous philosophers who had defied political and religious tyranny in their allegiance to the truth. It was an unlucky coincidence that Robert Southey should come across one of these entries, but no one could have been surprised that he spread the story when he got back to England, where it provided leverage for the *Quarterly Review* and for the *London Chronicle*, which fulminated:

Mr Shelley is understood to be the person who, after gazing on Mont Blanc, registered himself in the Album as Percy Bysshe Shelley, Atheist; which gross and cheap bravado he, with the natural tact of the new school, took for a display philosophic courage; and his obscure muse has been since constantly spreading all her foulness of those doctrines which a decent infidel would treat with respect, and in which the wise and honourable have in all ages found the perfection of wisdom and virtue.

The connection between the poem, the entries in the register, and the violence of this reaction is of crucial importance. Shelley's poem runs counter to a well-established tradition of finding in mountain scenery the evidence of the hand of God. This applies not only to fellow tourists like the writer of the entry at Chamonix but to fellow-poets. For instance, Gray wrote to West from the Grande Chartreuse in 1739: 'Not a precipice, not a torrent, not a cliff but is pregnant with religion and poetry. There are certain scenes that would awe an atheist into belief without help of other arguments.'[38] Perhaps the most pertinent example is Coleridge's 'Hymn before Sun-rise in the Vale of Chamouni', which was based on a German poem by Friederika Brun. This did not appear in book form till 1817 but it had been published in the *Poetical Register* for 1802 and in *The Friend* in 1809 where Shelley almost certainly read it; in any event, it represents exactly the kind of attitude against which he was reacting. Like Shelley, Coleridge finds that the natural scene prompts questionings but, unlike Shelley, he discovers the answers without any difficulty:

Motionless torrents! silent cataracts!
Who made you glorious as the Gates of Heaven
Beneath the keen full moon? Who bade the sun
Clothe you with rainbows? Who, with living flowers
Of loveliest blue, spread garlands at your feet?—
God! let the torrents, like a shout of nations,
Answer! and let the ice-plains echo, GOD!
GOD! Sing ye meadow-streams with gladsome voice!

The tone of this is very different from that of 'Mont Blanc', which displays a greater fear of the powers of nature and a greater hesitancy in finding a solution. Coleridge had noted that his poem was a 'Hymn in the manner of the Psalms' and he follows his model by praising the Lord in his creation; one could hardly find a more complete contrast to the self-sufficiency of Shelley's religion. Almost as if in premonition Coleridge had added an explanatory note which included the following exclamation: 'Indeed, the whole vale, its every light, its every sound, must needs impress every mind not utterly callous with the thought— Who *would* be, who *could* be an Atheist in this valley of wonders!' To that question, Shelley had provided a thoughtful and serious answer.

(iv)

Two years after writing 'Mont Blanc' Shelley embarked on *Prometheus Unbound*, which is probably the greatest and the most ambitious of all his achievements. Here he pursues the implications of 'Mont Blanc' among the snow and ice of a mountainous setting which is closely related both to that poem and to his experiences in the Alps. In this richly complex drama Shelley reshapes the Prometheus story closer to his heart's desire, since in his view Aeschylus had been untrue to the potential beauty of the myth when he reconciled Prometheus and Jupiter, the champion and the oppressor of mankind. Shelley's version endeavours to bring to fruition the truer pattern which he had sensed unawakened and unrealised within the depths of Aeschylus' play. He was attracted to the story not because of an irresistible predilection for Greek mythology as such but because he recognised the continuing relevance of the truths which it embodied. It was the responsibility of every age to reinterpret these myths for its own purposes: 'Of such truths / Each to itself must be the oracle'.

Given, then, this living relationship with the best that has been thought and said, the poet will reinterpret what he finds in terms of his own age. Thus, Shelley was able to see that the Zeus of *Prometheus Bound* (or Jupiter as Shelley calls him in *Prometheus Unbound*) was not simply the unfilial son of Saturn, the unfaithful husband of Hera, the capricious and vindictive Father of the Gods. He was all of those things but he was also only a symbol of the kind of divinity which man had duped himself into worshipping: as Aeschylus had put it, *pollōn onomatōn morphē mia* (the names are many, but the form is one)[39] a line which Shelley was fond of quoting. It followed that an interpretation of the Prometheus story which was valid for the revolutionary period of the early nineteenth century would recognise in Jupiter that daunting and vindictive God who ruled the hearts and minds of men by a combination of threats and promises. And, since the orthodox Christian view of God was a projection of man's own propensity to tyrannise over his fellows, since God was no more than the magnified image of an earthly tyrant, an attack on the power of Jupiter represented an attack on the reigning monarchies of Europe. That three of these had banded together for political purposes under the title of the Holy Alliance was a fact which seemed to endorse this point of view.[40] The theological premises of the argument implied the political and the political implied the theological: to release man from the bondage of his religious guilt and fears was to take another step toward abolishing the remaining vestiges of the *ancien régime*, while to unite men in free and brotherly love was to eliminate the system of hatred, self-contempt and retaliation on which the tyranny of religion was based. Therefore, it is wrong to see *Prometheus Unbound* simply as a poem which enacts a political revolution; likewise it is wrong to see it simply as a poem which readjusts the mental equilibrium. It does both of these things together and each readjustment or revolution implies and necessitates the other.

Once this has been understood, the peculiar potency of the language and the symbols can be seen in the appropriate focus. Throughout *Prometheus Unbound* Shelley employs the language of religion but he employs it to these heterodox and revolutionary ends. The old repressive religion is abandoned, the knots of superstition are unravelled (to use the image of Lucretius) and the new religion of love is established in its place. The negative world of the Decalogue is swept away and for it is substituted the positive injunction, 'Thou shalt love thy neighbour better than thyself'. This is in no sense an easy commandment to fulfil but one which requires constant vigilance and self-control as well as a proper recognition of one's own true dignity: Shelley makes this point in the 'Hymn to Intellectual Beauty' when he records how that beneficent spirit had taught him 'To fear himself, and love all human kind'.

Consider the opening speech of Prometheus in which, bound to his precipice, he turns his face to the torturing divinity who is his gaoler:

Monarch of Gods and Daemons, and all Spirits
But One, who throng those bright and rolling worlds
Which Thou and I alone of living things
Behold with sleepless eyes! regard this Earth
Made multitudinous with thy slaves, whom thou
Requitest for knee-worship, prayer and praise,

> And toil, and hecatombs of broken hearts,
> With fear and self-contempt and barren hope;
> Whilst me, who am thy foe, eyeless in hate,
> Hast thou made reign and triumph, to thy scorn,
> O'er mine own misery and thy vain revenge.

There is an obviously Miltonic ring to some of these lines ('Made multitudinous with thy slaves', 'Requitest for knee-worship') which immediately reminds us that one of Shelley's models for Prometheus was the Satan of *Paradise Lost*. Thus, the unjust gods of Aeschylus and Milton are fused in Jupiter, while the outspoken indignation of Prometheus and Satan burns behind the words of Shelley's hero. At the centre of this passage is the image of religious worship, a submission to divinity which is degrading and humiliating, not because worship is in itself damaging to humanity, but because the god in question is not worthy of our devotion. This system of religious worship has nothing to do with an acknowledgement of the spirit of good in the universe and everything to do with keeping the tyrant in power.

Jupiter here is a kind of Nobodaddy, a jealous, vindictive God, eager for sacrifice and self-abasement from his subjects. He is shaped, in part at least, by the Jehovah whom Shelley encountered in the Old Testament; yet the empire over which he rules is not a world of religious ceremonies and blood sacrifices, but a mental world. The hecatombs are not of oxen or of sheep but of 'broken hearts'. And the rewards of this service are 'fear and self-contempt and barren hope'. Shelley is thinking of the theological system of rewards and punishments, the system which promises requital in terms of eternal felicity in Heaven or eternal punishment in Hell. To hope for this kind of heaven after death is to be deceived by barren hope, that is, to withdraw oneself from the present possibilities of doing good for the illusory prospect of being rewarded with eternal happiness in another life. To subscribe to a belief in the reality of a hell of fire and flames is to submit to an illusory and degrading fear. This extortionate system of threats and promises leads man to undervalue himself, to misconceive his own potential, to trample on his own liberties: this is 'self-contempt'.

As Shelley saw it, any claim to virtue must be judged in terms of motivation. He explained the point in a letter of 1812: 'Paley's Moral Philosophy begins—Why am I *obliged* to keep my word? Because I desire Heaven and hate Hell. *Obligation* and duty therefore are words of no value as the criteria of excellence. So much for Obedience, Parents & Children. Do you agree to my definition of Virtue—Disinterestedness?'[41] (The reference to Obedience, Parents and Children acquires added point when one remembers that it was Paley whom Sir Timothy Shelley had beseeched his son to read in the hope of convincing him back into the fold.) Some years later he returned to the subject in his *Treatise on Morals*, where he attacks the conventional association of virtue and obligation:

Virtue is a law to which it is the will of the lawgiver that we should conform, which will we should in no manner be bound to obey, unless some dreadful punishment were attached to disobedience. This is the philosophy of slavery and superstition.

In fact, no person can be *bound* or *obliged* without some power preceding to bind and oblige. If I observe a man bound hand and foot, I know that some one bound him. But if I observe him returning self-satisfied from the performance of some action by which he has been the willing author of extensive benefit, I do not infer that the anticipation of hellish agonies, or the hope of heavenly reward, has constrained him to sacrifice ...[42]

These passages suggest that one way in which Prometheus is *unbound* is by being released from these obligations to behave virtuously, which are endorsed and supported by deterrent sanctions. The only authentic virtue is based on what can truly be described as free will.

In spite of this, Shelley did not discountenance Hell and Heaven: rather, he believed that they were potential in us here and now. To postpone them to the life after death was to submit ourselves to a belief in what was almost certainly illusory; it was also to avoid our serious responsibility to redeem ourselves and our society as far as was humanly possible. So, imagining the fall of Jupiter, Prometheus (as yet unregenerate) rejoices to think how he will suffer: 'How will thy soul, cloven to its depths with terror, / Gape like a hell within!' (I. 55-6). Conversely, if Hell is within man's reach, so too are the means of escape. Thus, in *Prometheus Unbound* the Spirit of the Hour describes regenerated man in terms of the internal Hell from which he has liberated himself, an *Inferno* of the mind which makes explicit reference to Dante:

None fawned, none trampled; hate, disdain, or fear,
Self-love or self-contempt, on human brows
No more inscribed, as o'er the gate of Hell,
'All hope abandon, ye who enter here'...

(III, iv. 133-6)

The reversal is portrayed even more positively in the final act, where it is made clear that revolutionary man has not only freed himself from Hell, but has created his own Heaven:

... Hate, and Fear, and Pain, light-vanquished shadows, fleeing,

Leave Man—who was a many-sided mirror,
Which could distort to many a shape of error
This true fair world of things—a sea reflecting Love;
Which over all his kind, as the Sun's Heaven
Gliding o'er ocean, smooth, serene, and even,
Darting from starry depths radiance and life, doth move ...

Man, one harmonious soul of many a soul,
Whose nature is its own divine control,
Where all things flow to all, as rivers to the sea;
Familiar acts are beautiful through love;
Labour, and Pain, and Grief, in life's green grove
Sport like tame beasts—none knew how gentle they could be!
(IV. 381–7, 400–5)

These last lines approach closer to the mere personification than is usual with Shelley but this song as a whole preserves a splendid image of harmony and unity between man and man, which is based on each man's discovery of the paradise which is latent within himself. The basic principle on which this passage is founded had been enunciated by Milton's Satan and cited both by Byron in *Manfred* and by Shelley in the *Defence of Poetry*: [43] 'The mind is its own place, and in it self / Can make a Heav'n of Hell, a Hell of Heav'n' (*Paradise Lost*, I. 254–5).

In order to realise this paradise, Prometheus has to conquer the evil tendencies in himself, to direct himself away from the potential Hell within. Through his ministers, Jupiter tries hard to persuade Prometheus of his own essential worthlessness and to force him to acquiesce in Jupiter's world of punishments and rewards. Jupiter's agent Mercury taunts Prometheus with the prospect of eternal punishment; the Furies try to impress on him the futility of human endeavour, bringing before his eyes two notable examples of idealism betrayed by the relentless process of history—the spread of Christianity and the French Revolution. The aim is to induce fear and self-contempt, a superstitious reluctance to improve on the existing state of things. This is the temptation of the Devil and in the fragmentary draft of *Hellas* it is rejected by Christ, who rebukes Satan for being a historical determinist: 'Obdurate spirit! / Thou seest but the Past in the To-come. / Pride is thy error and thy punishment' (*P.W.*, p. 452). (This might be Julian talking to Maddalo, insisting, even in the face of unsavoury realities, that 'this is not destiny / But man's own wilful ill' (lines 210–11).) What Christ implies here is that to take Satan's view of history is to put ourselves in bondage to the past; ultimately it is a denial both of free will and of moral responsibility. This, then, is the temptation to despair on the grounds that history inevitably repeats itself and that, since previous attempts to improve the human condition have notoriously failed, all future attempts are doomed to be equally unsuccessful.

Another subtle and insidious temptation to despair is to interpret the whole of history as a process of gradual degeneration from an imagined Golden Age. This doctrine is philosophically false: 'Later and more correct observations have instructed us that uncivilized man is the most pernicious and miserable of beings . . .'; it is also morally dangerous because it ministers to 'thoughts of despondency and sorrow'. It may, however, be turned to advantage: the 'imaginations of a happier state of human society' were 'the children of airy hope, the prophets and parents of mysterious futurity'.[44] The important distinction is that we must look forward not back, seeking for the New Jerusalem rather than the lost Eden. Or, as Shelley expressed it in one of his footnotes to the *Essay on Christianity*, 'Jesus Christ foresaw what these poets retrospectively imagined'. Once again Christ as prophet shows the way to later generations.

Like Christ and like Julian, Prometheus is alert to the dangerous pressures of despair: from experience he notes that 'Evil minds / Change good to their own nature'.[45] This fact is implicit in his opening speech where he acknowledges a close and subtle relationship between himself and Jupiter. In particular, this uncomfortable connection is mirrored in the richly ambivalent syntax of 'whilst me, who am thy foe, eyeless in hate, / Hast thou made reign'. Conventionally, *eyeless in hate* is taken to go with *thou*; even if the structure of this is rather jerky, no one can be surprised by such a description of the vigilant sadism of the Almighty. However, the syntax is awkward not because Shelley was too incompetent to iron it out but because it embodies a genuine ambiguity in the sense: *eyeless in hate* balances tantalisingly on the end of the line, poised between *me* (Prometheus) and *thou* (Jupiter). The hatred emanating from Jupiter has communicated itself to Prometheus: because he has allowed himself to respond in kind, he too is *eyeless in hate*. There may also be an allusive irony at work here, since one of the parallels for Prometheus as the enduring hero is Samson Agonistes who was also, notoriously, *eyeless*. If this allusion is intended, the implication might be that Prometheus, like Samson, has erred through indulging his baser passions. At any rate, this ambiguity seems to suggest that, at this point in the play, Prometheus and Jupiter are identified. It is therefore entirely appropriate that, when Prometheus asks to hear the curse which he once invoked on Jupiter, the words of that curse are spoken by the Phantasm of Jupiter himself. Prometheus cannot recall them since he has now cast out hatred but the Phantasm of Jupiter is more than an ironical dramatic device; its appearance actually suggests that in cursing Jupiter, Prometheus became identified with him.[46]

When the curse has been summoned from the recesses of conscious-ness and re-enacted in a therapeutic process well known to psycho-analysis, when hatred has been rejected and the vacuum filled by love (embodied in Asia), Jupiter necessarily falls. The suddenness of his dis-appearance should not be surprising since Jupiter is in fact a *nothing*, as the imagery of the play constantly proclaims. His disappearance follows logically from the end of 'Mont Blanc':

> And what were thou, and earth, and stars, and sea,
> If to the human mind's imaginings
> Silence and solitude were vacancy?

If man can populate the universe with the divinities he imagines to himself, he also has the power to recall those images and demythologise them.[47] So, in Act Three Prometheus has asserted his independence and dethroned the dark divinity of his own soul.

This psychological change is mirrored in imagery derived from religious ceremony and worship. Early in the play Mercury arrives to negotiate on behalf of Jupiter; the pressure he wishes to exert is an unsubtle one based on the threat of punishment. The best policy, he advises Prometheus, is submission:

> ... bend thy soul in prayer,
> And like a suppliant in some gorgeous fane
> Let the will kneel within thy haughty heart:
> For benefits and meek submission tame
> The fiercest and the mightiest.
>
> (I. 376–80)

To kneel would be for Prometheus to acknowledge Jupiter as the divinity of his own heart: it would be to collaborate with the forces of evil. Prometheus resists this invitation; later he is tempted with greater subtlety by a Fury who recommends a passive acquiescence in the *status quo*. She tells him that even the most lofty spirits are inhibited by misgivings which they would not openly acknowledge: 'Hypocrisy and custom make their minds / The fanes [temples] of many a worship, now outworn.'

When Prometheus has surmounted these temptations and his hope and endurance have been fortified by the vivifying love of Asia, the old religion of fear is abolished and 'thrones, altars, judgment-seats, and prisons' which 'imaged to the pride of kings and priests / A dark yet mighty faith' are unregarded and abandoned. Even more significantly:

> ... those foul shapes, abhorred by God and man,
> Which, under many a name and many a form,
> Strange, savage, ghastly, dark and execrable,
> Were Jupiter, the tyrant of the world;
> And which the nations, panic-stricken, served
> With blood, and hearts broken by long hope, and love
> Dragged to his altars soiled and garlandless
> And slain amid men's unreclaiming tears,
> Flattering the thing they feared, which fear was hate—
> Frown, mouldering fast, o'er their abandoned shrines.
>   (III, iv. 180–9)

Here the representative character of Jupiter becomes very clear: he is the deity of any false religion, Christian or otherwise; he is 'many fearful natures in one name' (I. 458). This false deity has been worshipped in pain and fear: even Love, which is potentially the redeeming agent, has been sacrificed to this dark idolatry.

Shelley's powerful image of 'love / Dragged to his altars soiled and garlandless' almost certainly had its origin in a famous passage where Lucretius describes how, on the advice of his soothsayer, Agamemnon agreed to sacrifice his daughter Iphigenia so that the winds might blow again and give his ships passage to Troy. Lucretius gives a very graphic description of how Iphigenia was crowned with the sacrificial fillet ordained by ritual and how, mutely imploring, she was sacrificed at the altar. His summary is uncompromising: *Tantum religio potuit suadere malorum* (an untranslatable sentence which means approximately 'So potent was Religion in persuading to evil deeds').[48] Shelley's own response is undoubtedly conditioned by his reading of Lucretius but he has added an important new dimension. For Lucretius, the moral of the story was the extent to which the demands of so-called religion could pervert the normal feelings of humanity; for Shelley, the moral also involved the dangerous influence of religion, but in his reading what has been so ruthlessly abandoned is not merely Iphigenia, a trembling and innocent girl, but love. This barbaric ritual is not merely a specific offence against the blood relationship binding the Atreidae one to another; it is also, and more important, an offence against the

F

spirit of love. Therefore, in Shelley's view it is a contradiction of all that is implied by true religion. It is a measure of the seriousness of the threat which he recognised in the history of organised religion that, even at this moment of supreme triumph, when Jupiter has been over-thrown and ordinary men are walking 'One with another even as spirits do', even at the end of this speech where he originally planned to finish the play, the image of man's inhumanity to man presents itself so forcibly.

Shelley, then, sees the sacrifice of Iphigenia as an offence against the spirit of love; in his version the brutal image is translated from the external world of dramatic action to the inner world of mental events. (To interpret this ritual murder as a specific allusion to execu-tions for adultery is to deprive the image of its generalising force and to turn a powerful indictment of man's inhumanity into a criticism of a mere social abuse.[49]) Yet the inner world does retain a vivid and tangible connection with physical actions. The adjective *soiled* im-mediately transmits to these mental happenings an unforgettable reality; and *garlandless* (a word which Shelley introduced into English from the Greek *astephanos*) derives much of its force from the incident in Lucretius.[50] This Iphigenia is not paid even the customary civility of being adorned for the sacrifice. Finally, *unreclaiming tears* is another phrase of particular resonance. On the literal level it means that, although the spectators at this sacrifice were grieved, they offered no objections, raised no voice in protest. In Lucretius it was Iphigenia herself who was struck dumb with fear (*muta metu*); in Shelley's new version this fear has transmitted itself to the acquiescing crowd.[51] Metaphorically, *unreclaiming tears* takes us to the heart of Shelley's thought. In a very practical way Shelley had devoted his own services to the process of reclamation; specifically, he had helped in the famous project for reclaiming land from the sea at Tremadoc. This in itself was an image, a living symbol of how man could reclaim the desert of his life and plant it with the flowers of progress. So the unreclaiming tears are not only the tears of cowardice and moral weakness but unpractical tears, tears which reject the possibilities of redemption which are open to the human race.[52] Since Jupiter has only reigned by the consent of man, love can still be rescued from the altar of sacrifice and the human condition can still be redeemed.

The same reversal can be observed in a later poem, *Hellas* (written late 1821, published 1822), which celebrates in advance the downfall of the Turkish hegemony and the recovery of Greek liberty. After one of the semi-choruses has reflected how, nourished in the guilty mind,

'Revenge and wrong bring forth their kind', the other semi-chorus responds:

> In sacred Athens, near the fane
>   Of wisdom, Pity's altar stood:
> Serve not the unknown God in vain,
> But pay that broken shrine again,
>   Love for hate and tears for blood.
>   (lines 733-7)

The details here are quite specific. The Athenians did indeed set up an altar to Pity in their market-place (a fact which Shelley could have discovered in Pausanias' *Description of Greece*).[53] The temple of Wisdom is presumably the Parthenon, which was sacred to Athene, patroness of Athens and goddess of Wisdom. The conjunction between Wisdom and Pity is crucial. Without love, wisdom is impotent, as the Fury tells Prometheus; likewise, without the capacity for pity, man cannot control his fate or achieve a proper mental or moral equilibrium. Thus, it is the refusal of Prometheus to cast out pity which finally delivers him from the temptations of the Furies (I. 634). Conversely, it is the failure of the spectators to respond with an active pity rather than a passive regret which permits Iphigenia to be sacrificed without complaint or intervention. With this in mind, Shelley allows his semi-chorus to wish that Pity could once again be recognised as a deity of moral significance. The basic message of the stanza is similar to that in Act Three of *Prometheus Unbound* but the reference to the unknown God deserves to be pursued further. St Paul had told the Athenians on Mars' Hill that they were 'too superstitious', that is, too narrowly devoted to a religious ritual whose significance they did not understand. The truth about God is not so simple but it is potentially liberating:

God that made the world, and all things therein, seeing that he is Lord of heaven and earth, dwelleth not in temples made with hands;
    Neither is worshipped with men's hands, as though he needed any thing, seeing he giveth to all life, and breath, and all things . . .
                                                        (Acts, 17: 24-5)

The emphasis on the state of man's soul rather than on external forms of worship comes close to Shelley's own attitude. Man must learn not to pay homage to divinities which are merely nebulous but to recognise within himself those truly divine potentialities which deserve his devotion and worship.

The final chorus of *Hellas* picks up once again the image of the altar:

Saturn and Love their long repose
   Shall burst, more bright and good
Than all who fell, than One who rose,
   Than many unsubdued;
Not gold, not blood, their altar dowers
But votive tears and symbol flowers.

For these lines Shelley provides a footnote of great specificity:

Saturn and Love were among the deities of a real or imaginary state of
innocence and happiness. *All* those *who fell*, or the Gods of Greece, Asia,
and Egypt; the *One who rose*, or Jesus Christ, at whose appearance the
idols of the Pagan World were amerced of their worship; and *the many
unsubdued*, or the monstrous objects of the idolatry of China, India, the
Antarctic islands, and the native tribes of America . . .

After discussing the Grecian Gods, he goes on to describe how 'the
sublime human character of Jesus Christ was deformed by an imputed
identification with a Power, who tempted, betrayed, and punished the
innocent beings who were called into existence by his sole will'; unfortunately this most 'benevolent of men has been propitiated with
myriads of hecatombs of those who approached the nearest to his
innocence and wisdom, sacrificed under every aggravation of atrocity
and variety of torture. The horrors of the Mexican, the Peruvian, and
the Indian superstitions are well known.' Thus Shelley, less than a year
before his death. It should be clear that what he was attacking here,
as in *Prometheus Unbound*, was a tangible evil, a concatenation of
systems based on torture and intolerance. Yet, this long footnote makes
it clear that the torture was also within: these evil gods 'reigned over
the understandings of men'. The instruments of oppression must be
replaced by love, sympathy and human understanding; the new object
of worship should be, not Jupiter in any of his guises, but man who was
potentially a god in his own right. In his attack on the oppressive
religio which entangled the minds of men, Lucretius had long ago
initiated this reversal of the hierarchy. As he informed his patron:

deus ille fuit, deus, inclute Memmi,
qui princeps vitae rationem invenit eam quae
nunc appellatur sapientia, quique per artem
fluctibus e tantis vitam tantisque tenebris
in tam tranquillo et tam clara luce locavit.
                (v. 8–12)[54]

By the exercise of his own faculties, man could liberate himself from the control of the supposed divinities. Shelley, too, sees Promethean man as his own god and his own ruler; once he is *Exempt from awe* (a phrase borrowed from Chapman's Homer) he becomes 'the king over himself'. As Blake had proclaimed in *The Everlasting Gospel*:

Thou art a Man, God is no more,
Thine own Humanity learn to Adore.

Notes to chapter five

1 *Letters of M.W.S.*, II. 139.
2 The review was actually based on *Laon and Cythna; or The Revolution of the Golden City*, the original and more direct version of *The Revolt of Islam* which was suppressed by the publisher and republished with alterations under the new title.
3 White, *The Unextinguished Hearth*, p. 142.
4 *Letters*, II. 128.
5 *Letters*, II. 204.
6 White, *The Unextinguished Hearth*, pp. 145–6.
7 White, *The Unextinguished Hearth*, p. 149.
8 Clark, *Prose*, p. 267.
9 Blake, *The Everlasting Gospel*.
10 *P.W.*, p. 156.
11 Medwin, *Life*, p. 255.
12 *Letters*, I. 265.
13 Bod. MS. Shelley adds. e. 8, pp. 166–56; Shelley adds. e. 9, pp. 1–8; *The Shelley Notebooks*, II. 118. Shelley read Tobit on 10 March and The Wisdom of Solomon on 2 April 1820 (*Journal*, pp. 130–1); he read St Luke in November or December of 1819 (*Journal*, p. 126) and St Matthew on 1 January 1820 (*Journal*, p. 127).
14 Clark, *Prose*, p. 269.
15 Clark, *Prose*, p. 123.
16 *Letters*, I. 125.
17 *De Rerum Natura*, iv. 6–7.
18 Clark, *Prose*, p. 269.
19 *Ibid.*
20 E. P. Thompson, *The Making of the English Working Class*, Penguin Books, Harmondsworth, 1968, p. 726.
21 Clark, *Prose*, p. 167.
22 *Letters*, II. 176.
23 Thompson, *The Making of the English Working Class*, pp. 726–30.
24 Clark, *Prose*, p. 269.
25 'It is this empire of terror which is established by Religion, Monarchy is its [sic] prototype, Aristocracy may be regarded as symbolising with its very essence' (*Letters*, I. 126).
26 Clark, *Prose*, p. 212. However, Shelley did believe in inherited wealth: see the fragment 'What men gain fairly' (*P.W.*, p. 574).
27 Clark, *Prose*, p. 210.
28 See especially *P.W.*, p. 277.
29 Clark, *Prose*, p. 214.
30 The draft is contained in Bod. MS. Shelley adds. e. 16, pp. 3–13. In the draft

l. 79 reads *In such wise faith* under which appear the words *But for*. Underneath this the line is rewritten in full: 'In such a faith with Nature reconciled'.

31   *The Works of Thomas Love Peacock*, ed. H. F. B. Brett-Smith and C. E. Jones, 10 vols., 1924–34, vii. 263 ff. For a summary of the Zoroastrian system, see VIII. 71–3.

32   'For of a surety a great dread holds all mortals thus in bond, because they behold many things happening in heaven and earth whose causes they can by no means see, and they think them to be done by divine power' (I. 151–4).

33   'For which reasons when we shall perceive that nothing can be created from nothing, then we shall at once more correctly understand from that principle what we are seeking, both the source from which each thing can be made and the manner in which everything is done without the working of the gods' (I. 155–8).

34   See the description of the *templa serena* in *De Rerum Natura*, II. 7 ff. Shelley introduces this concept in his translation of the Homeric 'Hymn to Venus' where he writes of 'Gods / Who live secure in their serene abodes'.

35   *Letters*, I. 497.

36   *Letters*, I. 499.

37   Sir Gavin de Beer, *On Shelley*, Oxford, 1938, pp. 35–54. There are slight variations in phrasing and word-order in Shelley's entries.

38   *The Correspondence of Thomas Gray*, ed. P. Toynbee and L. Whibley, Clarendon Press, Oxford, 1935, I. 125. Like Shelley, Gray recorded his feelings in a visitors' book: his entry, which was in a different spirit, was the famous Alcaic ode, 'Oh, Tu, severi religio loci'.

39   *P.V.*, 210; Bod. MS. Shelley adds. e. 11, cover.

40   For Shelley's view of the Holy Alliance, see *P.W.*, p. 448, a passage suppressed in the first edition (1822).

41   *Letters*, I. 200.

42   Clark, *Prose*, p. 188.

43   *Defence*, p. 56; *Manfred*, III, iv. 129–36.

44   Clark, *Prose*, p. 211.

45   *Prometheus Unbound*, I. 380–1.

46   The word 'phantasm' is sometimes used in eighteenth-century debates about the existence of God to describe the projection of a false deity. See for example this passage from D'Holbach's *Système de la Nature*: 'If men only had the courage to climb back to the source of the opinions which are most profoundly embedded in their minds, if only they allowed themselves a precise account of the reasons which had caused them to respect these opinions as sacred; if only they examined cold-bloodedly the motives behind their hopes and fears, they would discover that the objects and ideas capable of exciting them most violently had no reality at all and were only words devoid of meaning, phantasms born of ignorance and altered by a sick imagination' (translation cited from Frank E. Manuel, *The Eighteenth Century Confronts the Gods*, Harvard University Press, Cambridge, Mass., 1959, p. 231). Shelley may have had this kind of usage in mind when he introduced the phantasm of Jupiter.

47   The word *recall* brings together the summoning of the Phantasm of Jupiter and the passage in 'Mont Blanc' (lines 41–8) which deals with the creative power of the mind. The conjunction of these two passages seems to suggest that Jupiter is only a phantasm projected by the mind of Prometheus and ultimately subject to his control.

48   *De Rerum Natura*, I. 100. The passage in question runs from l. 80 to l. 101.

49 Cameron, *Shelley:The Golden Years*, p. 541, drawing on A. M. D. Hughes.
50 Used by Euripides, *Andromache*, 1020.
51 Cf. Shelley's account of the general failure to protest against the government's use of *agents provocateurs* in the case of the Pentridge rising: 'The public voice was overpowered by the timid and the selfish, who threw the weight of fear into the scale of public opinion ...' (Clark, *Prose*, p. 167). See also his lament in 1822: 'But all, more or less, subdue themselves to the element that surrounds them, & contribute to the evils they lament by the hypocrisy that springs from them' (*Letters*, II. 442).
52 See 'the unreclaimed fertility' (*Letters*, II. 202).
53 I. 17. i.
54 ... he was a god, noble Memmius, a god he was, who first discovered that reasoned plan of life which is now called Wisdom, who by his skill brought life out of those temptestuous billows and that deep darkness, and settled it in such a calm and in light so clear' (*De Rerum Natura*, v. 8–12).

CHAPTER SIX

THE CHRISTIAN MYTHOLOGY

(i)

Keats's friend Joseph Severn records that at Leigh Hunt's in 1817 Shelley retailed 'the plan of a poem he was about to write, being a comparison of the Blessed Saviour with a mountebank, whose tricks he identified with the miracles'.[1] Certainly, Shelley interpreted Christ's miracles in the spirit of eighteenth-century rationalism, but it is hard to believe that he ever spoke of Christ himself in terms so crude and dismissive. For most of his adult life he regarded Christ as the *beau idéal* of the reformer, misunderstood and persecuted as reformers always are: it was no accident that the archetypal Shelleyan hero, Prometheus, was closely identified with Christ at a number of points.

Shelley's interpretation of Christ is best approached through his *Essay on Christianity*. Christ, says Shelley, is 'the God of our popular religion' but clearly Shelley regards him not as God but as a godlike man, 'distinguished by the profound wisdom and the comprehensive morality of his doctrines'. He lived at a critical period in history when the great days of Rome were over, sentiments of liberty and heroism were dead and 'Accumulations of wealth and power were inordinately great'. 'All communication among human beings was vitiated and polluted in its sources' and the 'intercourse of man with man was that of tyrant with slave'.[2] The parallels with Shelley's own period in history are obvious. It did not escape Shelley, as it did not escape Blake or some of their more radical contemporaries, that Christ was an acute critic of the imperial system and a preacher of human liberty. As the Reverend Mark Wilks put it: 'Jesus Christ was a Revolutionist; and the Revolution he came to effect was foretold in these words, "He hath sent me to proclaim liberty to the captives".[3] As Blake put it: 'Jesus was all virtue, and acted from impulse, not from rules.'[4] As Shelley put it: 'Read the words themselves of this extraordinary person, and weigh their import well.

The doctrines, indeed, in my judgment, are excellent and strike at the root of moral evil. If acted upon, no political or religious institution could subsist a moment. Every man would be his own magistrate and priest . . .'⁵ In fact, 'Doctrines of reform were never carried to so great a length as by Jesus Christ'. Compared to what Christ proposed, Plato's *Republic* and Godwin's *Political Justice* are 'probable and practical systems'.

In this view Shelley was influenced by his perception that Christ was an inheritor of the great tradition of the biblical prophets. Shelley himself read the prophets and found in them outspoken confirmation of his own preconceptions. The parallels were inescapable: 'And these Israelites, believing intensely in clan brotherhood, hated intensely human slavery; the ownership of land; the vices of commerce and wealth; the collusion of the king, the aristocrat, the judge, the priest, and the military man; and all of the machinery of oppression.'⁶ The way in which this reading of the Bible intermeshed with Shelley's own conception of history can be traced in two notebook entries probably made in 1819 or 1820. The first seems to be a rudimentary plan for the 'Ode to Liberty':

> Isaiah Chap. 13. 14.
> The destruction of the French tyranny: then the destruction of the spirit of it surviving in Buonaparte—
> Ferdinand of Spain.
> The attempt in Italy.
> The fermentation of Germany.
> Greece & its liberty.
> *The Lord* hath broken the staff of the wicked & the sceptre of the rulers.⁷

Shelley's concerns here are familiar to readers of his poetry and to students of early nineteenth-century history. What is particularly interesting is the way in which he employs the biblical text to underline his own certainty that revolution is both justified and inevitable. It is worth while to place the quotation in its context in Isaiah. Chapter thirteen joyfully anticipates the destruction of the tyrants, a theme which is triumphantly developed in the following chapter:

> The LORD hath broken the staff of the wicked, and the sceptre of the rulers.
>   He who smote the people in wrath with a continual stroke, he that ruled the nations in anger, is persecuted, and none hindereth.
>   The whole earth is at rest, and is quiet: they break forth into singing.
>   And the firstborn of the poor shall feed, and the needy shall lie down in safety . . . (14: 5-7, 30)

This prophecy of violent revolution followed by ultimate peace is very close to the spirit of poems such as *The Revolt of Islam* and *Prometheus Unbound*: indeed, in its original version, *The Revolt of Islam* was actually subtitled *The Revolution of the Golden City*.

The second notebook entry occurs on the previous page and demonstrates very clearly how Shelley related Christ to this tradition of Biblical prophecy:

The people which sate in darkness saw great light: to those who sate in the region & shadow of death, light is sprung up.—

    Blessed are the poor in spirit—the mourners ye shall be comforted the meek ye shall inherit the earth, the poor in heart ye shall see god,

    the persecuted the reviled & the calumniated, ye rejoice, for great is your reward

The opening sentence is taken from a passage in Isaiah which prophesies that the Messiah will break the rod of the oppressor. However, Shelley was probably citing it from Matthew's gospel, where it is applied to Christ in the chapter which precedes the Sermon on the Mount, which is the source of the remaining sentences and 'for whose beneficent intentions he entertained the greatest reverence'.[8] Leigh Hunt recognised that this was one aspect of Christ's teaching to which Shelley responded with particular enthusiasm. In his reply to the *Quarterly*'s attack on Shelley, Hunt pointed out that Christ's spirit 'was a very general spirit, if it was anything, going upon the sympathetic excess, instead of the anti-pathetic—notoriously opposed to existing establishments, and reviled with every term of opprobrium by the Scribes and Pharisees then flourishing.'[9]

In Shelley's view, Christ was the enemy of all oppressive systems, which are based on force and fraud and the selfish passions. Yet his primary message was not one of defiance but of love and forgiveness. Contrary to standard doctrine, Christ did not believe in eternal punishment: 'He desires not the death of a sinner; he makes the sun to shine upon the just and upon the unjust.'[10] Christ did not subscribe to the old system of retaliation and retributive justice: far from asking us to derive a sadistic pleasure from seeing our enemies suffer in the name of justice, he exhorted us to love our enemies and to bless those who curse us. It was only at the courts of tyrants that the concept of justice had become separated from mercy. Julius Caesar, for example, was considered merciful because he refrained from murdering the noblest citizens of Rome, to do which would have made him guilty of yet another atrocity. That was not the exercise of true mercy; nor was it

true justice to invoke the laws in a mechanical and unfeeling way:
'This, and no other is justice. To consider under all the circumstances
and consequences of a particular case, how the greatest quantity and
purest quality of happiness will ensue from any action is to be just,
and there is no other justice.'[11] So much one might deduce from the
words of Christ, the enemy of tyrants, the opponent of systems, the
lover of mankind.

Such a reading of Christ was sufficiently revolutionary in the sense
that it offered justification for an attack on the systems of evil which
enslaved the contemporary world. But Shelley's response to Christ was
revolutionary in another, non-political way. Not only did he not believe that Christ was the Son of God; he was also convinced that Christ
himself did not believe in the existence of God. In his view, Christ
did not accept the orthodox implication of Judaism that God was at
one and the same time 'a limitless and inconceivable mystery' and 'a
being subject to passions'.[12] Certainly, he did not subscribe to the
general belief in a jealous and vindictive Jehovah. The word *God* as
he used it signified 'the interfused and overruling Spirit of all the energy
and wisdom included within the circle of existing things', or with
greater specificity, 'the overruling Spirit of the collective energy of the
moral and material world'.[13] Again, Shelley states: '... Jesus Christ
represents God as the fountain of all goodness, the eternal enemy of
pain and evil, the uniform and unchanging motive of the salutary
operations of the material world.'[14] In fact, when he speaks of God,
Christ is employing a useful metaphor which we must learn to translate for ourselves. Shelley applies this kind of interpretation to a number
of Christ's sayings, notably to 'Blessed are the pure in heart, for they
shall see God'. This expression, says Shelley, was 'the overflowing
enthusiasm of a poet' and 'prompted by the energy of genius' but, for
those reasons, 'it is the less literally true'. Here is Shelley's examination
of the text, his own heterodox variation on the common procedure of
the sermon:

'Blessed are the pure in heart, for they shall see God'—blessed are those
who have preserved internal sanctity of soul, who are conscious of no secret
deceit, who are the same in act as they are in desire, who conceal no thought,
no tendencies of thought from their own conscience, who are faithful and
sincere witnesses before the tribunal of their own judgement of all that
passes within their mind. Such as these shall see God. What! after death
shall their awakened eyes behold the King of Heaven? Shall they stand in
awe before the golden throne on which he sits, and gaze upon the venerable
countenance of the paternal Monarch? ... Jesus Christ has said no more

than the most excellent philosophers have felt and expressed—that virtue is its own reward.[15]

Shelley goes on to list the various ways in which one can see God, who is manifested in 'benignant visitings from the invisible energies by which [we] are surrounded'. For example, a man of pure and gentle habits will be aware of intimations of divinity in the fields and the woods and will derive from communion with his fellow men 'some intercourse with the Universal God':

Whoever has maintained with his own heart the strictest correspondence of confidence, who dares to examine and to estimate every imagination which suggests itself to his mind, who is that which he designs to become, and only aspires to that which the divinity of his own nature shall consider and approve—he has already seen God.[16]

This passage implies some uncertainty as to the source of these impulses to good. Shelley later employs the image of the Aeolian lyre and suggests that man's most imperial qualities are subject to the control of 'some higher and more omnipresent Power', which 'Power is God'; yet 'the divinity of his own nature' also suggests that God might be within man himself. Shelley was never able to resolve this problem but he retained an open mind and never denied those intimations of something greater than himself. Yet, ultimately the centre of his system was man rather than God. Christ's picture of Heaven was a delightful product of the poetic imagination, a beautiful idealism rather than a future reality. The rewards of the virtuous were here and now; God was the better part of our own nature and the real paradise was within. The *Essay on Christianity* sets it out with great clarity: 'That those who are pure in heart shall see God, and that virtue is its own reward, may be considered as equivalent assertions. The former of these propositions is a metaphorical repetition of the latter.'[17]

To Shelley it was obvious that Christ was a skilful orator who knew well how to handle a potentially hostile audience and to accommodate his doctrines to the prepossessions of those whom he addressed. Christ recognised that he was in danger (an uncomfortable position which Shelley knew that he would share if his own essay were published); he was attacking the very roots of the system of Jewish law.[18] The Sermon on the Mount shows him picking his way carefully towards the heart of the matter, reassuring his audience that he has come not to destroy but to fulfil, easing himself into the confidence of the multitude. Then, emboldened by his success, he finally declares in public 'the utmost singularity of his faith. He tramples upon all received opinions, on all the cherished luxuries and superstitions of mankind. He bids them cast aside the chains of custom and blind faith by which they have been encompassed from the very cradle of their being, and become the imitators and ministers of the Universal God.'[19] This approach to the reading of the Bible helps to explain how the 'atheist' Shelley could make Christ into one of his revolutionary heroes.

(ii)

If Shelley regarded Christ as a revolutionary hero, he was also haunted by images of the passion and his stricken heroes often bear a resemblance to this 'youth / With patient looks nailed to a crucifix' (P.U., 1. 585–6). He seems to have regarded Christ as the archetypal example of what could happen to the benevolent reformers, 'The wise, the mild, the lofty, and the just, / Whom thy slaves hate for being like to thee' (605–6). It is almost inevitable that the Prometheus who wishes 'no living thing to suffer pain' and whose meekness and patience are so cruelly put to the test should be associated with the figure of Christ. The parallel is first suggested when the cursing of Jupiter by Prometheus is fused with portents of the Crucifixion—'there stood / Darkness o'er the day like blood' (1. 101–2): by yielding to hate, Prometheus has disrupted the world of nature and crucified the potential redeemer within himself. Again, Prometheus is visited by a series of temptations which might remind us of how Christ was assailed in the wilderness; two of these temptations make particularly interesting use of the image of Christ.

First, there is a concise history of Christianity, projected in the mental theatre of Prometheus' consciousness by the tempting Furies.[20] This centres on the figure of Christ, a man 'of gentle worth' whose words 'outlived him, like swift poison / Withering up truth, peace, and pity', a sad process culminating in the wars of religion. As Prometheus watches, the chorus addresses him: 'And the future is dark, and the present is spread / Like a pillow of thorns for thy slumberless head.' Here Prometheus as spectator has been fused with Christ as victim of history. Secondly, there is the temptation to ultimate despair. The history of Christianity has been presented in a kind of montage in which it alternates with the history of the French Revolution; then a Fury draws the grim moral:

Behold an emblem: those who do endure
Deep wrongs for man, and scorn, and chains, but heap
Thousandfold torment on themselves and him.

Then, after some further description of the sufferings caused by war
and a closer focus on the face of Christ in his agony,[21] the last and
most dangerous of the Furies tells Prometheus that worse is yet to
come, 'Worse things unheard, unseen, remain behind'.

She then analyses the spiritual condition of society and finds nothing
but fear, greed and apathy: even the loftiest

... dare not devise good for man's estate,
And yet they know not that they do not dare.
The good want power, but to weep barren tears.
The powerful goodness want: worse need for them.
The wise want love; and those who love want wisdom;
And all best things are thus confused to ill.
Many are strong and rich,—and would be just—
But live among their suffering fellow men
As if none felt: they know not what they do.
                    (I. 623–31)

This diagnosis is grimly trenchant; however, it is important to remember
that it is not Shelley's last word but the dramatic utterance of a
character who is trying to persuade Prometheus to give up hope.
Prometheus recognises the truth of the analysis but he will not accept
that the conclusion is despair. He rejects apathy and he rejects despair:
he still has the capacity to be moved by these words of the Fury and
therefore his world is still redeemable. In this context, the Fury's final
phrase is splendidly ironical and insidiously tempting. It is based, of
course, on Christ's plea to his Father to forgive his persecutors ('for
they know not what they do'). Here, it is used by the Fury not in a
spirit of forgiveness, but as one of the counsels of despair. Where Christ
had seen in the ignorance of his enemies a reason why their wickedness
should not be held against them, a Fury sees in the general ignorance
of humanity a reason why we should give up all hopes of betterment.
Prometheus, being a Christ-like figure, is not deceived by this poisonous
talk but the temptation that speaks with the voice of Christ must have
been hard to resist.

   If man, through his representative Prometheus, can conquer temptation and repair the disunion in his soul, he can attain to a state which
is god-like. This was man's privilege before the fall. For example, Asia
describes the effect of music in that paradisal state, now lost:

And music lifted up the listening spirit
Until it walked, exempt from mortal care,
Godlike, o'er the clear billows of sweet sound...
(II, iv. 77–9)

In other words, man once walked on the water just as Christ walked on the Lake of Galilee (though in this case there was no storm, since all was harmonious in the Golden Age). Just in case the allusion is not clear enough, Shelley underlines it by using the word *Godlike*. The same image is later used by Asia in her love duet with Prometheus, where she sings of how she and Prometheus are borne on the wings of music and love to 'a diviner day', a paradise within:

A paradise of vaulted bowers
Lit by downward-gazing flowers,
And watery paths that wind between
Wildernesses calm and green,
Peopled by shapes too bright to see,
And rest, having beheld—somewhat like thee—
Which walk upon the sea, and chant melodiously!
(II, v. 104–10)

Thus, in moments of love and joy, man can achieve the state of divinity as imaged for us by the person of Christ.

Shelley's heterodoxy does not confine itself to suggesting that man should become the god of his own soul, the master of his own universe. Very daringly, and quite deliberately, he also introduces the figure of Satan. Thus, Prometheus is not only modelled on Christ but also on Satan, specifically on the Satan of *Paradise Lost*. Christ provided a pattern for the godlike potential of humanity, for long suffering, for the inevitable persecution of the reformer, for meekness and forgiveness. Satan provided a different perspective:

Nothing can exceed the energy and magnificence of the character of Satan as expressed in *Paradise Lost*. It is a mistake to suppose that he could ever have been intended for the popular personification of evil ... Milton's Devil as a moral being is as far superior to his God as one who perseveres in some purpose which he has conceived to be excellent in spite of adversity and torture is to one who in the cold security of undoubted triumph inflicts the most horrible revenge upon his enemy, not from any mistaken notion of inducing him to repent of a perseverance in enmity, but with the alleged design of exasperating him to deserve new torments. Milton has so far violated the popular creed ... as to have alleged no superiority of moral virtue to his God over his Devil.[22]

Shelley, of course, did not believe in the Devil as a historical character (as *On the Devil and Devils* fully demonstrates). However, he was eager to enter into the implications of the Biblical story and to identify himself with the sufferings and resistance of the Devil, who was the victim of malevolent tyranny. If used as a mythical analogue for Prometheus, the Devil could extend the scope and implication of his sufferings. But Shelley was also concerned with the necessity for resistance; and, since one of the most noble qualities of Milton's Satan was his heroic fixity of will, his unswerving refusal to yield, this made him a worthy prototype for Prometheus, who was faced with the need to 'defy Power which seems omnipotent'.

The Romantic 'misreading' or reinterpretation of *Paradise Lost* is a well known phenomenon. What is not so widely recognised is that Shelley's moral subtlety was sufficient to prevent him from feeling simple and unqualified satisfaction in a mere reversal of the conventional moral relations between God and the Devil. Shelley was no Satanist, nor did he delight in overturning orthodoxies simply to hear the sound of broken glass. His reinterpretation of *Paradise Lost* had a strong moral purpose; and when he found it was inadequate to his needs he explicitly said so:

The only imaginary being resembling in any degree Prometheus, is Satan; and Prometheus is, in my judgement, a more poetical character than Satan, because, in addition to courage, and majesty, and firm and patient opposition to omnipotent force, he is susceptible of being described as exempt from the taints of ambition, envy, revenge, and a desire for personal aggrandisement, which in the Hero of *Paradise Lost*, interfere with the interest. The character of Satan engenders in the mind a pernicious casuistry which leads us to weigh his faults with his wrongs, and to excuse the former because the latter exceed all measure.[23]

Shelley was to take a similar attitude towards the character of Beatrice Cenci, whose murder of her father we can sympathetically understand but which we cannot condone:

It is in the restless and anatomizing casuistry with which men seek the justification of Beatrice, yet feel that she has done what needs justification; it is in the superstitious horror with which they contemplate alike her wrongs and their revenge, that the dramatic character of what she did and suffered, consists.[24]

Thus, we may be drawn into sympathy for the sufferings of Satan and the sufferings of Beatrice at the hands of their respective tyrannical fathers, one in Heaven, the other in the Palace of the Cenci; but we must not allow the intensity of their suffering or the magnitude of their injuries to arouse in us the desire for revenge. That would be to perpetuate the (quite literally) vicious circle, since 'Force from force must ever flow'. Beatrice Cenci exemplifies the road which Prometheus might have taken and did not; so in a slightly different way does Satan; Prometheus is a more admirable character than either because he resists the temptations. Shelley calls him 'more poetical', a phrase which might easily be misunderstood; by it he means that Prometheus is a character more in keeping with those ideal standards which poetry sets before itself, an archetypal figure who comes closer to that best self which poetry attempts to embody for its readers.

Shelley offered yet another identification of this challenging kind in his description of the poet in *Adonais*:

> He answered not, but with a sudden hand
> Made bare his branded and ensanguined brow,
> Which was like Cain's or Christ's—Oh! that it should be so!
> (lines 304–6)

Nor surprisingly, this brought down further curses on his head. The *Literary Gazette*, for example, commented on this 'passage of memorable and ferocious blasphemy' with memorable and ferocious inhumanity:

What can be said to the wretched person capable of this daring profanation. The name of the first murderer—the accurst of God—brought into the same aspect image with that of the Saviour of the World! We are scarcely satisfied that even to quote such passages may not be criminal . . . That any man who insults the common order of society, and denies the being of God, is essentially mad we never doubted. But for the madness, that retains enough of rationality to be wilfully michievous, we can have no more lenity than for the appetites of a wild beast. The poetry of the work is *contemptible* . . .[25]

Here, as usual, it will be observed that religion goes together with politics ('insults the common order of society'), and politics and religion go together with literary values ('The poetry of the work is *contemptible*'). The reaction is extreme but it does give an unequivocal indication of the challenging nature of Shelley's poetry; even today the conjunction of Cain and Christ is likely to give the reader pause for thought.

Shelley's intentions here are worth some consideration. He defended himself in a letter to his Irish friend John Taafe, who apparently had objected:

The introduction of the name of *Christ* as an antithesis to *Cain* is surely any thing but irreverence or sarcasm.—I think when you read the passage again, you will acquit it of any such tendency.... But be it observed that I speak as Milton would have spoken in defence of the great cause whose overthrow embittered his declining years.[26]

First of all, then, Christ and Cain are not interchangeable names: Christ is the 'antithesis' to Cain. What Shelley seems to have in mind here is a progressive scale of torture and punishment. Cain is the first example of the outcast, a figure who typifies the alienation implicit in the whole stanza, where we are told that the poet sings 'in the accents of an unknown land'. Shelley was sympathetic to Byron's inter- pretation of Cain (his play on the subject was 'apocalyptic . . . a revela- tion not before communicated to man')[27] but the whole cast of his mind would have prevented him from condoning the murder of Abel. Much as in the case of Satan, Shelley could sympathise with Cain because of the way he was treated by the orthodox. The suffering of Cain is there- fore intense, unpardonable in those who caused it, but in one sense justifiable. The suffering of Christ offers a clear-cut contrast. Far from suggesting that Christ was a murderer like Cain, Shelley's point is pre- cisely that Christ was not guilty of blood but the harmless benefactor of humanity. Therefore, his punishment is all the more horrifying, a more extreme instance of human brutality, an offence against the spirit of love which bears some resemblance to the ritual murder of Iphigenia. Obviously, the conjunction of Cain and Christ, even as colleagues in suffering, is a challenging gesture in the face of the orthodox: but Shelley's intentions are essentially moral rather than blasphemous.

In fact, the introduction of Christ in this context is not a random association of ideas but can be related very closely to the concept which underlies the whole poem. Keats, like the poet himself, like Cain and like Christ, has been exiled and hounded to death, as if he were a criminal; but the real murderers are the critics who 'produced the most violent effect on his susceptible mind' and hastened his death. Whether this was literally true or not is of little importance; what matters is that it provides a potent myth and a moral frame of reference for Shelley's poem. The reviewers are men who publicly espouse the basic principles of Christianity, but whose actions are informed by a different spirit:

It may well be said that these wretched men know not what they do. . . As to *Endymion*, was it a poem, whatever might be its defects, to be treated contemptuously by those who had celebrated with various degrees of complacency and panegyric, *Paris*, and *Woman*, and a *Syrian Tale*, and Mrs Lefanu, and Mr Barrett, and Mr Howard Payne, and a long list of the illustrious obscure? Are these the men who, in their venal good nature, presumed to draw a parallel between the Rev. Mr Milman and Lord Byron? What gnat did they strain at here, after having swallowed all those camels? Against what woman taken in adultery dares the foremost of these literary prostitutes to cast his opprobrious stone?[28]

Here, as so often, Shelley is quoting the Bible against those who profess to live by it, and to great effect. Underlying the whole passage is Christ's message of forgiveness and love of our fellow men, which these reviewers have failed to put into practice. Once again, Shelley refers to Christ's plea that his enemies should be forgiven, for they 'know not what they do'. There is, too, the obvious reference to the woman taken in adultery; underlying this story there is a suggestion not only of the need for forgiveness but of the basic corruption of those who set themselves up as arbiters of morality. The savage indignation of Shelley's preface is directly related to Christ's uncompromising denunciation of the Scribes and Pharisees in Chapter 23 of Matthew:

Woe unto you, scribes and Pharisees, hypocrites! for ye pay tithe of mint, and anise, and cummin, and have omitted the weightier matters of the law, judgment, mercy, and faith: these ought ye to have done, and not to leave the other undone.
  Ye blind guides! which strain at a gnat, and swallow a camel. . . .
  Woe unto you, scribes and Pharisees, hypocrites! for ye are like unto whited sepulchres, which indeed appear beautiful outward, but are within full of dead men's bones, and of all uncleanness . . .
  Ye serpents, ye generation of vipers! how can ye escape the damnation of hell!
  Wherefore, behold, I send unto you prophets, and wise men, and scribes: and some of them ye shall kill and crucify; and some of them shall ye scourge in your synagogues, and persecute them from city to city:
  That upon you may come all the righteous blood shed upon the earth . . .
                                                            (23-4, 27, 33-5)

Shelley not only quotes from this attack in his Preface; he also bases the whole symbolic structure of *Adonais* on its implications. For instance, this passage, which could be seen as mere Gothic melodrama, acquires a new moral resonance if we bear in mind Christ's characterisation of the scribes and Pharisees as serpents and vipers:

Our Adonais has drunk poison—oh!
What deaf and viperous murderer could crown
Life's early cup with such a draught of woe?
                                    (lines 316-18)

Again, Christ's image of the whited sepulchres gives extra resonance to Shelley's imagery of corpses and charnels, which more obviously derives from the central theme of death and immortality.

Finally, it is interesting that in this battle with the establishment, religious, literary and political, Shelley invokes the example of Milton ('I speak as Milton would have spoken'). 'The great cause' in which Milton was enlisted, was, in the narrow sense, republicanism, in the wider sense, human liberty. In the preface to *Prometheus Unbound* Shelley wrote:

We owe the great writers of the golden age of our literature to that fervid awakening of the public mind which shook to dust the oldest and most oppressive form of the Christian religion. We owe Milton to the progress and development of the same spirit: the sacred Milton was, let it ever be remembered, a republican, and a bold inquirer into morals and religion.

It was all the more satisfactory to be able to claim Milton as a standard-bearer in that the pious had always regarded *Paradise Lost* as the great pillar of orthodoxy in English poetry. Shelley did not go so far as to claim with Blake that Milton was 'of the Devil's party without knowing it' but he did claim that 'Milton's poem contains within itself a philosophical refutation of that system of which, by a strange and natural antithesis, it has been a chief popular support'. This gives special point to the fourth stanza of *Adonais*, which is devoted to Milton, who had written one of the models for Shelley's poem in *Lycidas*:

> He died,
> Who was the Sire of an immortal strain,
> Blind, old, and lonely, when his country's pride
> The priest, the slave, and the liberticide
> Trampled and mocked with many a loathèd rite
> Of lust and blood; he went, unterrified,
> Into the gulf of death; but his clear Sprite
> Yet reigns o'er earth; the third among the sons of light.
>
> (lines 29–36)

Here Shelley portrays the disillusionment of Milton after the shameful reversal involved in the Restoration; but Milton remained true to himself and faced death, not with the terror proper to the Christian who literally believed in hell, but with the calm and self-content which belongs to 'the kings of thought'. He is 'the third among the sons of light' because he is the inheritor of the epic tradition of Homer and Dante; but this phrase, too, has a heterodox implication. According to the New Testament, the children of light' are the followers of the Lord; in the Shelley version 'the sons of light' are those who transcend the loathèd rites of lust and blood and who are reborn in the spirit of poetry. This light was not the light of revealed religion but the light which could reveal the true potentiality of man: 'Imagination is as the immortal God which should assume flesh for the redemption of mortal passion'. Therefore, Milton is a martyr and hero; but the calendar of saints which includes him is not that of orthodox belief and his dispensation is not that of the law and the prophets but the new dispensation of humanity.

(iii)

Christ, then, was an important figure in Shelley's poetic world. On the one hand, he was a revolutionary hero who had challenged the prevailing orthodoxies and who had suffered death for his refusal to compromise with authority. In this way he provided Shelley with a powerful symbol both for the defiant revolutionary and for the virtuous man who is seemingly defeated in this life by enemies who do not recognise his worth. It was this aspect of Christ he had in mind when he copied out the following verses from The Wisdom of Solomon:

Let us examine him with despitefulness and torture, that we may know his meekness, and prove his patience.
   Let us condemn him with a shameful death: for by his own saying he shall be respected.
   Such things they did imagine, and were deceived: for their own wickedness hath blinded them (2: 19–21)[29]

On the other hand, Christ was also important for being a profound moral teacher who expressed his meaning with the imagistic force of a great poet. Shelley frequently speaks of Christ as a poet who followed in the great tradition of the Biblical prophets. In particular, since he was a poet employing a system of metaphors and since he was also an orator who recognised the necessity for communicating through indirection, his message was not to be interpreted literally. To take him at his word was to be guilty of a vulgar and dangerous error; indeed, 'The advocates of literal interpretation have been the most efficacious enemies of those doctrines whose institutor they profess to venerate'.[30]
   With such authority to support him, Shelley began to employ the terminology of orthodox Christianity for metaphorical purposes which were often directly opposed to the basic doctrines of orthodoxy. Taking

his cue from Christ both as revolutionary and as poet, he evolved an elaborate metaphorical system which challenged many received ideas and subtly adapted others to its own purposes. The most radical of his re-orderings was his re-location of the centre of power in man rather than God, the enthronement of man as his own divinity. Shelley systematically develops the implications of this new religion through the imagery of *Prometheus Unbound*. One of the most notable instances is the way in which Shelley enlists the old cardinal virtues in alliance with others of his own invention under the banner of the religion of humanity. The full import can be seen in Demogorgon's last words, which bring the play to an end:

> This is the Day, which down the void abysm
> At the Earth-born's spell yawns for Heaven's despotism,
>   And Conquest is dragged captive through the deep;
> Love, from its awful throne of patient power
> In the wise heart, from the last giddy hour
>   Of dread endurance, from the slippery, steep,
> And narrow verge of crag-like agony, springs
> And folds over the world its heading wings.
>
> Gentleness, Virtue, Wisdom, and Endurance,—
> These are the seals of that most firm assurance
>   Which bars the pit over Destruction's strength;
> And if, with infirm hand, Eternity,
> Mother of many acts and hours, should free
>   The serpent that would clasp her with his length,
> These are the spells by which to re-assume
> An empire o'er the disentangled Doom.
>
> To suffer woes which Hope thinks infinite;
> To forgive wrongs darker than Death or Night;
>   To defy Power, which seems omnipotent;
> To love, and bear; to hope, till Hope creates
> From its own wreck the thing it contemplates;
>   Neither to change, nor falter, nor repent:
> This, like thy glory, Titan, is to be
> Good, great and joyous, beautiful and free;
> This is alone Life, Joy, Empire, and Victory.

(IV. 554–78)

The vigorous images of Love's activity in these lines derive in the first place from the physical setting of *Prometheus Bound*, the 'eagle-baffling' mountain to which Prometheus has been nailed by Jupiter. This unwelcoming natural setting with its suggestions of fear, isolation, cold and pain is brilliantly translated into an image of mental reality, the unredeemed mind of humanity awaiting its liberator, just as Prometheus awaits his liberator on the bleak precipice. But it is a mistake to expect that liberation to arrive conveniently from some unspecified outward source. There can be no god descending from a machine. The liberation must come from within ourselves; we are the masters of our own fate. Man's nature is 'his own divine control'. The agent of regeneration is love, love who is enthroned within the 'wise heart', love who is associated with patience and endurance. If recognised and encouraged, this power can deliver us from our captivity; like the Blessed Virgin it comes to us in the hour of our death ('the last giddy hour / Of dread endurance'); like the Holy Ghost it 'folds over the world its healing wings'. How close this last image approaches the expressions of orthodoxy becomes clear if we think of Hopkins' lines in 'God's Grandeur'; 'the Holy Ghost over the bent / World broods with warm breast and with ah! bright wings'.

Yet this release is not easily won and man's freedom can only be maintained with difficulty. The second stanza introduces the image of Destruction, a grim presence which seems to bear some relation to the Dragon of Revelation. Shelley's apocalyptic poem does not suggest that man's victory cannot be reversed: instead it implies that man must be eternally vigilant or the serpent will uncoil itself and rise out of the pit. The price of this eternal vigilance is Gentleness, Virtue, Wisdom and Endurance—a characteristically Shelleyan and uncanonical list of virtues. Shelley here combines mental cultivation and self-knowledge (Wisdom) with the moral virtues of Gentleness (sympathy, love of our neighbour) and Endurance (the willingness to suffer for our beliefs so that the world may be constantly redeemed from the grasp of evil). Virtue is hard to define in this context but here as often in Shelley it accompanies Wisdom, of which ideally it should be the inevitable result.

The final stanza extends the list of necessary qualities and attributes: endurance, forgiveness, resistance, love and fortitude, hope and constancy. Here there are a number of similarities to the Sermon on the Mount where, together with the Epistle of St James, Shelley went for 'his Christianity in the proper sense of the word'.[31] For instance, Christ says 'Blessed are they which are persecuted for righteousness' sake: for theirs is the kingdom of heaven'; Shelley's version is 'To suffer woes which Hope thinks infinite . . . is alone Life, Joy, Empire, and Victory'. In the Sermon on the Mount the emphasis is on passivity, on the peacemakers, the meek, the merciful, the persecuted, those that mourn.

Shelley also inculcates the virtues of passivity and endurance but in his case there is a greater emphasis on the need for defiance and unyielding resistance ('To defy Power, which seems omnipotent'). Above all, where Christ offers a reward in the life after death ('for theirs is the kingdom of heaven'), Shelley offers the reward in the here and now, the world in which we find our happiness, or not at all ('This . . . is to be / Good, great and joyous, beautiful and free'). The kingdom of heaven is potential within each one of us now.

'Blessed are the meek' was another beatitude to which Shelley subscribed after his own fashion. Earlier in the play Asia and Panthea have to descend into the realm of Demogorgon, to penetrate into the very depths of the mind itself, from which, through their willed acquiescence in the process of historical necessity, the fall of Jupiter will be effected. On their journey a chorus of spirits advises them:

> Resist not the weakness:
> Such strength is in meekness
> That the Eternal, the Immortal,
> Must unloose through life's portal
> The snake-like Doom coiled underneath his throne,
> By that alone!
>
> (II, iii. 93–8)

The choice of the word *meekness* is not accidental; Asia and Panthea do 'inherit the earth' because they have learnt the virtue of conquering self-love and surrendering themselves to the power of a love which is universal. So we humble ourselves to be exalted, are weak that we may be strong. The presence of *strength* here should not be overlooked. Yet the emphasis on non-resistance suggests the need for suffering and endurance; as Julian tells Maddalo

> We know
> That we have power over ourselves to do
> And suffer—what, we know not till we try;
> But something nobler than to live and die—
> So taught those kings of old philosophy
> Who reigned, before Religion made men blind;
> And those who suffer with their suffering kind
> Yet feel their faith, religion.
>
> (lines 184–91)

Somehow, we must hold on, even in the face of suffering; this belief in the potential of humanity is true religion.

It is interesting that Shelley uses the word *faith* here, since of the three virtues set forth in Corinthians it is the only one which does not feature in Demogorgon's catalogue. This is because, in the orthodox sense, Shelley did not accept the necessity of faith. In so far as it signified a blind submission to providence in the certainty that one would be justified by faith alone, it was a pernicious doctrine; this may help to explain Shelley's predilection for the Epistle of St James which is very blunt on this subject: 'Yea, a man may say, Thou hast faith, and I have works: shew me thy faith without thy works, and I will shew thee my faith by my works' (2: 18). It is clear that in the world of *Prometheus Unbound* faith is used in a pejorative sense. It is presented as an integral part of the system of tyranny which helps to maintain Jupiter in power. Jupiter himself recognises this and openly admits that his empire is built 'On eldest faith, and Hell's coeval, fear' (III, i. 10).

On this subject Leigh Hunt tells a revealing anecdote, which is probably based on a memory of Shelley on the day before he was drowned: 'He assented warmly to an opinion which I expressed in the cathedral at Pisa, while the organ was playing, that a truly divine religion might yet be established, if charity were really made the principle of it, instead of faith.'[32] Consequently, it is no surprise that Demogorgon has nothing to say about faith. Charity, however, is prominent in its Shelleyan manifestation of *love*. It is interesting that Shelley links love and endurance ('To love, and bear') since this is directly in accordance with what St Paul says to the Corinthians: 'Charity suffereth long, and is kind ... Beareth all things, believeth all things, hopeth all things, endureth all things' (1 Corinthians, 13: 4, 7).

Apart from love, perhaps the most important virtue for Demogorgon, as for Shelley, is hope. It is mentioned twice in the final stanza where it is closely connected with love ('Charity ... hopeth all things'). In the *Defence of Poetry* it appears in an impassioned description of how civilisation had recovered from the Dark Ages: 'But mark how beautiful an order has sprung from the dust and blood of this fierce chaos! how the world, as from a resurrection, balancing itself on the golden wings of knowledge and of hope, has reassumed its yet unwearied flight into the heaven of time.'[33] We may note here how, once again, Shelley is deliberately employing religious imagery in a secular context—there is the 'resurrection' which may be roughly the equivalent of the Renaissance, and the world itself appears in the guise of an angel flying tirelessly into the 'heaven of time'. Most significantly, the wings on which this world is balanced, the fulcrum of civilisation, are knowledge and hope. Knowledge may be identified with the Wisdom which Demogorgon refers to, or rather it is the beginning of that Wisdom, the fruits of philosophical and scientific enquiry. But this exercise of the calculating faculty will be the enemy of human progress unless it is moderated and harnessed by the power of the imagination; in the case of the Renaissance, man was able to avoid this danger and to improve his condition because he recognised the progressive implications of rational inquiry.

Shelley clarifies the implications of hope as he understood it in a letter to Mrs Gisborne, in which for all his light-heartedness he is very serious:

Let us believe in a kind of optimism in which we are our own gods. It is best that Mr Gisborne should have returned, it is best that I should have overpersuaded you & Henry, it is best that you should all live together without any more solitary attempts—it is best that this one attempt should have been made, otherwise one other thing which is best might not have occurred, & it is best that we should think all this for the best even though it be not, because Hope, as Coleridge says is a solemn duty which we owe alike to ourselves & to the world—a worship to the spirit of good within, which requires before it sends that inspiration forth, which impresses its likeness upon all that it creates, devoted & disinterested homage.[34]

The reference here is to Coleridge's characterisation of hope as 'an awful duty . . . a nurse of all other, the fairest virtues . . .' (The Friend). Wordsworth, too had written of hope as 'the paramount duty that Heaven lays, / For its own honour, on man's suffering heart'.[35] The Wordsworth version in particular serves to bring out exactly what is special in Shelley's formulation. Hope is a duty but it is a duty which we owe not to heaven but 'to ourselves & to the world'; it is not imposed from above but is 'a worship to the spirit of good within'. Where Wordsworth looks upward, Shelley looks inward.

Finally, it should be noted that Shelley wished to inculcate these secular virtues in his readers in the hope that, through their influence, society might eventually be transformed. The Revolt of Islam was written 'in the view of kindling within the bosoms of my readers a virtuous enthusiasm for those doctrines of liberty and justice, that faith and hope in something good, which neither violence nor misrepresentation nor prejudice can ever totally extinguish among mankind'.[36] And Prometheus Unbound was composed in the knowledge that 'until the mind can love, and admire, and trust, and hope, and endure, reasoned principles of moral conduct are seeds cast upon the highway of life which the unconscious passenger tramples into dust, although they would bear the harvest of his happiness'.[37] This is Shelley's version of the parable of the sower and it is evident that, if the virtues he would inculcate are the secularised equivalents of faith, hope and charity and the other patterns of orthodox virtue, so too is *Prometheus Unbound* the gospel which bears within it the seeds of man's liberation.

In fact, not only does *Prometheus Unbound* promulgate its own version of St Paul and of the Sermon on the Mount, but its whole structure is as intimately based on certain Biblical patterns as it is on Aeschylus' play. M. H. Abrams has recently shown in great and convincing detail how many of the Romantics undertook 'radically to recast, into terms appropriate to the historical and intellectual circumstances of their own age, the Christian pattern of the fall, the redemption, and the emergence of a new earth which will constitute a restored paradise'.[38] Shelley's play is an excellent example of this. Like many of the Romantics, he did not believe in sin in its strictly theological sense, but he recognised the existence of evil: in his interpretation, the fall resulted from man's yielding to his own selfish faculties and from his failing to achieve the internal harmony of which he was capable. Shelley fuses the pagan myth of a lost Golden Age with the biblical pattern; and further extends the implications of the fall or lapse from felicity by separating Prometheus from Asia, that is, heroic endurance from love or man from his own best self. As in Revelation, which provided the paradigm for much Romantic mythmaking, there is a millennial return to lost felicity and a final consummation of love in the unification of Asia and Prometheus, a bridal at which the whole universe is in attendance. Finally, the dragon is returned to his den; though there is always the possibility that he may come again.

(iv)

During the time when he was working on the last act of *Prometheus Unbound* Shelley wrote the 'Ode to the West Wind', another poem which trespasses on the preserves of orthodoxy. This ode has a strong religious flavour which relates it to the religious poetry of more than one culture. As has often been pointed out, the structure of the poem bears an obvious similarity to that of Greek hymns to the Gods (such as the Homeric *Hymns*, seven of which Shelley translated). There is the same pattern of prayer-invocation, sanction and treaty. Again, there are similarities to the Vedic hymns (notably those to the Maruts or Storm-gods) and more obviously to the Psalms.[39] There is the usual abasement of the supplicant before the divinity: 'I fall upon the thorns of life! / ... A heavy weight of hours has chained and bowed / One too like thee.' Such is the despair of the weak mortal that he strives with his god 'in prayer in my sore need'; this he acknowledges as a weakness, remembering perhaps that Job had been specifically warned against it (33: 13).

Behind all this, there is a sense of religious awe, in that Shelley acknowledges the majesty and the force of the wind. But, for all its acknowledgement of the numinous, there is no sense of a personal deity; nor is there any sense of a transcendental world. The poet's concern is that the Spirit of the wind should be manifested now, in the inspiration which will enable him as a poet to play his part in the transformation of society. There is even an almost mischievous wit at the expense of established religion when Shelley says to the wind:

> Thou dirge
> Of the dying year, to which this closing night
> Will be the dome of a vast sepulchre
> Vaulted with all thy congregated might
>
> Of vapours, from whose solid atmosphere
> Black rain, and fire, and hail will burst: O hear!

In the 'vaulted' dome and the 'congregated' might of vapours there is a slight suggestion of a form of religion which is dangerously subversive. This is borne out by the earlier description of loose clouds as 'Angels of rain and lightning': Shelley had in mind the Greek original of the word *angel*, which means messenger, but in its context the word also implies a species of angel which is less beautiful and ineffectual than usual. These angels are messengers of rain and lightning and they appear in close proximity to a notoriously unrestrained devotee in the shape of 'some fierce Maenad'.

All of this is particularly daring when one considers that it runs counter to a deeply-rooted Christian response, which must have been familiar to all of Shelley's readers. The Psalmist had claimed the wind for God, 'who maketh the clouds his chariot; who walketh upon the wings of the wind' (104: 3), and the poets had followed suit. 'In 'A Hymn to the Seasons' James Thomson had paid his homage:

> On the whirlwind's wing
> Riding sublime, thou bidst the world adore,
> And humblest nature with thy northern blast.
> (lines 18–20)

Robert Burns recorded:

There is scarcely any earthly object gives me more—I don't know if I should call it pleasure, but something which exalts me, something which enraptures me—than to walk in the sheltered side of the wood or high plantation, in a cloudy, winter day, and hear a stormy wind howling among the trees & raving o'er the plain. It is my best season for devotion;—my mind is rapt up in a kind of enthusiasm to Him who, in the pompous language of Scripture, 'walks on the wings of the wind'.[40]

'Ode to the West Wind' also discovers in the wind the pressure of some 'unseen presence', terrifying in its power and in its destructive potential, yet benevolent too and ultimately fructifying. However, the presence that Shelley recognises in the force of the wind cannot be equated with the God of orthodox Christianity, and his hymn is far from conventional in its intentions. In its structure, its language and much of its imagery, the 'Ode to the West Wind' may appear to be observing the conventions of religious poetry but the deity it celebrates is a radical one and the heaven to which it looks forward is nothing less than a social and political revolution.

Consider first the general pattern of the imagery. The marvellously impetuous first stanza presents a world in dissolution, the wind driving the dead leaves before it like pestilence-stricken multitudes. This leads on to an image of the great winter of the world, the darkness which waits for a redeemer: the wind impels

to their dark wintry bed

The wingèd seeds, where they lie cold and low,
Each like a corpse within its grave . . .

But spring promises a resurrection:

Thine azure sister of the Spring shall blow

Her clarion o'er the dreaming earth, and fill
(Driving sweet buds like flocks to feed in air)
With living hues and odours plain and hill . . .

Though the phrasing is characteristically Shelleyan, the suggestions both of resurrection and of the Last Judgement are clearly derived from the Scriptures. The most likely source can be found in 1 Corinthians in the passage so unforgettably set to music in Handel's *Messiah*:

In a moment, in the twinkling of an eye, at the last trump: for the trumpet shall sound, and the dead shall be raised incorruptible, and we shall be changed. (15:52)

However, there are significant differences between Shelley's account and the Authorised Version. First, in Shelley the agent of resurrection is female (though the soft west wind of Spring was traditionally the masculine Zephyrus or Favonius) and a natural force rather than a supernatural one.[41] Secondly, Shelley's apocalypse is without the transcendental implications of the New Testament. Admittedly, the Millenium as imaged in Revelation is a state of felicity on this earth which has been restored and renewed after the return of Christ and the defeat of the old serpent: but St John seems to imply something more than this though his meaning here is not easy to follow. He sees 'the holy city, new Jerusalem, coming down from God out of heaven' and hears a voice saying, 'Behold the tabernacle of God is with men and he will dwell with them';[42] both of these passages seem to prophesy a new earth which somehow has become transcendental. In contrast, Shelley's vision like that of Isaiah is much less mystical and much more explicitly based on the hope of regeneration in society. Though Shelley was undoubtedly influenced by Revelation his apocalypse is resolutely unmystical: there is no suggestion that man will be translated to Heaven when the Millenium is over or that the new Jerusalem will come down to earth. For Shelley, the terms of reference are much more practical: Heaven can only be realised on earth and the one way to realise it is to create the ideal society. Politics have been substituted for mysticism; the natural for the supernatural.

At the end of the poem the trumpet sounds again when Shelley prays to the wind:

Be through my lips to unawakened Earth

The trumpet of a prophecy! O Wind,
If Winter comes, can Spring be far behind?

In the Bible the trumpet is often associated with the destruction of enemies or of the old way of life. There is also the 'great voice, as of a trumpet' of Revelation, the prophetic voice which Shelley was to invoke specifically in his own 'Ode to Liberty' in the following year.[43] In the 'Ode to the West Wind' Shelley wants to play the role of the Biblical prophet who announces the advent of the new heaven and new earth or, to use his own phrase, the 'new birth' (which also suggests the birth of a redeemer such as Christ). In the closing lines of his ode Shelley is specifically relating himself to this tradition of Biblical prophecy. This helps to make explicit another traditional conception which underlies the whole poem. Shelley's west wind is not only the wind of Greek and Roman myth, destructive or animating in its alternative manifestations, but it is also the creative spirit or breath of wind (*ruach*) of God which moved on the face of the waters in Genesis and which God breathed into the nostrils of man, so that he became a living soul. According to the Bible, too, the wind can destroy, and it can reanimate the dead. Above all, this animating spirit, this principle of life was the source of inspiration for religious oracles and for prophetic poetry. This is acknowledged alike in the Book of Job and in the story of Pentecost as told in the Acts. Therefore, as M. H. Abrams has said, Shelley 'may seem radically innovative. But from a philological point of view Shelley was reactionary . . .'[44]

This is perfectly true; and Abrams has performed a valuable service in showing how (like Wordsworth and Coleridge) Shelley was reviving an older religious attitude to the mysterious power which informed the wind. It is important to recognise this, otherwise we may fall into the error of reading the 'Ode' as thinly disguised autobiography, and the thorns of life on which the poet falls and bleeds as an allegorical concealment for Lord Eldon, or the *Quarterly Review* or even Sir Timothy Shelley. As we have seen in an earlier chapter, Shelley is consciously making use of the prophetic tradition and his poem must be interpreted accordingly. Calling this procedure *reactionary* quite properly draws attention to Shelley's literary sophistication; but the label also gives a false impression, since Shelley is employing this literary device not for fear of innovation but for purposes which are distinctly revolutionary. As we have seen, the prophecies on which he draws are prophecies with serious political implications: as in the case of Blake, Isaiah and Revelation are being directed at contemporary English society in a critical spirit.

The Biblical trumpet which announces radical change makes another notable appearance in the Third Act of *Prometheus Unbound*. There the Spirit of the Earth reports on the moment when society is radiantly transformed after the reunion of Prometheus and Asia and the downfall of Jupiter:

Well, my path lately lay through a great city
Into the woody hills surrounding it.
A sentinel was sleeping at the gate—

When there was heard a sound, so loud, it shook
The towers amid the moonlight, yet more sweet
Than any voice but thine, sweetest of all,
A long, long sound, as it would never end:
And all the inhabitants leapt suddenly
Out of their rest, and gathered in the streets,
Looking in wonder up to Heaven, while yet
The music pealed along. I hid myself
Within a fountain in the public square,
Where I lay like the reflex of the moon
Seen in a wave under green leaves—and soon
Those ugly human shapes and visages
Of which I spoke as having wrought me pain
Passed floating through the air, and fading still
Into the winds that scattered them, and those
From whom they passed seemed mild and lovely forms
After some foul disguise had fallen; and all
Were somewhat changed: and after brief surprise
And greetings of delighted wonder, all
Went to their sleep again; and when the dawn
Came—wouldst thou think that toads, and snakes, and efts
Could e'er be beautiful? yet so they were,
And that with little change of shape or hue:
All things had put their evil nature off.

From earlier in the play we know that this sound has been produced
by the Spirit of the Hour who has breathed into a mysterious conch
'A voice to be accomplished' (III, iii. 67). This conch was a wedding
gift to Asia from Proteus, which suggests that it may be related to the
infinite potentialities of nature. It has been suggested that this peal of
music was probably a remembrance of the mysterious and mournful cry
which announced the passing of the pagan gods; but for Shelley this
is a supremely joyful moment, not an occasion for regret. Surely this
'long, long sound' is, yet again, the trumpet of Corinthians which
signifies that death and corruption have been vanquished and that all
shall be changed?

(v)

The previous sections have attempted to show how Shelley suggested,
by his unconventional use of orthodox imagery, that revolutionary
man could attain to a godlike control over the empire of his own mind
and over the external world. The heroic man is often identified with
Christ in his sufferings and in his ultimate ability to resist his enemies

and transcend their threats and tortures. The poet himself may be crowned with thorns but, like Christ, he acknowledges his prophetic responsibility and dedicates himself to the regeneration of society. Finally, it is sometimes suggested that man can achieve a limited but important kind of immortality which has nothing to do with the Christian system of reward and punishment. This immortality, Shelley suggests, while it cannot be attained completely in this life, can be prefigured and even briefly enjoyed in advance, under special conditions. Those conditions apply particularly in the cases of poetic inspiration and of love, when it is possible to transcend the limits of mortality and to be, however briefly, divine.

Here it is worth recalling Shelley's explication of Christ's words 'for they shall see God' in the *Essay on Christianity*. As we have seen, he provides a rich variety of intepretations which translate Christ's prophecy into secular terms. One of these interpretations has to do specifically with inspiration:

We live and move and think, but we are not the creators of our own origin and existence... we are not the masters of our own imaginations and moods of mental being. There is a Power by which we are surrounded, like the atmosphere in which some motionless lyre is suspended, which visits with its breath our silent chords at will. Our most imperial and stupendous qualities—those on which the majesty and the power of humanity is erected—are, relatively to the inferior portion of its mechanism, indeed active and imperial; but they are the passive slaves of some higher and more omnipresent Power. This Power is God.[45]

In this case Shelley is obviously writing out of his own experience of inspiration; indeed, the image of the Aeolian lyre and the generally sacramental tone bear a close relation to the 'Hymn to Intellectual Beauty'. However, although he acknowledged the possibility of an external force which was greater than ourselves, Shelley (no more than Coleridge) did not like to regard the mind as a kind of barrel organ, a mere mechanism in the hands of a controlling master. The *Essay on Christianity* itself suggests another way of seeing things when it refers to 'the divinity of his [man's] own nature'.[46] This may seem like a confusion on Shelley's part but it is not: it reflects two kinds of experience. It is impossible to be sure whether the inspiration comes from without or within; if it comes from without, it requires man's collaboration if it is to be realised within him; if it comes from within, man is his own divinity. In either case, his destiny is a high one; in either case, he may be said to be god-like.

The same ambivalence is further developed in Shelley's translation of Plato's *Ion* and in the *Defence of Poetry*. In his version of the *Ion* he writes that poets 'do not compose according to any art which they have acquired but from the impulse of the activity within them'[47] where Plato actually said that poets are inspired to write *theiai dunamei* (by a divine force). In itself this might appear to be a careless slip on Shelley's part but the accompanying evidence demonstrates beyond doubt that he wished to qualify the unreserved affirmation of the original. For instance, where Plato speaks of poets who are inspired and possessed (*entheoi ontes kai katechomenoi*) Shelley says they are 'in a state of inspiration and, as it were, *possessed* by a spirit not their own'. He wants it to be quite clear that, in his view, Plato is speaking metaphorically, just as Christ is in the Sermon on the Mount.

The same cautiousness is evident in the *Defence of Poetry* where he describes the evanescent visitations of thought and feeling, which constitute poetic inspiration:

It is as it were the interpenetration of a diviner nature through our own; but its footsteps are like those of a wind over the sea, which the coming calm erases, and whose traces remain only, as on the wrinkled sand which paves it.[48]

Thus, we seem to experience the vanishing apparitions of a divinity which visits us from without, but can it be that we project these deities from within? Shelley catches the ambiguity with great skill when he claims: 'Poetry redeems from decay the visitations of the divinity in man.'[49] At first sight, he might seem to be referring to the visits of the divinity *to* man, but, as soon as this sentence is placed alongside his variation on Plato, we can see that Shelley does not intend anything so simple. He means the divinity which manifests itself in man but which may originate either from without or from within.

This image of divinity is extended in the 'Ode to Liberty'. An unused passage in the manuscript draft reads as follows:

Within [the temple] a cavern of [the mind of man]
   man's inmost spirit
Is throned [an Idol], so intensely fair
That the adventurous thoughts which wander near it
Worship—and as they kneel, and tremble [like votaries] wear
The splendour of its presence—and the light
Penetrates their dreamlike frame
Till they become charged with the strength of flame
  . . .
They change and pass but it remains the same.[50]

Shelley discarded this intriguing, if too elaborate, passage (though the final line seems to have found its way into *Adonais*). He compressed the basic idea and used it in stanza xvi where he wishes that men could release themselves from the superstitious fears induced by religion 'Till human thoughts might kneel alone, / Each before the judgement-throne / Of its own aweless soul, or of the Power unknown!' Here again we meet calculated ambiguity of definition. The religious image here is probably a development of an image from Bacon's *Advancement of Learning* which Shelley refers to in the *Essay on Christianity*:

Every human mind has what Lord Bacon calls its *idola specus*, peculiar images which reside in the inner cave of thought. These constitute the essential and distinctive character of every human being, to which every action and every word bears intimate relation . . .[51]

This idol throned within Shelley refers to in his letters as 'the ruling spirit' and 'the god of my own heart';[52] in another letter, he identifies it with 'the Imagination, who is the master of them both [the passions and the understanding], their God, and the Spirit by which they live and are'.[53] The last phrase is Shelley's version of St Paul's declaration to the Athenians, 'For in him we live, and move and have our being . . .',[54] a passage used to describe the effects of 'the grand elementary principle of pleasure' by Wordsworth in the Preface to *Lyrical Ballads*. Here Shelley seems to be claiming that the poet is the Creator and that his imagination performs the work of the Holy Spirit. In the preface to *The Cenci*, as we have seen, he invoked Christ ('blasphemously and senselessly', said the *Literary Gazette*)[55] and so completed an identification between the powers of poetry and all three persons of the Holy Trinity.

The claim that 'Imagination is as the immortal God which should assume flesh for the redemption of mortal passion' is not idly made. It sees the human condition as redeemable and it recognises that the imagination, acting through poetry, can be the agent of that redemption. Poetry can deliver us from the bondage of selfishness, disperse the dull vapours of the little world of self, defeat the 'curse' which separates man from man (Shelley's equivalent to the Christian redemption from the effects of the Fall). Above all, poetry is opposed to the principle of self, which in the effects of the Industrial Revolution and the tightening grip of capitalist economics has 'added a weight to the curse imposed on Adam'. Poetry is the potential saviour of mankind enlisted on the side of God against Mammon: 'Poetry and the principle of Self, of which money is the visible incarnation, are the God and Mammon of the world'.[56] But Poetry and its informing spirit, Imagination, carry out their primary functions in this sacred war not by attacking Mammon in its external manifestations (war, poor pay, bad housing conditions, repressive government policies, etc.) but by attempting to redeem the world within:

All things exist as they are perceived; at least in relation to the percipient. 'The mind is its own place, and of itself can make a heaven of hell, a hell of heaven.' But poetry defeats the curse which binds us to be subjected to the accident of surrounding impressions. And whether it spreads its own figured curtain, or withdraws life's dark veil from before the scene of things, it equally creates for us a being within our being. It makes us the inhabitant of a world to which the familiar world is a chaos. It reproduces the common universe of which we are portions and percipients, and it purges from our inward sight the film of familiarity which obscures from us the wonder of our being. It compels us to feel that which we perceive, and to imagine that which we know. It creates anew the universe, after it has been annihilated in our minds by the recurrence of impressions blunted by reiteration. It justifies the bold and true word of Tasso: *Non merita nome di creatore, se non Iddio ed il Poeta.*[57]

Thus the poet redeems the fallen world, by creating a new one. The curse of being subject to sense impressions is lifted and the wonder of life is recreated out of the common universe, just as God summoned the universe out of the primal chaos in 'the great morning of the world'.

(vi)

Shelley uses almost precisely the same imagery in his attempts to convey the essence of love. Perhaps the best example of how this works can be found in *Epipsychidion*. Here Shelley is describing the effects of the philosophy of true love: it is

> the eternal law
> By which those live, to whom this world of life
> Is as a garden ravaged, and whose strife
> Tills for the promise of a later birth
> The wilderness of this Elysian earth.
>   (lines 185–9)

The final line presents much the same paradox that we find in his assessment of Italy as the 'Paradise of exiles'. The earth has Elysian possibilities, it can be transformed into a garden of paradise but it must await its redeemer ('a later birth'). In *Epipsychidion* the sages who believe in true love, 'that deep well whence [they] draw / The unenvied light of hope', are the secular equivalent of those who reverently expected the coming of the Messiah. When the Messiah does come he will appear as a liberator, rising again from his tomb, harrowing hell, releasing from their bondage the living and the dead:

> For it can burst his charnel, and make free
> The limbs in chains, the heart in agony,
> The soul in dust and chaos.
>
> (lines 405–7)

In the world of *Epipsychidion*, the Messiah is female and represents the redemptive possibilities of love within the mental world of the poet. The poet is granted a vision which transforms his life but which is suddenly withdrawn; however, nothing can

> uncreate
> That world within this Chaos, mine and me,
> Of which she was the veiled Divinity,
> The world I say of thoughts that worshipped her...
>
> (lines 242–5)

The poem makes constant use of the attendant imagery of religion: temples, veils, and the rituals of worship. Perhaps the most interesting example is the image of the veiled divinity, which seems to imply that behind the veil there is a presence too bright for mortal eyes. This becomes quite explicit in the passage where Shelley describes the poet's vision:

> on an imagined shore,
> Under the grey beak of some promontory
> She met me, robed in such exceeding glory,
> That I beheld her not.
>
> (lines 197–200)

Behind this, there is a memory of the Transfiguration (which Shelley also uses in Panthea's vision of Prometheus and later in Prometheus' song to Asia). Even more appropriately, there is probably also a memory of how Beatrice appeared to Dante in Paradise:

Without answering I lifted up mine eyes and saw her, making to herself a crown as she reflected from herself the eternal rays.

From that region which thundereth most high, no mortal eye is so far distant, though plunged most deep within the sea,

as there from Beatrice was my sight...[58]

The framework of *Epipsychidion* is largely based on Dante and here, as elsewhere, Shelley seems to be providing his own secularised version of the *Vita Nuova* and the *Divina Commedia*. Shelley agreed with Dante on the importance of love but he did not see it as a step towards a higher felicity, to be found only in heaven: he regarded true love as a heaven in itself and for him the condition of the lover represented an experience of beatitude which was available to human beings on this earth. This heterodoxy is made more explicit in a prose fragment where he is describing the effect of beauty on the beholder and claiming the necessity of a sympathetic sharer:

... if ... you can pour forth into another's most attentive ear the feelings by which you are entranced, there is an exultation of spirit in the utterance —a glory of happiness which far transcends all human transports, and seems to invest the soul as the saints are with light, with a halo, untainted, holy, and undying.[59]

The terms which Shelley employs to describe this experience of intimate understanding in the presence of beauty are unmistakably borrowed from the orthodox Christian conception of the happiness of the blessed in the Divine Presence. Here he is developing to their logical conclusion those concepts which underlie his metaphorical interpretation of the Beatitudes: 'Blessed are the pure in heart, for they shall see God.'

Surprising though it may seem, Shelley was much concerned with the state of beatitude. It was this concern which led him to rate that 'perpetual hymn of everlasting love', the *Paradiso*, as the crowning achievement of the *Divina Commedia*.[60] Later in his life he specified an appreciation of the opening of the *Paradiso* as one of the touchstones of true literary taste.[61] Conversely, it was Michelangelo's failure to transcend the horrors of Hell and to rise to his subject in his portrayal of Heaven, that betrayed a lack of 'the essence of the creative power of mind' in the Sistine Chapel. Shelley expressed his disappointment very bluntly:

On one side of this figure are the Elect, on the other the host of Heaven, they ought to have been what the Christians call *glorified bodies*, floating onward, & radiant with that everlasting light (I speak in the spirit of their faith) which had consumed their mortal veil. They are in fact very ordinary people.[62]

This criticism is very instructive for what it tells us of Shelley. Far from criticising Michelangelo for being too deeply involved in a religious faith which he cannot accept, Shelley finds him wanting because he is not able to embody satisfactorily the ultimate premises of that faith.

There can be no doubt that Shelley was particularly responsive to the portrayal of states of beatitude. His letters provide several revealing glimpses into the way he investigated this subject. Take for example this sentence from a description of Correggio's 'Christ Beatified' at Bologna, a painting which Shelley considered 'inexpressibly fine':

... the whole figure seems dilated with expression, the countenance is heavy as it were with the weight of the rapture of the spirit, the lips parted but scarcely parted with the breath of intense but regulated passion, the eyes are calm and benignant, the whole features harmonized in majesty & sweetness.[63]

Even in this impassioned description Shelley insists on the sceptical reservation of 'as it were'; yet the passage reveals a remarkable ability to feel *into* the state of beatitude. The impression of the almost overwhelming weight of rapture is also found in a word picture of a Madonna lattante by Guido which Shelley saw in the same gallery:

Her eyes are almost closed, her lip deprest; there is a serious and even a heavy relaxation as it were of all the muscles which are called into action by ordinary emotion. But it is only as if the spirit of a love almost insupportable from its intensity were brooding upon and weighing down the soul, or whatever it is without which the material frame is inanimate and inexpressive.[64]

Here again we have the recognition of experiences which transcend the limits of mortality and here again we find that sceptical refusal to assent to the supernatural in Shelley's cautious periphrasis about the soul. This may serve as an emblem of the way in which Shelley handles this kind of imagery: undoubtedly man had his intimations of immortality but, in all probability, these were emanations from the deity within, the power that was enthroned in his own heart.

Notes to chapter six

1   Cameron, *Shelley: The Golden Years*, p. 58.
2   Clark, *Prose*, pp. 197–8.
3   M. H. Abrams, 'English Romanticism. The Spirit of the Age' in *Romanticism Reconsidered*, ed. Northrop Frye, Columbia University Press, New York and London, 1963, p. 37.
4   *The Marriage of Heaven and Hell*.
5   Clark, *Prose*, p. 214. Shelley's comment on Luke I. 52 is 'Jacobinism' (Bod. MS. Shelley adds e. 9. p. 1).
6   Bennett Weaver, *Toward the Understanding of Shelley*. University of Michigan Press, Ann Arbor, 1932, p. 60.

7 Bod. MS. Shelley adds. e. 9, p. 211.
8 Hunt, *Autobiography*, p. 269.
9 Brimley Johnson, *Shelley–Leigh Hunt*, p. 34.
10 Clark, *Prose*, p. 204.
11 Clark, *Prose*, p. 203.
12 Clark, *Prose*, p. 201.
13 Clark, *Prose*, p. 202.
14 Clarke, *Prose*, p. 204. Cf. *Adonais*, ll. 379–87.
15 Clark, *Prose*, p. 201.
16 Clark, *Prose*, p. 202.
17 *Ibid.*
18 Clark, *Prose*, pp. 199–200.
19 Clark, *Prose*, p. 200.
20 Godwin used the phrase 'the theatre of mind' in *Thoughts on Man* (1831) cited by C. E. Pulos, *The Deep Truth*, p. 59.
21 I. 546–63. See *Letters*, II. 50 for the description of a Crucifixion by Guido Reni which may have influenced *Prometheus Unbound*.
22 *Defence*, pp. 46–7.
23 *P.W.*, p. 205.
24 *P.W.*, pp. 276–7.
25 White, *The Unextinguished Hearth*, pp. 288–9.
26 *Letters*, II. 306.
27 *Letters*, II. 388.
28 *P.W.*, p. 431.
29 Bod MS. Shelley adds e. 8, p. 166.
30 Clark, *Prose*, p. 202.
31 Hunt, *Autobiography*, p. 269.
32 Hunt, *Autobiography*, p. 330.
33 Clark, *Prose*, p. 288. Cf. *Revolt of Islam*, ll. 3692–3 for a similar image.
34 *Letters*, II. 125.
35 September 14 1809; *Works*, III. 140. Cf. *Letters*, I. 504.
36 *P.W.*, p. 32.
37 *P.W.*, p. 207.
38 *Natural Supernaturalism*, p. 29.
39 See Coleman Parsons, 'Shelley's Prayer to the West Wind', *K.-S.J.*, XI (1962), pp. 31–7.
40 Geoffrey Grigson, *The Romantics*, Routledge, 1947, p. 77.
41 Cf. the role of Love in *Prince Athanase* which 'as soft air / In spring ... moves the unawakened forest' (ll. 290–1). See also the function of Venus at the opening of Lucretius' *De Rerum Natura*.
42 Revelation, 21 : 2–3.
43 See also his description of poets as 'trumpets which sing to battle and feel not what they inspire' (*Defence*, p. 59).
44 'The Correspondent Breeze : A Romantic Metaphor', *English Romantic Poets*, ed. M. H. Abrams, p. 44.
45 Clark, *Prose*, p. 202.
46 *Ibid.*
47 Notopoulos, *The Platonism of Shelley*, p. 473.
48 *Defence*, pp. 54–5.
49 *Defence*, p. 55.
50 Bod. MS. Shelley adds. e. 6, p. 105. Compare this to the passage from the Inner Light Protestants quoted in Abrams, *Natural Supernaturalism*, pp. 46 ff.
51 Clark, *Prose*, p. 199.

52 *Letters*, II. 437, 394. Cf. 'O thou Immortal Deity / Whose throne is in the [Heaven] depth of Human thought . . .' (Bod. MS. Shelley adds. e. 6, p. 33).

53 *Letters*, II. 152.

54 Acts, 17 : 28.

55 White, *The Unextinguished Hearth*, p. 169.

56 *Defence*, p. 52.

57 *Defence*, p. 56. See *Letters*, II. 30.

58 *Paradiso*, XXXI. 70–6, cited from the Temple Classics Edition, Dent, 1912.

59 Clark, *Prose*, p. 337.

60 *Defence*, p. 45.

61 *Letters*, II. 436.

62 *Letters*, II. 81.

63 *Letters*, II. 49–50.

64 *Letters*, II. 51.

CHAPTER SEVEN

THE GREEK EXAMPLE

(*i*)

Shelley never visited Greece but for him it was always the most alluring of the countries of the mind. Towards the end of his life he was planning an expedition but, like his projected visits to Spain and to India, this came to nothing. The nearest he could approach to the country of Homer, Plato and the Greek tragedians was the Greek cities of southern Italy; like Winckelmann, who so imaginatively and influentially recaptured the glories of Greek sculpture for the late eighteenth century, his image of the Greek landscape was formed largely on Greek literature, with the help of Italian settings. Shelley's version of the Greek landscape is rich and lush, inhabited by small delicate creatures:

> The wind in the reeds and the rushes,
> The bees on the bells of thyme,
> The birds in the myrtle bushes,
> The cicadae above in the lime,
>   And the lizards below in the grass ...
>   ('Hymn of Pan', lines 6–10)

This Theocritean world of forests and highlands, of moist river-lawns, islands and dewy caves is recognisably the world of *Prometheus Unbound*, of *Epipsychidion*, *Adonais* and *The Witch of Atlas*, a beautiful, animated setting for human activity, still fresh it seems with the dew of creation. In that world under 'the roof of blue Ionian weather' the waters of fountain, rivulet and pond are 'clear as elemental diamond' and the air is 'heavy with the scent of lemon flowers'. Shelley's richly detailed letters from Italy show that he was peculiarly responsive to 'the warm and radiant atmosphere which is interfused through all things' and to the brightness and clarity of the air. Once he had settled in Italy Shelley was able to give full indulgence to his preference for writing poetry in the open air: 'S[helley] says he always "writes best in the air,"—under a tree—in a garden or on the bank of a river; there is an undivided spirit reigns abroad, a mutual harmony among the works of Nature, that makes him better acquainted with himself and them.'[1]

So he composed 'With a Guitar, to Jane' sitting under a tree in a pine forest; *Prometheus Unbound* in the flowering ruins of the Baths of Caracalla; *The Cenci* in a sort of glass-house at the top of his summer villa near Leghorn, 'an airy cell' where he basked in the dazzling sunlight and the heat, like a salamander or, to use another of his own similes, like an exotic; *The Triumph of Life* on the deck of his yacht, the *Don Juan*. He also read continually in a variety of outdoor settings. Trelawny describes him on board the *Don Juan* with Plato in one hand and the tiller in the other; his hat is knocked overboard and he almost follows, causing Trelawny to say: 'You will do no good with Shelley, until you heave his books and papers overboard . . .'.[2] At the Bagni di Lucca he found a transparent pool in the middle of a forest:

My custom is to undress and sit on the rocks, reading Herodotus, until the perspiration has subsided, and then to leap from the edge of the rock into this fountain—a practice in the hot weather exceedingly refreshing. This torrent is composed, as it were, of a succession of pools and waterfalls, up which I sometimes amuse myself by climbing when I bathe, and receiving the spray over all my body, whilst I clamber up the moist crags with difficulty.[3]

This activity gave rise to a striking image in *Prometheus Unbound* where Panthea, who has been listening to a love-duet between the Moon and the Earth, tries to convey what she has experienced: 'I rise as from a bath of sparkling water, / A bath of azure light, among dark rocks, / Out of the stream of sound', to which Ione replies 'Your words fall like the clear soft dew / Shaken from a bathing wood-nymph's limbs and hair' (IV. 503–5, 508–9). This is a good instance of how Shelley can give material presence to the activities of the mind and shows how profitably he could employ his personal experiences for poetic purposes. The introduction of the bathing wood-nymph is particularly interesting since it also shows how he could translate such experiences into a mythological realm, into the predominantly Greek world of *Prometheus Unbound*. The combination of Herodotus and scrambling up a waterfall is also indicative not only of an unstuffy attitude to classical literature but of the way in which the Italian landscape informed Shelley's reading and experience of the great Greek writers.

Shelley had no doubt that an exposure to the benignant influences of the open air was one of the formative principles of Greek civilisation. In January 1819 he visited Pompeii and recorded his impressions in a long and rapturous letter to Peacock, which tells us much about his view of Greek society. First, there is a detailed description of the streets, theatres, private houses and temples, and a careful appraisal of mosaics, paintings and other works of art. Then Shelley recreates the view from the temple of Jupiter:

Above & between the multitudinous shafts of the columns, was seen the blue sea reflecting the purple heaven of noon above it, & supporting as it were on its line the dark lofty mountains of Sorrento, of a blue inexpressibly deep, & tinged towards their summits with streaks of new-fallen snow. Between was one small green island. To the right was Capua, Inarime, Prochyta and Miseno. Behind was the single summit of Vesuvius rolling forth volumes of thick white smoke whose foamlike column was sometimes darted into the clear dark sky & fell in little streaks along the wind. Between Vesuvius & the nearer mountains, as thro a chasm was seen the main line of the loftiest Apennines to the east. The day was radiant & warm. Every now & then we heard the subterranean thunder of Vesuvius; its distant deep peals seemed to shake the very air & light of day which interpenetrated our frames with the sullen & tremendous sound. This scene was what the Greeks beheld. (Pompeii you know was a Greek city.) They lived in harmony with nature, & the interstices of their incomparable columns, were portals as it were to admit the spirit of beauty which animates this glorious universe to visit those whom it inspired. If such is Pompeii, what was Athens? What scene was exhibited from its Acropolis? The Parthenon and the temples of Hercules & Thesus & the Winds? The islands of the Aegean Sea, the mountains of Argolis & the peaks of Pindus & Olympus, & the darkness of the Boeotian forests interspersed?[4]

This evocation of 'the city disinterred' is nicely representative of Shelley's response to the Italian scene in several ways. To begin with, it provides a good example of that particularly close relation between the natural world and the history of human civilisation which Shelley discovered throughout Italy. The natural world is important in and for itself because of its beauty, its fertility, its fierce energies: but it also provides a significant setting for the drama of human history, a moral landscape against which man works out his salvation. Dominating the whole scene is the cone of Vesuvius, a potent and haunting presence and a symbol of dark and radical forces; like Ozymandias, the people of Pompeii were overshadowed by forces greater than themselves, the inexorable patterns of history. Yet, in the day of its glory, Pompeii came close to bodying forth the ideal city of the imagination, its portals open to receive the spirit of beauty:

I now understand why the Greeks were such great Poets, & above all I can account, it seems to me, for the harmony the unity the perfection the uniform excellence of all their works of art. They lived in a perpetual commerce with external nature and nourished themselves upon the spirit of its forms. Their theatres were all open to the mountains & the sky. Their columns that ideal type of a sacred forest with its roof of interwoven tracery admitted the light & wind, the odour & the freshness of the country pene-trated the cities. Their temples were mostly upaithric; & the flying clouds the stars or the deep sky were seen above. O, but for that series of wretched wars which terminated in the Roman conquest of the world, but for the Christian religion which put a finishing stroke to the ancient system; but for those changes which conducted Athens to its ruin, to what an eminence might not humanity have arrived![5]

Shelley may not have shared the Wordsworthian view of natural religion but this letter certainly indicates that he regarded the natural environment as one of the most significant factors in the development of a civilisation. The word *upaithric* is credited to Shelley by the Oxford Dictionary; in fact, he probably found it in Peacock who in turn derived it from the Greek word *hupaithrios* meaning 'open to the air' or 'having no roof'. Not the least interesting part of this passage is the final sen-tence, a characteristic mixture of lament and invective, which suggests quite clearly that, although hostile outside forces played an impor-tant part, Greek civilisation was ultimately responsible for its own downfall.

Shelley's admiration for Greece was balanced by an understanding of its weaknesses. Women, for example, were treated by the Greeks as inferior to men: 'This invidious distinction of humankind as a class of beings [of] intellectual nature into two sexes is a remnant of savage barbarism which we have less excuse than they for not having totally abolished.'[6] Athenian society also depended upon the underprivileged existence of a large slave class. Finally, for all its idealism and the spleandour of its monuments, even the Greek achievement was ulti-mately undermined by that very system of revenge and retribution against which Aeschylus had warned his countrymen so often. These shortcomings in Greek civilisation should not be denied, nor should they be concealed by a pretence that the Greeks were really much the same as us: Shelley criticises Barthélemy, the author of *Anacharsis*, for writing from the viewpoint of a Frenchman and a Christian and, while he recognises that Wieland makes 'a very tolerable Pagan', he regrets that 'he cherishes too many political prejudices and refrains from diminishing the interest of his romances by painting sentiments in which no European of modern times can possibly sympathise'. Here Shelley is referring specifically to the significant role of homosexuality in that male-oriented society, yet the point has a wider application:

Let us see their errors, their weaknesses, their daily actions, their familiar conversation and catch the tone of their society. When we discover how far the most admirable community ever formed was removed from that perfection to which human society is impelled by some active power within each bosom to aspire, how great ought to be our hopes, how resolute our struggles.[7]

These words are taken from *A Discourse on the Manners of the Ancient Greeks Relative to the Subject of Love*, an essay whose intention was to make Plato more acceptable to the English reader, in particular by a sympathetic explanation of the Greek attitude to homosexuality.

Yet, whatever the limitations of Greek civilisation, it was still to be lamented that darker influences had intervened to thwart its direct continuance. Like Milton, Shelley regretted the passing of the old Greek deities but unlike Milton he blamed Christianity for distorting what was essentially beautiful:

The sylvans and fauns with their leader, the great Pan, were most poetical personages and were connected in the imagination of the Pagans with all that could enliven and delight. They were supposed to be innocent beings not greatly different in habits from the shepherds and herdsmen of which they were the patron saints. But the Christians contrived to turn the wrecks of the Greek mythology, as well as the little they understood of their philosophy, to purposes of deformity and falsehood.[8]

One of the side-effects of this crude misrepresentation was that it destroyed the 'power of producing beauty in art',[9] a power which was only rediscovered after the Renaissance. Since the condition of art is directly related to the health of society, this crudeness in aesthetic forms was also uncomfortably evident in the shape of politics. If only the Greeks had managed to perpetuate themselves in their most glorious manifestations:

Were not the Greeks a glorious people? What is there, as Job says of the Leviathan, like unto them? If the army of Nicias had not been defeated under the walls of Syracuse, if the Athenians had, acquiring Sicily, held the balance between Rome & Carthage, sent garrisons to the Greek colonies in the south of Italy, Rome might have been all that its intellectual condition entitled it to be, a tributary not the conqueror of Greece; the Macedonian power would never have attained to the dictatorship of the civilized states of the world. Who knows whether under the steady progress which philosophy & social institutions would have made, (for in the age to which I refer their progress was both rapid & secure,) among a people of the most perfect physical organization, whether the Christian Religion would have arisen, or the barbarians overwhelmed the wrecks of civilization which had survived the conquests & tyranny of the Romans.—What then should we have been?[10]

Shelley then goes on to offer an acute piece of self-analysis in which, without exonerating himself, he suggests that the loss of Greek civilisation has subjected him and others like him to a frustrating situation in which one is bound to be in error, whether by speaking out or by holding one's peace. The harmonising possibilities of life have been largely withdrawn:

As it is, all of us who are worth any thing spend our manhood in unlearning the follies, or expiating the mistakes of our youth; we are stuffed full of prejudices, & our natural passions are so managed that if we restrain them we grow intolerant & precise because we restrain them not according to reason but according to error, & if we do not restrain them we do all sorts of mischief to ourselves & others. Our imagination & understanding are alike subjected to rules the most absurd . . .

There is here a note of tired resignation, almost of apathy, which seems to look forward to Matthew Arnold's lament for 'the weariness, the fever and the fret' of the 1850s. But a more significant comparison can be made with German Romantics such as Schiller and Hölderlin and with some of Shelley's English contemporaries such as Leigh Hunt and Keats. All of these poets mourned for the passing of the Greek gods and the world of antique mythology 'When holy were the haunted forest boughs, / Holy the air, the water, and the fire'. For the most part they concentrated their attention on the loss of 'happy pieties', looking after rather than before (even though Keats, for one, was beginning to develop a theory of evolution in *Hyperion*).

What distinguishes Shelley's attitude is two features, both political and closely related to one another. In the first place, though Shelley's comments on the history of art leave no doubt that he was concerned with a loss of beauty, this letter in which he speculates on what we might have been had Greek civilisation not gone under makes it clear that his primary concern is not aesthetic but political. Certainly, he was responsive to the aesthetic attractions of Greek life, but he also looked towards Greece as a political model, an intimation of the ideal society.

The letter is very concrete in its references to specific historical facts and events; there are no images of lost gods wandering in the lonely woods. Secondly, there is Shelley's view that, though we must lament the downfall of Greece, we should be encouraged by what it achieved. Though in his own day it could be claimed that justice and the true meaning of society were, if not more accurately, yet more generally understood, and though perhaps men *knew* more, it would require 'a universal and an almost appalling change in the system of existing things' if contemporary society were to approach the condition of ancient Greece. In spite of this, perhaps even because of it, we ought to give our attention to the study of Greek society:

The study of modern history is the study of kings, financiers, statesmen, and priests. The history of ancient Greece is the study of legislators, philosophers, and poets; it is the history of men, compared with the history of titles. What the Greeks were was a reality, not a promise. And what we are and hope to be is derived, as it were, from the influence and inspiration of these glorious generations.[11]

To those who believed in the capacity of man to create an ideal society (or an approximation to it), ancient Greece, and Athens in particular, was both proof and encouragement. What had been done once, could be done again—though Shelley was under no illusions as to the difficulty of the struggle. In Plato's *Republic*, and especially in Book Six, the theoretical basis had been laid down with incomparable understanding:

His speculations on civil society are surely the foundations of true politics, & if ever the world is to be arranged upon another system than that of the several members of it destroying & tormenting one another for the sake of the pleasures of sense, or from the force of habit & imitation; it must start from some such principles.[12]

Plato had also established the principle of the forgiveness of injuries and had explained the error of revenge and the 'immorality and inutility of punishment considered as punishment' (that is, the doctrine of retributive justice).

Not only did the *Republic* offer a worthy ideal for the social reformers but the great Greek philosophers, whom Shelley studied in his carefully annotated copy of Diogenes Laertius,[13] offered noble examples both in their doctrines and in their own lives. For instance, there was Crates' pithy definition of one of the goals of philosophy, which Shelley copied into a notebook: 'He said that we should study philosophy to the point of seeing in generals nothing but donkey-drivers.' Another sentence which occurs in a notebook is Antisthenes' brave statement: 'It is better to be with a handful of good men fighting against all the bad, than with hosts of bad men against a handful of good men.' Most significant of all is this passage about Diogenes, which Shelley marked in his copy and which Leigh Hunt noted as characteristic of his unfailing delight 'in a gird at things aristocratical': 'He would ridicule good birth and fame and all such distinctions, calling them showy ornaments of vice. The only true commonwealth was, he said, that which is as wide as the universe.'[14] These sentences were quoted by Shelley in the *Essay on Christianity*, where he attempts to explain Christ's views on the equality of mankind and finds that they were very similar to those of the most enlightened Greek philosophers.[15]

Finally, Shelley recognised that the philosophers were men of courage who were not afraid to die for their beliefs. The wise man is his own legislator, and according to another passage which Shelley marked, 'is guided not by the laws but by virtue': therefore, he is usually 'anti-tyrannical' and often exposed to danger. One of Shelley's comments on Plato's *Apology* recorded: 'Socrates *alone* in the Senate opposed the condemnation of the ten captains, & ran great risk of his life——'[16] Thus, not only did the Greek philosophers offer clear and unprejudiced approaches to the great problems of morals and of politics, but they were also emblems of human courage, clarity of intellect and self-knowledge. As Shelley said of Socrates: 'I conceive him personally to have presented a grand & simple model of much of what we can conceive, & more than in any other instance we have seen realized, of all that is eminent & excellent in man.'[17]

(ii)

What the Greeks had achieved was 'a reality, not a promise' but that reality was in itself a promise, an intimation of human potential. Shelley was well aware of the gap between this glorious achievement and the condition of contemporary Greek society, which was sadly degraded by 'moral and political slavery', as he noted in the Preface to *Hellas*. Corruption of the best might produce the worst; yet Shelley sensed that even this darkness could be dispersed and that Greece could become an independent nation once again. It is this recovery of freedom which *Hellas* enacts in advance and prophesies, projecting 'upon the curtain of futurity, which falls upon the unfinished scene, such figures of indistinct and visionary delineation as suggest the final triumph of the Greek cause as a portion of the cause of civilisation and social improvement'.[18]

This 'lyrical drama' illustrates very conveniently the uses of history. Aeschylus, of course, provides the basic pattern in his play the *Persae* which presents the effects of defeat in the battle of Salamis (480 B.C.) on the Persian court and emperor. The angle of vision here is somewhat surprising since we might have expected Aeschylus to concentrate on celebrating the Athenian victory rather than on investigating the morale of the defeated. Yet, for Shelley's purposes this inherited framework provided an ideal perspective since it allowed him to adumbrate the possibilities of another Greek victory over the oriental enemy (in this case the Turks) without compromising his fundamental pacifism. *Hellas*, like the *Persae*, focuses on the psychology of defeat and is suffused with a sense of loss and of transience which seems to contradict Shelley's declared intention to celebrate the imminent recovery of Greek liberty. Temperamentally, Shelley was always liable to align himself with the defeated rather than with the conqueror, particularly if victory involved bloodshed and loss of life, a cost which conflicted with his profoundest humanitarian ideals. So Shelley sided with Milton's Satan rather than with God the Father, with the prostrated Persians rather than with the triumphant Greeks. Any victory which was based on physical force rather than on psychological adjustment and an intellectual acknowledgment of mutual rights, as in *Prometheus Unbound*, was probably founded on an illusion. Force begets force; therefore, the 'security of triumph' can be undermined at any moment by that very force which gave it power and sustains its kingdom. This explains the sceptical and melancholy modulation with which the final chorus comes to its heavily qualified end :

Another Athens shall arise
    And to remoter time
Bequeath, like sunset to the skies,
    The splendour of its prime,
And leave, if nought so bright may live,
All earth can take or Heaven can give.

Saturn and Love their long repose
    Shall burst, more bright and good
Than all who fell, than One who rose,
    Than many unsubdued;
Not gold, not blood, their altar dowers
But votive tears and symbol flowers.

O cease! must hate and death return?
     Cease! must men kill and die?
Cease! drain not to its dregs the urn
     Of bitter prophecy.
The world is weary of the past,
O might it die or rest at last!

Here, Shelley acknowledges the haunting possibility that the cyclical view of history may be the true one; more correctly, one might say that his revolutionary optimism is tempered by the recognition that revolutions which are based on blood will, in their turn, give rise to other revolutions and further bloodshed. This recognition provides a dourly realistic substratum even to such an optimistic creation as *Prometheus Unbound*. Yet, although he recognised the difficulties and was often sobered and dejected by that record of crimes and errors which was history, Shelley did believe that it was ultimately possible to escape from the treadmill. To believe that history unfolded itself in a pattern of recurring cycles was ultimately to deny the freedom and responsibility of the individual. There was such a thing as historical necessity—'The viewless and invisible Consequence' which 'Watches thy goings-out and comings-in' as Aeschylus described it in a fragment which Shelley translated.[19] Yet, man is free in the way in which he relates himself to this force:

     tho all the past could not have been
Other than as it was—yet things foreseen
Reason and Love may force beneath their yoke
Warned by a fate foregone.[20]

Thus, in *Prometheus Unbound* the process of historical necessity is embodied in Demogorgon, who is both a 'mighty Darkness' and a 'living Spirit'. Demogorgon is activated by the Spirit of the Hour, who represents a precise point in the continuum of history: but the course taken by Demogorgon and the Spirit of the Hour is conditioned by the actions of Prometheus and Asia. Were it not for the heroic resistance of the one and the enduring love of the other, Demogorgon would not be able to bring about the downfall of Jupiter. Thus, it is possible for the human race to initiate a new historical pattern. If man can recognise his own full potential, then he can break free from the vicious circle which has characterised so much of European history and which is the fundamental pattern of the power-struggles of Greek mythology and of Aeschylean drama (the blood feuds of the Oresteian trilogy).

This shift of historical perspective is implied by the imagery of *Prometheus Unbound*. The world of Jupiter, the old order of blood, violence and usurpation is symbolised by the serpent who devours his own tail, the *drakōn ouroboros*: as a rule, this serpent is interpreted as the Neoplatonic emblem for Eternity, with particular reference to Hermes Trismegistus and to the Platonic formula *hen to pan* (all is one). This concentration on sources has diverted attention from the function of the serpent in this specific context where Shelley seems to imply that the success of the new society depends upon man's ability to 'bar the pit over Destruction's strength', to keep the dragon under control. A new vigilance is required if peace is to be perpetuated. Something of what this involves is suggested by another serpent, the amphisbaenic snake which yokes the chariot of the Spirit of the Hour to its team of marble horses, in a monument to the glorious moment of regeneration. Traditionally the amphisbaena is a snake with a head at either end; so Shelley's image suggests both the heightened consciousness associated with the regeneration of society and a potentiality totally different from the self-enclosed system represented by the *ouroboros*. The vicious circle is replaced by the open-ended system; the cycle of history is superseded by a new sense of responsibility which enables man to accept that he is his own master though yoked to the chariot of time. Shelley recognises that the new system can never be more than provisional, in the sense that, unless man exercises constant vigilance and self-control, it is always possible to slide back into the old patterns, to release the *ouroboros* from his den. *The Cenci* demonstrates how easily Prometheus can find himself behaving like Jupiter. For the serpent can never be eliminated: he is held in preventive detention only at our own discretion.

So Shelley approached the record of Greek history with a clear sense of its shortcomings but believing also that its true message was the infinite potentiality of man. In the cancelled Prologue to *Hellas* he presented a debate between Christ and Satan which owes something to the Prolog to Goethe's *Faust* but whose main importance consists in the exploration of conflicting attitudes to history. Satan represents a kind of historical nihilism not unlike that with which the last Fury tempts Prometheus. Satan attempts to blunt Christ's revolutionary optimism by claiming that everything beneath the empyrean is subject to his control and that, far from being regenerated by the intervention of Christ, Greece will suffer from Famine, Pestilence, Superstition, War, Fraud and Change. To this Christ replies: 'Obdurate spirit! / Thou seest but the Past in the To-come.' There can be no doubt that

Shelley endorses this criticism. Christ is here presented as an inheritor of the Greek tradition, moulded and influenced 'by Plato's sacred light, / Of which my spirit was a burning morrow',[21] and like Shelley himself a believer in the solemn duty of hope. Satan is guilty of interpreting history as an end-stopped system, a pattern which can only repeat itself. But the future need not duplicate the past: man may transcend the limitations of history and realise his full potential.

The epigraph to *Hellas*, which is taken from *Oedipus at Colonus*, underlines this duty of historical optimism: it reads *mantis eim' esthlōn agōnōn* (I am a prophet of fortunate contests).[22] Shelley's use of this quotation illustrates very clearly his general view of history and his belief in the importance of Greece. Where many writers would simply have directed their gaze towards the future ('O Wind, / If Winter comes, can Spring be far behind?'), Shelley bases his optimism on the record of history. Sophocles is cited not because he is an authority but because he offers a message which links the future meaningfully to the past. For all its limitations—its attitude to women and to slaves, its militarism, the bloodiness of its warfare as recorded by Homer in the *Iliad* and by Thucydides in his history of the Peloponnesian War—it was Greece more than any other country which had recognised the potential of man and embodied it in images of lasting power and beauty:

The human form and the human mind attained to a perfection in Greece which has impressed its image on those faultless productions, whose very fragments are the despair of modern art, and has propagated impulses which cannot cease, through a thousand channels of manifest or imperceptible operation, to ennoble and delight mankind until the extinction of the race.[23]

Or, as a chorus of Greek captives expresses it in *Hellas*:

> Temples and towers,
>   Citadels and marts, and they
> Who live and die there, have been ours,
>   And may be thine, and must decay;
> But Greece and her foundations are
> Built below the tides of war,
> Based on the crystàlline sea
> Of thought and its eternity;
> Her citizens, imperial spirits,
>   Rule the present from the past,
> On all this world of man inherits
>   Their seal is set.
>   (lines 692–703)

Shelley was acutely aware that the great artistic creations of Athens could not have come into existence without fostering from the general climate of political life, yet here he seems to be saying that once they had been created, they transcended the limitations of the political realm and had their being in the inviolate world of ideas. In their turn, these works of art could influence the shape of politics: in the 'Ode to Liberty' Shelley describes how Athens 'Gleamed with its crest of columns, on the will / Of man, as on a mount of diamond, set . . .', a potent and enduring image of Liberty and an inspiration to political leaders in later times. Yet, as both these passages make clear, though Greece and Athens in particular was a historical fact, its primary significance was that it provided an energising image of what man could achieve. Athens was crowned by its crest of columns formed by the temples of the Acropolis, the *mount* which provides a concrete geographical foundation for Shelley's description; but, as Shelley suggests, it was also a city of the mind founded firmly on the will of man, a thought-based monument to human potentiality. These complex lines also yield us the image of Athens as an ornament of civilisation set on its mount of diamond, a picture of permanence and beauty which is closely related to 'the crystàlline sea / Of thought and its eternity'. Athens is always there; it is our duty and responsibility to relate ourselves to it and to potentiate its implications in our own lives. To do this is to transcend the darker possibilities of history, to reject the temptations of Satan and of the Furies, the dangerous complacency of Malthusianism, the pessimism of the Wordsworths and Coleridges who could not recover from the failure of the French Revolution, the cynical despair of the Byrons who could not bring themselves to think well of human nature. It is to make an act of faith in man, to believe that after the dark winter of the world *Il buon tempa verra* (the good time will come).[24]

(iii)

No one was more responsive than Shelley to the beauty of Greek literature and Greek art, to the harmonious forms of Greek civilisation:

Homer and the cyclic poets were followed at a certain interval by the dramatic and lyrical poets of Athens, who flourished contemporaneously with all that is most perfect in the kindred expressions of the poetical faculty; architecture, painting, music, the dance, sculpture, philosophy, and we may add, the forms of civil life. For although the scheme of Athenian society was deformed by many imperfections which the poetry existing in chivalry and Christianity has erased from the habits and institutions of modern Europe; yet never at any other period has so much energy, beauty and virtue, been developed; never was blind strength and stubborn form so disciplined and rendered subject to the will of man, or that will less repugnant to the dictates of the beautiful and the true, as during the century which preceded the death of Socrates.[25]

Yet, for all this enthusiasm, Shelley's attitude to the Greek achievement, and especially his attitude to Greek literature, was never inhibited by an undue sense of reverence, a fear lest he should intrude on a beauty which was sacrosanct. Shelley admired Greek literature because he recognised that it was endlessly potential, a rich matrix of energising possibilities rather than a rigid pantheon of unrivalled perfections. As he wrote in the *Defence of Poetry*:

All high poetry is infinite; it is as the first acorn which contained all oaks potentially. Veil after veil may be undrawn, and the inmost naked beauty of the meaning never exposed. A great poem is a fountain for ever overflowing with the waters of wisdom and delight; and after one person and one age has exhausted all its divine effluence which their peculiar relations enable them to share, another and yet another succeeds, and new relations are ever developed, the source of an unforeseen and an unconceived delight.[26]

It can be seen at once that Shelley was not the kind of man who thought of those masterpieces of Greek and Latin literature which we have been fortunate enough to inherit as monuments of 'classical' literature. For him, the notion of 'classicality' had ugly connections. In 1812 he told Godwin, who had encouraged him to read widely in Greek and Latin:

Nor can I help considering the vindicators of ancient learning . . . as the vindicators of a literary despotism, as the tracers of a circle which is intended to shut out from real knowledge, to which this fictitious knowledge is attached, all who do not breathe the air of prejudice, & who will not support the established systems of politics, Religion & morals . . . Did Greek & Roman literature refine the soul of Johnson, does it extend the thousand narrow bigots educated in the very bosom of *classicality*[?][27]

To accept the great works of Greek and Latin literature as unassailable 'classics' and to impose them as models which we must humbly and unoriginally follow was to establish a tyranny which denied alike the rights of the individual writer and of his readers. This was to cut literature off from life, to make it a system not of 'things' but of 'words'. It short-circuited the vital relationship between the writer and the society of which he was a part; it diverted his attention from the problems of his own day ('real knowledge') to the less electric atmosphere of the past, thus reducing the danger of 'change in our social condition or the opinions which cement it'.[28] The process of imitation fostered and encouraged by a classical education was no substitute for an imaginative commitment to one's material. This applied to the borrowing of techniques both from Greek and Latin and from one's own contemporaries:

Thus a number of writers possess the form, whilst they want the spirit of those whom, it is alleged, they imitate; because the former is the endowment of the age in which they live, and the latter must be the uncommunicated lightning of their own mind.[29]

The lightning must be *uncommunicated* in the sense that it cannot be derived from anybody else, far less from literary tradition; every word must be an energy, a pure and original impulse from within.

This uncompromising attitude towards tradition can be traced clearly in Shelley's letters to Byron. Writing in May 1821 he explained his views on the Pope controversy, in which Byron had played a leading part:

I certainly do not think Pope, or *any* writer, a fit model for any succeeding writer; if he, or they should be determined to be so, it would all come to a question as to under *what forms* mediocrity should perpetually reproduce itself; for true genius vindicates to itself exemption from all regard to whatever has gone before . . .[30]

Several months later he was encouraging Byron to claim for himself this exemption of genius. Privately he believed that Byron affected 'to patronize a system of criticism fit only for the production of mediocrity' and that all his best poems and passages had been produced 'in defiance of this system';[31] in the letter he tactfully suggests that Byron has not yet achieved his true potential:

I still feel impressed with the persuasion that you *ought*—and if there is prophecy in hope, that you *will* write a great and connected poem, which shall bear the same relation to this age as the 'Iliad', the 'Divina Commedia', and 'Paradise Lost' did to theirs; not that you will imitate the structure, or borrow from the subjects, of any of these, or in any degree assume them as your models.

This, perhaps, is an extreme formulation but it shows clearly enough Shelley's belief that while, as Dr Johnson once put it, 'No man ever yet became great by imitation' on the other hand 'A noble emulation is the source of every excellence'.[32]

Undoubtedly, the great literature of the past provided examples of what the writer of genius could achieve. To some extent it also provided a quarry of raw material. But it did not offer a cut and dried method by imitating which the young writer could automatically produce his own works of literature. Though Shelley was addicted to the reading of Greek, especially to Homer, Plato and the Greek dramatists, he recognised that to follow humbly in their footsteps would be to deprive his own poetry of the social relevance which he so firmly believed in. Every poem was a beginning and every poem was an end; therefore, although the poet himself might be profoundly influenced by his read- ing of classical literature, it was his responsibility to create something 'wholly new & relative to the age'.[33] Though, as a reader, Shelley con- sidered Greek 'the only sure remedy for diseases of the mind', as a writer he could never have agreed with Hogg's practice of employing it as a narcotic to blur his perception of contemporary social realities. Nor would he have agreed with the valuation implied in Dr Johnson's observation that 'Greek is like fine lace; a man gets as much of it as he can'. Shelley allotted to Greek a far more significant function; for him it was not a mere decoration, an elegant frill at the cuff or neck but a direct route to the heart of the matter, whether psychological, moral or political.

One of the most exciting features of his own poetry is the way in which he discovers in Greek literature (and sometimes in Greek art) new meanings which are applicable to his own day and age. If he inherits a framework he never feels constrained to accept it gratefully while cramping his own imaginings within its limits. The best example is *Prometheus Unbound*, whose very title is sparked off by an energising conflict with the premises of the original play by Aeschylus. Shelley underlines his dissatisfaction with his predecessor and model by intro- ducing the play with an aggressive epigraph from Cicero, *Audisne haec, Amphiarae, sub terram abdite?* (Do you hear these words, Amphiaraus, hidden under the ground?) This provocative cry is clearly directed towards Aeschylus, whose treatment of the relations between rebel and tyrant left Shelley angry and frustrated: 'The moral interest of the fable, which is so powerfully sustained by the sufferings and endurance of Prometheus, would be annihilated if we could conceive of him as unsaying his high language and quailing before his successful and perfidious adversary.'[34] For the noble and high-minded revolu- tionary, the founder of human civilisation, to compromise with the tyrant and the oppressor of mankind was to invalidate the moral worth of his resistance. The trimmings of political expediency had no place in a play which should have been devoted to expressing the potentialities of moral excellence and which should have inculcated the virtues of honourable defiance rather than the cruder benefits of 'composing the affair by arbitration'. So, in one of the drafts, Asia tells Prometheus:

> One sung of thee, who left the tale untold,
>   Like the false dawns which perish in the bursting;
> Like empty cups of wrought and daedal gold,
>   Which mock the lips with air, when they are thirsting.[35]

Of course Shelley was perfectly aware that Aeschylus had completed his trilogy on the subject of Prometheus; *untold* here suggests not that Aeschylus left the conclusion of his work unwritten but that the conclusion he found for it was not satisfactory—not satisfactory by Shelley's standards and not satisfactory if one judged it by the standards implicit in *Prometheus Bound*. Aeschylus had been finally untrue to his own conception: the shape of the Promethean trilogy is not consistent with its own better implications. In holding this view Shelley was not guilty of arrogance: the Preface to *Prometheus Unbound* makes it clear that he was keenly aware of his own inferiority to Aeschylus. Yet, if great poetry was infinite, the acorn which contained all oaks potentially, every poet was justified in exploring its special meaning for his own age. As Shelley said of Dante: 'His very words are instinct with spirit; each is as a spark, a burning atom of inextinguishable thought; and many yet lie covered in the ashes of their birth, and pregnant with a lightning which has yet found no conductor.'[36] It was his duty, not only as a reader but as a writer, to play the role of lightning conductor and activate these latent forces. Poems (or poetic plays like *Prometheus Bound*) contained the possibilities of their own regeneration: 'It [Poetry] is the faculty which contains within itself the seeds at once of its own and of social renovation.'[37] Believing this as firmly as he did, Shelley must have felt that he was doing homage to Aeschylus and to the essential significance of his message by helping to uncover the 'true' meaning of the Promethean trilogy and thus enabling it to realise its own best self.

Greek literature was not, then, a rigid or static system but was capable of endless development. Shelley used it not only to reinterpret itself (as in the case of *Prometheus Unbound*) or to provide a starting point (as in the case of *Adonais* or *Hellas*) but he also employed it as a means for reinterpreting his own society. Thus, *Prometheus Unbound* is a critique of the politics of violent revolution, the crude instinct to hit back as soon as one is hurt—a reaction which will only help to perpetuate the meaningless cycle of violence; it is also a critique of the gloom and misanthropy which overcame so many intellectuals and reformers after the failure of the French Revolution—a response which leads to apathy, passivity, and acquiescence in the *status quo*, and provides a fertile ground for sophists like Malthus, who 'lull the oppressors of mankind into a security of everlasting triumph'.[38] This critique is based not only on the best implications of Aeschylus himself but on the record of Greek society as perpetuated both in literature and in art, a rich reservoir of images which celebrate the virtues of man. The Platonic dialogues, for example, provide a number of touchstones by which the society of early nineteenth-century England (and of most other European countries) could be found wanting. Shelley was so affected by them that he translated all of the *Symposium* and the *Ion* and a variety of shorter passages from the other dialogues. In particular he was attracted by Plato's investigation and celebration of love in the *Symposium* and his rhapsodic account of poetic inspiration in the *Ion*. Behind it all was the figure of Socrates, whom Shelley often associated with Christ as the most perfect of men, an example by which we might learn to live our own lives with courage, clarity of mind and self-control. Other, less idealised, images were provided by Homer and Pindar and the dramatists.

(iv)

As soon as Shelley had explored the great galleries in Florence and Rome, the images of literature were reinforced by the images of Greek sculpture. Shelley had strong views on the significance of these statues and their relation to the pattern of Greek society :

The men of Greece corresponded in external form to the models which they have left as specimens of what they were. The firm yet flowing proportion of their forms; the winning unreserve and facility of their manners; the eloquence of their speech, in a language which is itself music and persuasion; their gestures animated at once with the delicacy and the boldness which the perpetual habit of persuading and governing themselves and others; and the poetry of their religious rites, inspired into their whole being—rendered the youth of Greece a race of beings something widely different from that of modern Europe.[39]

For Shelley, these statues were significant influences on human behaviour. 'The mind becomes that which it contemplates'; therefore,
in the exultant hymn in which the Earth celebrates the powers of
regenerated man, language, sculpture and painting are all acknowledged
as important factors in the maintenance of man's new-found status.
In particular,

> All things confess his strength. Through the cold mass
> Of marble and of colour his dreams pass—
> Bright threads whence mothers weave the robes their children wear . . .
> (P.U., IV. 412–14)

Here Shelley seems to be suggesting that sculpture (and painting?)
can even be an important prenatal influence. Although this particular
variation is Shelley's own, the underlying idea can be found in a number
of his predecessors—notably Shaftesbury, Winckelmann and Lessing.
Lessing, for example, had said: 'As beautiful men produced beautiful
statues, so the latter reacted upon the former and the state became
indebted to beautiful statues for beautiful men.'[40] And Winckelmann,
whom Shelley had studied carefully, had stressed the Greek attitude
to the naked body which, in his view, was largely responsible for the
nobility of their statues. The Greeks reverenced the human body, trained
it for athletic contests, clothed it simply and freely and provided
generous public facilities for keeping it clean and free from disease.
The Greeks had no false shame: they were constantly exposed to the
beauties of the human body in the gymnasia and the bath-houses. 'Then
every solemnity, every festival, afforded the artist opportunity to
familiarize himself with all the beauties of nature.'[41] Even Sophocles
considered it no indignity to dance naked in the theatre.[42] As a result,
Greek art was inevitably superior to ours, in its treatment of the human
body; 'they enjoying daily occasions of seeing beauty (suppose even not
superior to ours), acquired those ideal riches with less toil than we,
confined to a few and often fruitless opportunities, ever can hope
for.'[43] Shelley acknowledged the importance of these daily occasions.
Writing from Florence, where he had spent three hours contemplating
the statues of Niobe and Apollo, he reflected regretfully:

. . . all worldly thoughts & cares seem to vanish from before the sublime
emotions such spectacles create: and I am deeply impressed with the great
difference of happiness enjoyed by those who live at a distance from these
incarnations all that the finest minds have conceived of beauty, & those who
can resort to their company at pleasure. What should we think if we were

forbidden to read the great writers who have left us their works.—And yet, to be forbidden to live at Florence or Rome is an evil of the same kind & scarcely of less magnitude.[44]

However, Shelley did have at least one reservation. Though he shared Winckelmann's admiration for the Greek sculptors, he did not have the same interest in the naked male body. In his essay on Greek art and literature he proposes an important connection between these images of the idealised male and the Greek attitude towards homosexuality:

If my observation be correct, the word *kalos* (beautiful) is more frequently applied to the male sex, while *eueidēs* (handsome) denoted the attractiveness of a female. Whether the cause is to be sought in the climate, in the original constitution of the peculiar race of the Greeks, or in the institutions and system of society, or in the mutual action of these several circumstances, such is the effect. And as a consequence of those causes, beautiful persons of the male sex became the object of that sort of feelings, which are only cultivated at present as towards females.[45]

Though Shelley admired the artistic excellence of these statues and though they provided food for his imagination and for his poetry, he regarded their concentration on male beauty as a moral deficiency. One of the most notable ways in which his version of the Prometheus story differs from that of Aeschylus is in the central role played by Asia, a character invented by Shelley to replace the less particularised and much less formidable Oceanides. Flanked by Panthea and Ione, Asia is an essential presence in the world of *Prometheus Unbound*: without her love and support, the virtues of Prometheus would not be sufficient in themselves to bring about the overthrow of Jupiter. Asia is complementary to Prometheus: without her he is incomplete. Here the son-in-law of Mary Wollstonecraft acknowledges the female principle and the social and moral significance of love between men and women. It was no accident that, when Shelley produced his own version of the Homeric *Hymn to Mercury*, the delightful child god of the original was made to undergo a sex-change and reappeared in the feminine guise of the Witch of Atlas.[46]

Given these important reservations, Shelley was an enthusiastic student of Greek art (which means statues and architecture, since there is no evidence that he ever saw any Greek pottery or even studied it in prints as Keats did). Leigh Hunt has recorded how 'He used to sit in a study adorned with casts, as large as life, of the Vatican Apollo and the Celestial Venus'.[47] By his own account, one of his chief aims in Italy was to observe in statues and painting 'the degree in which, &

the rules according to which, that ideal beauty of which we have so intense yet so obscure an apprehension is realized in external forms'. Here he is, for example, making observations in Monte Cavallo:

On each side on elevated pedestals stand the statues of Castor & Pollux, each in the act of taming his horse, which are said, but I believe, wholly without authority, to be the work of Phidias & Praxiteles. These figures combine the irresistible energy with the sublime & perfect loveliness supposed to have belonged to the divine nature. The reins no longer exist, but the position of their hands & the sustained & calm command of their regard seem to require no mechanical aid to enforce obedience ... the sublime and living majesty of their limbs & mien, (the nervous & fiery animation of the horses they restrain), seen in the blue sky of Italy, & overlooking the City of Rome, surrounded by the light & the music of that chrystalline fountain, no cast can com[m]unicate.[48]

This combination of energy and control, of calmness and vitality, represented Shelley's own ideal in art and literature. In this case his experience of the work of art is influenced by the Italian environment but that is entirely appropriate for statues which were intended to be viewed not in a museum but in the bright light of a Mediterranean country. However, most statues had to be visited indoors and Shelley devoted much time and care to exploring the collections in Rome and in Florence. Armed with a copy of Winckelmann's *History of Ancient Art*, he examined the statues with great attention and produced a series of sixty notes and descriptions. Some of these are perfunctory, mere shorthand for his own convenience, but the majority provide a revealing insight into his views on Greek art and on Greek civilisation in general.

One of the most extensive and the finest of these notes concerns the statue of Niobe at Florence:

This figure is probably the most consummate personification of loveliness with regard to its countenance as that of the Apollo of the Vatican is with regard to its entire form that remains to us of Greek Antiquity. It is a colossal figure—the size of a work of art rather adds to its beauty, because it allows the spectator the choice of a great number of points of view in which to catch a greater number of the infinite modes of expression of which any form approaching ideal beauty is necessarily composed—of a mother in the act of sheltering from some divine and inevitable peril, the last, we will imagine, of her surviving children.[49]

The emphasis here on the kinetic experience and the infinite number of ways in which the statue can be approached comes very close to

Shelley's view on the inexhaustible potentiality of great literature with which 'new relations are ever developed'. After a detailed description of mother and child, Shelley focuses on the face of the mother:

There is embodied a sense of the inevitable and rapid destiny which is consummating around her as if it were already over. It seems as if despair and beauty had combined and produced nothing but the sublime loveliness of grief. As the motions of the form expressed the instinctive sense of the possibility of protecting the child and the accustomed and affectionate assurance that she would find protection within her arms, so reason and imagination speak in the countenance the certainty that no mortal defence is of avail.
    There is no terror in the countenance—only grief—deep grief. There is no anger—of what avail is indignation against what is known to be omnipotent? There is no selfish shrinking from personal pain; there is no panic at supernatural agency—there is no adverting to herself as herself—the calamity is mightier than to leave scope for such emotion . . .

Here he approaches a statue with the same kind of moral concern with which he would have approached a work of literature (this method of interpretation runs through most of his descriptions and is particularly noticeable in his reaction to the *Laocoon*). Shelley found it difficult to respond in terms which were merely aesthetic; since the work of art could subtly influence the quality of our lives, every artist had a moral responsibility which should not be shirked. Yet his analysis of the *Niobe* leaves no doubt that he was also interested in the technical means by which the effects were achieved. His note ends with a remarkably detached example of calculated observation, a technical appraisal which tempers the subjective flavour of what has come before: 'Compare for this effect the countenance as seen in front and as seen from under the left arm, moving to the right and towards the statue, until the line of the forehead shall coincide with that of the wrist.' This is a coolly objective note which contrasts with the empathetic fervour of the main word-picture. However, when one considers his response as a whole, it appears that he was as much concerned with detail and technique as with the feelings embodied in the figures; from his point of view, form and content were inextricably interwoven or, to use a word which Shelley seems to have coined, they interpenetrated one another. A formal or technical deficiency would blur or obliterate the underlying moral significance. For example, there was in Florence a Bacchus by Michelangelo. Shelley admired its 'workmanship': 'The arms are executed in the most perfect and manly beauty; the body is conceived with great energy, and the lines which describe the sides and thighs, and the manner in which they mingle into one another are of the highest order of boldness and beauty.' On the other hand: 'The lower part of the figure is stiff, and the manner in which the shoulders are united to the breast, and the neck to the head, abundantly inharmonious'. The overall effect is, therefore, unfortunate: 'It wants as a work of art unity and simplicity', a result which can be traced to a lack of sympathy with the Greek concept of Bacchus on the part of a Catholic.[50] Thus, the technical excellence of certain parts cannot redeem the lack of imaginative unity which characterises the whole. Shelley was applying here the standards of Winckelmann who had declared that '...Michelangelo, compared with Raphael, is what Thucydides is to Xenophon' (that is, his essential nobility is vitiated by his complexity and superfluity of detail). Winckelmann goes on to generalise in a sentence which seems to have left its mark on Shelley's aesthetics: 'All beauty is heightened by unity and simplicity, as is everything which we do and say; for whatever is great in itself is elevated, when executed and uttered with simplicity'.[51]

Without simplicity and, more particularly, without unity, a work of art must be deficient; local excellences can not compensate for a general lack of harmony. Thus, technique must collaborate with the total imaginative conception of the poet or the sculptor. You could not produce a significant work of art without an adequate technique; on the other hand, mere technical excellence had a very limited value unless it was deployed in the service of the imagination.

However, it was possible for a statue to present a subject which was morally repellent but, by means of its aesthetic excellence, to transform the material and make it acceptable. Take for example the *Laocoon*:

Intense physical suffering, against which he pleads with an upraised countenance of despair, and appeals with a sense of its injustice, seems the predominant and overwhelming emotion, and yet there is a nobleness in the expression and a majesty that dignifies torture.[52]

Or consider this relief depicting four Maenads on an altar dedicated to Bacchus:

The tremendous spirit of superstition aided by drunkenness and producing something beyond insanity seems to have caught them in its whirlwinds and to bear them over the earth as the rapid volutions of a tempest bear the ever-changing trunk of a waterspout, as the torrent of a mountain river whirls the leaves in its full eddies. Their hair loose and floating seems caught in the tempest of their own tumultuous motion, their heads are thrown back leaning with a strange inanity upon their necks, and looking up to Heaven, while they totter and stumble even in the energy of their tempestuous dance. . . .

This was indeed a monstrous superstition only capable of existing in Greece because there alone capable of combining ideal beauty and poetical and abstract enthusiasm with the wild errors from which it sprung.

Shelley concludes that, unlike the Romans, the Greeks 'turned all things —superstition, prejudice, murder, madness—to Beauty'.[53]

In these passages Shelley seems to be softening his characteristically rigorous moral attitude; the focus of attention is aesthetic rather than moral, the image rather than the meaning, the medium rather than the message. Both in the *Niobe* and in the sculpture of the Maenads there is an energy allied to formal beauty which, if it does not make all disagreeables evaporate, can transcend them by incorporating them into a greater aesthetic scheme. This theory is once again derived from Winckelmann. Appraising the *Niobe*, for example, Winckelmann speaks of an 'equilibrium of feeling' and remarks that the sculptor understood 'the secret of uniting the anguish of death with the highest beauty'.[54] Of the *Laocoon* he says:

The last and most eminent characteristic of the Greek works is a noble simplicity and sedate grandeur in gesture and expression. As the bottom of the sea lies peaceful beneath a foaming surface, a great soul lies sedate beneath the strife of passion in Greek figures.[55]

This image is remarkably similar to some of Shelley's own but, though Shelley shares Winckelmann's appreciation of the need for an 'active tranquillity', he puts stronger emphasis both on the disagreeables and on the vitality of the sculpture.

(*v*)

Perhaps the most important function which Greek art and literature performed for Shelley was that it provided glimpses of an alternative society, radiant images of what man could be and of what he could achieve. Central to the Greek achievement was the fact that it had taken place outside the orbit of Christianity and central to Shelley's reaction was the opportunity it seemed to present of discovering an antidote to a system founded on 'fear and self-contempt and barren hope'. In fact, it was the study of Greek and Latin which first prompted Shelley to probe the inadequacies of the Christian system:

The first doubts which arose in my boyish mind concerning the genuineness of the Christian religion as a revelation from the divinity were excited by a contemplation by [of] the virtues & genius of Greece & Rome. Shall Socrates & Cicero perish while the meanest hind of modern England inherits eternal life? I mean not to affirm that this is the first argument with which I would combat the delusions of superstition, but it certainly was the first that operated to convince me that they were delusions.[56]

Seven years later he developed his view of Socrates with ironical effect: 'I conceive that many of those popular maxims which under the name of Christianity have softened the manners of modern Europe are channels derived from the fountain of his profound yet overflowing mind. These sentiments are with me a kind of religion . . .'[57]

Here Shelley indirectly admits that some of the fundamental points in Christ's teaching were positive and life-enhancing; in particular he is thinking of the doctrine of the equality of man which eventually led to the 'abolition of personal and domestic slavery, and the emancipation of women from a great part of the degrading restraints of antiquity'.[58] These ideas could be traced back as far as Socrates and Plato while some of them were even implied in the doctrines of the pre-Socratic philosophers: 'Jesus Christ divulged the sacred and eternal truths contained in these views to mankind, and Christianity, in its abstract purity, became the exoteric expression of the esoteric doctrines of the poetry and wisdom of antiquity.'[59] Christ followed in the footsteps of the Greek philosophers; but his doctrines were quickly distorted and, in spite of the positive influence of the Christian belief in the brotherhood of man, by Shelley's time the Church had been transmogrified into an oppressive organisation which largely ignored the teaching of its founder. The Christian religion which had been intended to liberate man, to encourage him to love his neighbour as himself, had become another link in the nexus of privilege and power.

In Shelley's view of politics (as in that of the biblical prophets) Priest and King were, almost indissolubly, connected. Thus, the angry sonnet 'Feelings of a Republican on the Fall of Bonaparte', recognises that the deposition of Napoleon does not automatically signify the restoration of liberty since, though the individual has fallen, the system of power remains intact:

> I know
> Too late, since thou and France are in the dust,
> That Virtue owns a more eternal foe
> Than Force or Fraud: old Custom, legal Crime,
> And bloody Faith the foulest birth of Time.

This may be rather too emphatically abstract but its analysis of the structure of power is central to Shelley's thinking; 'bloody' is not a general epithet of denunciation but refers specifically both to the sacrificial basis of Christianity and to the wars of religion (one of the temptations to despair which Prometheus has to transcend).[60] Thus, in *Prometheus Unbound* Jupiter is both the tyrannical god and the unjust king and the effects of the Promethean revolution are manifested not only in the political and social spheres but also in the conduct of religion.

In this resistance to the tyranny of superstition Shelley consciously marched under the banners of Socrates, Plato and the other Greek philosophers whom he had read about in Diogenes Laertius. One of his notebooks contains an unpublished defence of atheism, which helps to explain the closeness of his relation to the Greeks:

In the first place the word *atheos* does not mean atheist. It's [*sic*] literal translation is 'godless' and its accepted meaning among the Greeks was 'an impious person'—it was a mere term of reproach and revilement. Atheist on the contrary expresses a person who denies certain opinions concerning the cause of the Universe. It expresses neither blame nor praise but simply defines an opinion. Thus all those persons who deny that this great system of things was arranged by one intellectual being in the same manner as we perceive other thinking agents arrange such portions of it as are submitted to their power, are called Atheists. All the Greek philosophers until the time of Anaximander were in this sense atheists. . . . It is the last insolence in the advocates of an upstart and sanguinary superstition to use the word Atheist as a name of reproach. The assertion that these mighty geniuses were men of impious hearts, and limited understandings is intolerable.[61]

It was perhaps in this spirit that he described himself in the visitors' book at Chamonix as democrat, lover of mankind and atheist. The same air of proud defiance can also be recognised in his answer to Trelawny's asking why he continued to call himself an atheist in spite of the social consequences:

It is a word of abuse to stop discussion, a painted devil to frighten the foolish, a threat to intimidate the wise and good. I used it to express my abhorrence of superstition; I took up the word, as a knight took up a gauntlet, in defiance of injustice. The delusions of Christianity are fatal to genius and originality: they limit thought.[62]

These passages are crucial for a proper understanding of Shelley's attitude to religion. His 'atheism' was essentially a refusal to acquiesce in the acknowledged systems of belief with their unfortunate consequences both in morals and in politics. Ranging himself alongside the Greek philosophers, supported and encouraged by the example of Lucretius and by the sceptical philosophers of the eighteenth century, Shelley resisted the accepted notions of divinity. One might ask why, if Shelley did not believe in 'God', did he spend so much energy in resisting him? The solution to this apparent contradiction seems to be that what Shelley was fighting against was not God but those distorted projections of our own darker passions which are imposed on us in the name of religion: what he was defying was not the idea of God but those unjust fantasies which had taken its place. In this holy war against the false gods, Shelley found his strongest support in Greek philosophy and literature.

The outstanding example was that of Socrates who was condemned to death because the authorities regarded him as a disruptive influence but whose courage in the face of death, as recorded by Plato in the *Apology* and the *Crito*, was as admirably unswerving as his devotion to the truth. Socrates was 'by his death approved', like the poet Lucan;[63] he went 'unterrified, / Into the gulf of death', like Milton; he provided an inspiring lesson of how the good man should prepare himself for death. Two passages which Shelley copied out in his notebooks help to indicate the strength of this influence.[64] In the first, Socrates is teasing his friend Crito who is overcome by the fear of death and cannot come to terms with the fact that the Socrates who is now calmly discussing his own death will soon be a corpse: 'I cannot persuade Crito, my friends, that the Socrates who is now conversing and arranging the details of the argument is really I; he thinks I am the one whom he will presently see as a corpse, and he asks how to bury me.' Secondly, there is a brave and clear-headed declaration in the *Apology*: 'For to fear death is nothing else than to think one is wise when one is not; for it is thinking one knows what one does not know. For no one knows whether death be not the greatest of all blessings to man, but they fear it as if they knew that it is the greatest of evils. And is not this the most reprehensible form of ignorance, that of thinking one knows what one does not know?'

The significance of these passages is their suggestion that it is possible for man to conquer the fear of death. To do so may require courage of a high order but the example of Socrates shows that it can be done. To liberate onself from the fear of death is to blunt one of the strongest weapons of the tyrant, a weapon frequently employed by religious orthodoxy to cow the rebel and frighten him into submission. In the case of Christianity there is also the fear of eternal punishment after death, a fear which is based on a false image of god as a tyrant in human shape, lord of the dungeons and master of everlasting fire. Against such false gods the example of Socrates was a powerful antidote.

There were other influences on Shelley's attitude to the Gods which were more literary than philosophical. The most notable of these was Euripides, whose heterodoxy greatly appealed to Shelley. The manuscript draft of the last two stanzas of 'Ode to the West Wind' shares a page with a quotation from the *Hercules Furens: aretēi se nikō thnētos ōn theon megan* (By virtue I, a mortal, vanquish thee, a mighty god).[65] This line comes from a speech where Amphitryon reproaches Zeus, who has been visiting Amphitryon's wife in his absence, and confronts him with the consequences of his behaviour. The speech ends with Amphitryon describing Zeus as 'a rather stupid god or else unjust'. The spirit of this defiance is very characteristic of Shelley: indeed, the line which he has written out in his notebook might have served as a useful epigraph to *Prometheus Unbound*. It is by virtue rather than by force that Prometheus is finally able to conquer Jupiter; the lesson is self-reliance, self-knowledge and unswerving adherence to one's own highest principles.

Euripides provided another model for defiance of the gods in his satyr play *The Cyclops*, which Shelley translated in full, probably during the summer of 1819. It would seem that one of the main attractions for Shelley was the character of Polyphemus himself; certainly Shelley responds admirably to the hubristic self-reliance of this speech:

Stranger, I laugh to scorn Jove's thunderbolt;
I know not that his strength is more than mine.
As to the rest I care not. When he pours
Rain from above, I have a close pavilion
Under this rock, in which I lay supine,
Feasting on a roast calf or some wild beast,
And drinking pans of milk, and gloriously
Emulating the thunder of high Heaven.
And when the Thracian wind pours down the snow
I wrap my body in the skins of beasts,
Kindle a fire, and bid the snow whirl on.
The earth by force, whether it will or no,
Bringing forth grass fattens my flocks and herds
Which, to what other God but to myself
And this great belly, first of deities,
Should I be bound to sacrifice? Know this
That Jupiter himself instructs the wise
To eat and drink during their little day

> Forbidding them to plague him; as for those
> Who complicate with laws the life of man,
> He has appointed tears for their reward.
>
> (lines 305–25)

Though the ascetic, water-drinking poet could never have endorsed this programme for hedonism, there can be no doubt that he was stirred by the conception of the rebellious outcast, who bears similarities both to Frankenstein's monster and to Prometheus. His translation subtly alters the meaning in several places so that Shelley's Cyclops is even more triumphantly independent than the original in Euripides.[66]

(vi)

Thus, in various ways and from various sources, the ancient Greeks provided fuel for the fire of Shelley's indignation. Not only did they inspire his resistance to tyranny and superstition; they also helped to suggest how the old religion could be replaced by a new one which was centred not on God but on man. We can see this process at work in *Prometheus Unbound*, which places considerable emphasis on the religious basis of Jupiter's power.

At the beginning of Act Three, just before his fall, we see Jupiter for the one and only time in his own right (in a previous manifestation in the first act he was merely a phantasm). Now he addresses the assembled Deities and in a speech from the throne reviews the state of his kingdom with some complacency:

> All else has been subdued to me; alone
> The soul of man, like unextinguished fire,
> Yet burns towards Heaven with fierce reproach, and doubt,
> And lamentation, and reluctant prayer—
> Hurling up insurrection, which might make
> Our antique empire insecure, though built
> On eldest faith, and Hell's coeval, fear . . .

Yet even man is soon to fall with the arrival of Demogorgon's chariot bearing the 'fatal child, the terror of the earth'; the dramatic irony of this misconception is known to the audience and will soon be revealed to Jupiter. The latter openly admits to his fellow deities that his empire has been based on 'faith' and 'fear'; he is well aware that his power and authority is founded on his ability to impose these mental conditions on his subjects. Even he can see that this religious devotion is far from happy: it is characterised by 'fierce reproach, and doubt, / And lamentation, and reluctant prayer'.

Significantly, Jupiter's image of the soul of man 'Hurling up insurrection' associates human rebellion with volcanic activity, which is one of the controlling metaphors of the whole play. The cave of Demogorgon is located in the crater of a volcano and the action by which he brings about the downfall of Jupiter can be equated with a volcanic eruption which has been energised by Asia and Prometheus. (Jupiter actually refers to the 'earthquake of his [Demogorgon's] chariot'). Further resonance is added to this image by the fact that Prometheus is himself a Titan. According to Greek mythology, many of the Titans were imprisoned under mountains; volcanic activity was therefore associated with their violent efforts to break out and to overthrow the divine establishment. Polyphemus was also related to this tradition; thus, the phrase 'Hurling up insurrection' brings together a long history of rebellion against the Gods.

After Jupiter has fallen, the Spirit of the Hour provides an extensive description of the regenerated world. The Spirit is very specific about the relation between political power and religious worship, and shows how the downfall of one has involved necessarily the downfall of the other:

> Thrones, altars, judgement-seats, and prisons—wherein
> And beside which, by wretched men were borne
> Sceptres, tiaras, swords, and chains, and tomes
> Of reasoned wrong, glozed on by ignorance—
> Were like those monstrous and barbaric shapes,
> The ghosts of a no-more-remembered fame,
> Which, from their unworn obelisks, look forth
> In triumph o'er the palaces and tombs
> Of those who were their conquerors, mouldering round.
> These imaged to the pride of Kings and Priests
> A dark yet mighty faith, a power as wide
> As is the world it wasted, and are now
> But an astonishment; even so the tools
> And emblems of its last captivity,
> Amid the dwellings of the peopled earth,
> Stand, not o'erthrown, but unregarded now.
> And those foul shapes, abhorred by God and man—
> Which, under many a name and many a form,
> Strange, savage, ghastly, dark and execrable,
> Were Jupiter, the tyrant of the world . . .
> Frown, mouldering fast, o'er their abandoned shrines.
>   (III, iv. 164–83, 89)

Behind these lines lies the same appreciation of the ironies of history which informs 'Ozymandias'; but where the earlier poem refers exclusively to the emblem of political power, the Spirit of the Hour also devotes much attention to the monuments of religion. Shelley suggests that in the new society the monuments of the old will be as monstrously irrelevant as obelisks and pyramids are for us—the relics of a barbarous superstition, degrading to humanity. The religion which has been bypassed by history can not be identified specifically with Christianity; rather it is any form of worship which prevents man from fully realising himself, by thwarting his best capacities and by distorting him after its own disfigured image. Jupiter is plural; not an individual god, he is a religious system to which all individual gods in their various ways belong: 'those foul shapes ... / Were Jupiter, the tyrant of the world'. These evil deities are 'abhorred by God and man', a puzzling phrase in which *God* must be understood metaphorically as representing not a specific divinity but the general spirit of goodness in the world, a spirit which is offended by such brutalities as the ritual murder of Iphigenia (see pp. 149–50).

This, then, is the religion which has become obsolete along with Jupiter, a religion based on the perversion of all that is good in man. The despair of hell has been replaced by the felicity of heaven; and just as the first had manifested itself in religious practices, so now the second gives rise to a new religion, based not on God but on man: 'By virtue I, a mortal, vanquish thee a mighty god.' The old religion of Jupiter, that 'dark yet mighty faith' with its altars, shrines and misshapen gods is replaced by a new religion with its own temples and statues.

There can be no doubt that Shelley's basic model for the new religion of man was his reconstruction of Greek civilisation. As he put in one of his essays: 'The period which intervened between the birth of Pericles and the death of Aristotle is undoubtedly, whether considered in itself or with reference to the effects which it had produced upon the subsequent destinies of civilized man, the most memorable in the history of the world.'[67] Much more pointedly: 'Of no other epoch in the history of our species have we records and fragments stamped so visibly with the image of the divinity in man'. For example there is the temple of Prometheus:

> ... Beside the windless and crystalline pool,
> Where ever lies, on unerasing waves,
> The image of a temple, built above,
> Distinct with column, arch, and architrave,

And palm-like capital, and over-wrought
And populous with most living imagery—
Praxitelean shapes, whose marble smiles
Fill the hushed air with everlasting love.
It is deserted now, but once it bore
Thy name, Prometheus . . .

(III, iii, 159–68)

Near to this temple is the cave to which Prometheus will withdraw, having shown humanity how to escape from its bondage. It has been suggested that Shelley is locating this temple in the Academy where Socrates and Plato once taught, while he places the cave of Prometheus in the nearby grove of Colonus, which was sacred to the Furies and from which Oedipus was mysteriously translated in Sophocles' play. If this is so, the implications are highly appropriate: guilt and pain have been tamed, even if they can never be banished for good, and, through the exercise of self-knowledge, man has come to terms with his own possibilities and with his limitations. Whether Shelley intended these associations to affect his readers we cannot be sure; the most important implications of the description depend not on our recognition of specific locations but on our response to this calm and beautiful image of a Greek temple. Like the 'abandoned shrines' of Jupiter's religion, it too is deserted, since the religion of the Greeks has no modern congregation; yet Shelley implies that, unlike Jupiter's temples, it is always relevant if we are ready to open our minds to its influence. The 'Praxitelean shapes, whose marble smiles / Fill the hushed air with everlasting love' are, presumably, images of the 'divinity in man', statues which may have a beneficial effect on the way men live their lives. The synaesthesia is characteristic and highly effective: 'marble smiles' which 'Fill the hushed air' suggest not only the holy silence of the temple and of the observer, breathless with adoration, but also a pervasive and complex influence which goes far beyond an effect at the level of the merely visual.

Thus, while the temples of Jupiter are obsolete and unregarded, the temples of Greece with their marble statues are perpetual indications of beautiful possibility. The Acropolis for example, surmounted by its crest of columns, is a jewel of European civilisation, an unshakable reality in the minds of men:

For thou [Liberty] wert, and thine all-creative skill
Peopled, with forms that mock the eternal dead
In marble immortality, that hill

Which was thine earliest throne and latest oracle.
...
Within the surface of Time's fleeting river
  Its wrinkled image lies, as then it lay
Immoveably unquiet, and forever
  It trembles, but it cannot pass away!
           ('Ode to Liberty', lines 72–9)

Here Shelley insists on that direct and intimate connection between the quality of political life (Liberty) and the quality of art which he expounds in the *Defence of Poetry*. The spirit of Liberty which animated all Athenian life informs its statues and its public buildings and provides for later generations an enduring emblem of what man can achieve if he can only shake off his chains. Since some recent interpreters have imported Yeatsian ironies into the first four lines, it is worth observing perhaps that 'mock' does not mean 'deride' but 'imitate' as in 'Ozymandias'. The eternal dead are probably not the artists ironically outlived by the work of their own hands but the Athenian heroes or demigods whose immortality is bodied forth in these statues. Far from introducing irony, these lines present an image of art as something transcendent and immortal and, far from including dolphin-torn and gong-tormented seas, they suggest a permanence, calm and quiet which transcends 'all that man is, / All mere complexities, / The fury and the mire of human veins'. The calm reflections of the buildings in the water (here the Ilissus becomes the river of Time) is a very close parallel to the temple of Prometheus, whose image 'ever lies, on unerasing waves'.

That Shelley is rejecting the troubled variety of life in favour of an ideal tranquillity becomes even more certain when we compare his lines with Wordsworth's 'Elegiac Stanzas' on Peele Castle. Here Wordsworth describes the image of the castle reflected in the sea—'It trembled, but it never passed away'—a formulation which was obviously the source of Shelley's own line. But the point of Wordsworth's poem is that this picture of lasting ease and Elysian quiet without toil or strife is no longer adequate to his emotional or moral needs. Now that a deep distress has humanised his soul, he finds that he is drawn to Beaumont's picture of Peele Castle which portrays it not as reflected in a smiling sea but braving the elements of a storm. Wordsworth welcomes 'this rueful sky, this pageantry of fear' and the spirit of resistance embodied in the old castle; his old thoughtless happiness was blind and unrealistic and it has been replaced by a kind of stoical optimism. There *was* a place for stoical optimism in Shelley's philosophy (the endurance of Prometheus embodies it nobly and defiantly) but in the 'Ode to Liberty' he is concerned not with the spirit of resistance but with the perpetuation of a mental reality. The image of Athens reflected in the water is an image which suggests the continuing relevance of what Athens has been to those who come after; it concerns the transmission through time and space of a civilising idea whereas Wordsworth is more concerned with the embodiment of a moral attitude. The difference in approach is further underlined by the fact that Wordsworth's image is a local one, chosen from the native tradition, while Shelley's takes him back to Hellenic culture.

Thus, Greece in general and Athens in particular provided Shelley with images of civilisation in full flower which are often concentrated either on temples or on the statues with which they are adorned. In the regenerated world the temples of Jupiter are replaced by the temples of Greece, emblems of a supremely humanistic civilisation and shrines to the human spirit. The implications of this process become particularly clear at the beginning of the last act of *Prometheus Unbound* when Shelley introduces a triumphant paean sung by the Hours and the Spirits of the Human Mind. These Spirits had previously appeared in the First Act when they had been summoned to encourage Prometheus and had appeared 'Like flocks of clouds in Spring's delightful weather, / Thronging in the blue air'; now that Prometheus has been released from his rock, they come to celebrate the effects of his unbinding:

> We come from the mind
> Of humankind,
> Which was late so dusk, and obscene, and blind;
> Now 'tis an ocean
> Of clear emotion,
> A heaven of serene and mighty motion ...

Man's mind is no longer clouded with fears and superstitions and he now constitutes a harmonious universe within himself; later in the act this harmony within is fully mirrored and complemented by the harmony of the macrocosm without.

The Spirits go on to catalogue more precisely their sources within the range of human potentiality:

> From the azure isles,
> Where sweet Wisdom smiles,
> Delaying your ships with her siren wiles;

From the temples high
Of man's ear and eye
Roofed over Sculpture and Poesy;
From the murmurings
Of the unsealed springs
Where Science bedews her daedal wings.

The first three lines are obviously based on the *Odyssey* and the azure isles suggest the Aegean seascape in general; this is the homeland and origin of human wisdom or philosophy. But it is the next stanza which is particularly significant in the context we have been considering. The Spirits have turned the human mind into a temple. It is informed by the senses (ear and eye) and at its centre are sculpture and poetry which, together with science, represent the pinnacle of human achievement. Thus, it is implied that the temples of humanity are more enduring and more significant than the shrines of Jupiter, which are now 'But an astonishment', a mere curiosity to point the finger at.

Shelley quietly develops the implications of this religious imagery. For example, when the Spirits first appear, Panthea marks them out for us: 'See, where the Spirits of the human mind / Wrapped in sweet sounds, as in bright veils, approach.' This daring piece of synaesthesia presents the Spirits to us in the guise of priestesses as on some Athenian frieze; they have come from the temple of the human mind and they celebrate the powers of regenerated, Promethean, man who, as we learn later, is now his own divinity or, as the Earth expresses it, 'Man . . . / Whose nature is its own divine control'. More precisely, the new object of worship is not so much man himself as the power of Love in man (Shelley's models here may have been either Pausanias or Athenaeus both of whom recorded that the Greeks had once set up an altar to Eros in the Academy).[68] In Shelley's mythology the altar of the new religion is contrasted to the sacrificial altar of the old system: there are no more mutely imploring Iphigenias. So in his revolutionary 'Ode to Naples' Shelley addresses the city in terms which recall the past but reject it in favour of a happier future:

Bright Altar of the bloodless sacrifice,
Which armèd Victory offers up unstained
To Love, the flower-enchained!

Thus, hatred and fear are expelled: there is 'no quarter given to Revenge, or Envy, or Prejudice', and 'Love is celebrated everywhere as the sole law which should govern the moral world'.[69]

Notes to chapter seven

1   Maria Gisborne and Edward E. Williams, *Journals and Letters*, ed. F. L. Jones, Norman, Oklahoma, 1951, p. 106.
2   Trelawny, *Records*, p. 139.
3   *Letters*, II. 26.
4   *Letters*, II. 73–4.
5   *Letters*, II. 74–5.
6   Clark, *Prose*, p. 223.
7   Clark, *Prose*, p. 219.
8   Clark, *Prose*, p. 274.
9   *Letters*, II. 322.
10   *Letters*, II. 156.
11   Clark, *Prose*, p. 219.
12   *Letters*, II. 360.
13   For the details, see Roy R. Male, Jr. and James A. Notopoulos, 'Shelley's Copy of Diogenes Laertius', *Modern Language Review*, LIV (1959), pp. 10–21.
14   Brimley Johnson, *Shelley–Leigh Hunt*, p. 83.
15   Clark, *Prose*, p. 209.
16   Bod. MS. Shelley adds. e. 10, p. 219r.
17   *Letters*, II. 145–6.
18   *P.W.*, p. 446.
19   Bod. MS. Shelley adds. e. 9, p. 368.
20   G. M. Matthews, ' "Julian and Maddalo": the Draft and the Meaning', *Studia Neophilologica*, XXXV (1963), p. 72.
21   *P.W.*, p. 450.
22   L. 1080. Shelley asked Peacock to order him two seals bearing the device of a dove with outspread wings encircled by this motto. (*Letters*, II 276–7).
23   *P.W.*, p. 447.
24   See *Letters*, I. 277.
25   *Defence*, p. 34.
26   *Defence*, pp. 48–9.
27   *Letters*, I. 318.
28   *P.W.*, p. 206.
29   *P.W.*, p. 206.
30   *Letters*, II. 290.
31   *Letters*, II. 309.
32   Hume's phrase.
33   *Letters*, II. 323.
34   *P.W.*, p. 205. In the draft Shelley actually directed the epigraph *To the ghost of Aeschylus* (Bod. MS. Shelley adds. e. 11, p. 215).
35   Bod. MS. Shelley adds. e. 12, p. 4.
36   *Defence*, p. 48.
37   *Defence*, p. 40.
38   *P.W.*, p. 34.
39   Clark, *Prose*, p. 221.
40   Quoted in Stephen A. Larrabee, *English Bards and Grecian Marbles: the relationship between Sculpture and Poetry, especially in the Romantic Period*, Columbia University Press, New York, 1943, p. 184.
41   *On the Imitation of the Painting and Sculpture of the Greeks*, translated by Fuseli, cited from David Irwin, *Winckelmann: Writings on Art*, Phaidon, 1972, p. 64.
42   *Ibid.* Athenaeus recounted this story and Shelley made notes on it (Bod.

MS. Shelley adds. e. 6, pp. 67–9) which seem to be connected with his preface to the *Symposium* and his essay on the Ancient Greeks.

43 *Ibid.*, p. 67.
44 *Letters*, II. 313.
45 Clark, *Prose*, p. 221.
46 On the cover of Bod. MS. Shelley adds. e. 10, Shelley notes *andros kai gunaikos ē autē aretē* (The virtue [i.e. scope and potential] of man and woman is the same).
47 *Autobiography*, p. 267.
48 *Letters*, II. 88–89.
49 Clark, *Prose*, p. 352.
50 Clark, *Prose*, p. 352.
51 *The History of Ancient Art*, cited from Irwin, pp. 118–19.
52 Clark, *Prose*, p. 344.
53 Clark, *Prose*, p. 349.
54 *The History of Ancient Art*, p. 133.
55 *On the Imitation of the Painting and Sculpture of the Greeks*, cited from Irwin, p. 72.
56 *Letters*, I. 307.
57 *Letters*, II. 146.
58 *Defence*, p. 44.
59 *Defence*, p. 44.
60 See *P.U.*, I. 546–63.
61 Bod. MS. Shelley adds. c. 4, f. 2.
62 Trelawny, *Records*, p. 107.
63 *Adonais*, l. 404.
64 Bod. MS. Shelley adds. e. 6, p. 144v; e. 10, p. 219r. See James A. Notopoulos, 'New Texts of Shelley's Plato', *K.–S.J.*, XV (1966), pp. 99–115.
65 L. 342; Bod. MS. Shelley adds. e. 6, p. 137v.
66 For the details, see my *The Violet in the Crucible*, pp. 106–7.
67 Clark, *Prose*, p. 217; *Defence*, p. 34.
68 Pausanias, I. 30. i; Athenaeus, *Deipnosophistae*, 561 e. Shelley must have read this passage of Athenaeus since he quotes two passages from the same book (13) in his notebooks: the speech of Ephippus (571 f) and the story of Zariadres and Odates (beginning at 575). For Pausanias, see p. 151.
69 *P.W.*, p. 37.

CHAPTER EIGHT

THE ANIMATION
OF DELIGHT

(i)

Writing from Milan in the spring of 1818, Shelley characterised himself as one 'whose chief pleasure in life is the contemplation of nature'.[1] The truth of this description is fully corroborated by his letters from Italy. From the Bagni di Lucca he reports:

The atmosphere here, unlike that of the rest of Italy, is diversified with clouds, which grow in the middle of the day and sometimes bring thunder and lightning, and hail about the size of a pigeon's egg, and decrease towards the evening, leaving only those finely woven webs of vapour which we see in English skies, and flocks of fleecy and slowly moving clouds, which all vanish before sunset; and the nights are for ever serene, and we see a star in the east at sunset—I think it is Jupiter—almost as fine as Venus was last summer; but it wants a certain silver and aerial radiance, and soft yet piercing splendour, which belong, I suppose, to the latter planet by virtue of its once divine and female nature. I have forgotten to ask the ladies if Jupiter produces on them the same effect. I take great delight in watching the changes of the atmosphere.[2]

The observing eye behind this passage is recognisably that of 'Ode to the West Wind', of 'The Cloud' and of those lines in 'To a Skylark' which describe how Venus seems to fade out in the morning sky: 'that silver sphere, / Whose intense lamp narrows / In the white dawn clear / Until we hardly see—we feel that it is there.'

Shelley's habit of close scrutinising and detailed description is applied not only to the sky and the planets but to many other manifestations of nature. Here, for example, he tries to convey an impression of the waterfall at Terni, a phenomenon so extraordinary that 'The very imagination is bewildered in it':

Stand upon the brink of the platform of cliff which is directly opposite. You see the ever-moving water stream down. It comes in thick & tawny folds flaking off like solid snow gliding down a mountain. It does not seem hollow within, but without it is unequal like the folding of linen thrown carelessly down. Your eye follows it & it is lost below, not in the black rocks which gird it around but in its own foam & spray, in the cloudlike vapours boiling up from below, which is not like rain nor mist nor spray nor foam, but water in a shape wholly unlike any thing I ever saw before. It is as white as snow, but thick & impenetrable to the eye.[3]

These are not the words of a man who 'had no eyes', as William Morris once remarked of Shelley, but of a poet who trained himself to observe the processes of nature as closely as he could. There is an obvious connection between Shelley's analysis of the waterfall and his description of mists, water vapours and clouds in a number of poems; the apparent intangibility of the subject matter should not deceive us into diagnosing vagueness on the part of the observer. A waterfall may be tenuous and the spray it throws up may be almost impalpable but these are undeniable facts of nature to which Shelley is responding with an excited attention supported and informed by analytical scrutiny. The whole passage demonstrates a scrupulous search for definition: the water is like snow and yet unlike it; it cannot be hollow within and yet its uneven appearance suggests that it ought to be; the vapour is not like rain nor mist nor spray nor foam. Clearly Shelley is fascinated by the way in which water can take on so many appearances and transform itself into the semblance of so many varieties of matter.

Shelley's letters from Italy make it clear that, in so far as he does ignore the yellow bees in the ivy bloom, it is neither through blindness nor incapacity nor through an insensitivity to the charms of nature.

(ii)

The moth fluttering from the mown grass,[4] the bat beating its wings against the wired window of the dairy,[5] the slow, soft toads creeping out of their damp corners,[6] the exact gradations of a sunset—he had an eye which 'used to notice such things' and was capable of recording them in his poetry yet he could not remain satisfied for long with the minute particular in itself. Unquestionably, the streaks on the tulip were beautiful but this beauty was meaningless unless it led you on to something greater. So much is evident from the two Italian letters, which reveal an unmistakable urge to penetrate beyond the phenomena of the natural scene. This tendency can be observed in the celebrated address to the skylark. Shelley is so enraptured by the bird's singing that he evolves a verse form which reproduces 'in the delicate hesitant poise of each stanza upon its prolonged floating last line, the lark-song with its extended trill';[7] yet, he also announces immediately that his concern is not ornithological ('Hail to thee, blithe Spirit! / Bird thou never wert').

It seems obvious that Shelley was scanning the natural world for traces of some underlying purpose, the fingerprints of a creator perhaps or, if this was too crudely anthropomorphic, the intimations of im-mortality. To this end, he devoted himself in earlier days to scientific investigation. A rather tortuously argumentative letter of 1811 gives us some indication of the driving motive behind his studies when he declares:

I will say then, that all nature is animated, that microscopic vision as it hath discovered to us millions of animated beings whose pursuits and passions are as eagerly followed as our own, so might it if extended find that Nature itself was but a mass of organized animation . . .[8]

It is almost as if Shelley purchased his microscope and his telescope so that he could thoroughly investigate any clues which the Divinity or organising principle of the universe had left behind, threads which might lead him out of the labyrinth of unknowing towards the secret truth; he passionately desired evidence that we were not a random collection of atoms. There is a paradox here which Sir Timothy Shelley would have done well to appreciate; once you remove the premises of orthodoxy, Shelley's approach to the inquisition of truth is not unlike that of Bishop Butler or of William Paley, whom Sir Timothy tried to persuade his renegade son into reading, with unhappy results. All three were searching for proofs of something which raised man above the level of the beasts and gave meaning to his existence; all three looked to nature for the solution.

Like Butler and like Paley, Shelley wanted to believe in man's signi-ficance, to discover that man was not born merely to die. Not long before his own death he left the following record of his beliefs in one of the notes to *Hellas*:

That there is a true solution of the riddle, and that in our present state that solution is unattainable by us, are propositions which may be regarded as equally certain: meanwhile, as it is the province of the poet to attach him-self to those ideas which exalt and ennoble humanity, let him be permitted to have conjectured the condition of that futurity towards which we are all impelled by an unextinguishable thirst for immortality. Until better arguments can be produced than sophisms which disgrace the cause, this desire itself must remain the strongest and the only presumption that eternity is the inheritance of every thinking being.[9]

Here Shelley is substituting hope for the more orthodox virtue of faith. This kind of sceptical probabilism, in which man's ignorance is interpreted as a possible source of hope rather than despair, is typical of Shelley's posture in face of the problems of philosophy. Yet, if his ultimate commitment to an optimistic outlook was related to his own need to believe that all was for the best, it was supported by his scientific investigations and by his contemplation of the natural world. For, although what he saw there could not be regarded as a positive proof that man was destined to immortality, far less that he was the creature of a ruling intelligence, the natural world was undeniably beautiful and its processes seemed to suggest that natural objects did not function at random but according to certain identifiable principles of action.

In the early essay 'On a Future State' we see him setting out to explore the facts of nature. In particular he is fascinated by the problem of death, which he examines from the perspective of the scientist or, as he prefers to say, the natural philosopher. Dismissing all religious beliefs as totally foreign to the subject, he concentrates on the physical facts of death with a clinical detachment which only occasionally flares up into images of Gothic melancholy:

By the word *death* we express that condition in which natures resembling ourselves apparently cease to be that which they were. We no longer hear them speak, nor see them move. If they have sensations and apprehensions, we no longer participate in them. We know no more than that those external organs and all that fine texture of material frame, without which we have no experience that life or thought can subsist, are dissolved and scattered abroad. . . . How can a corpse see or feel? Its eyes are eaten out, and its heart is black and without motion. . . . When you can discover where the fresh colours of the faded flower abide, or the music of the broken lyre, seek life among the dead.[10]

These are the facts which all of us must face, though 'the popular religion' and man's desire to be forever as he is now often hinder us from seeing them objectively. Assuming the disinfected robe of the natural philosopher, Shelley then proceeds to dissect the cadaver to see if he can isolate any unidentified substances:

It is probable that what we call thought is not an actual being, but no more than the relation between certain parts of that infinitely varied mass of which the rest of the universe is composed and which ceases to exist so soon as those parts change their position with regard to each other. Thus colour, and sound, and taste, and odour exist only relatively. But let thought be considered as some peculiar substance which permeates and is the cause of the animation of living beings. Why should that substance be assumed to be something essentially distinct from all others and exempt from subjection to those laws from which no other substance is exempt?[11]

There is no scientific evidence to show that the mysterious principle of life can survive the moment of death. If it were to survive a redistribution among other forms but deprived of its normal properties of consciousness, memory and desire, such life after death would not be meaningful in any sense acceptable to man. Even if the intellectual and vital principle in man is quite different from all other substances, that fact in itself offers no solid ground for believing that it survives after death. Shelley then goes on to ask if we existed before our birth (a question which must remind us of Hogg's story of how he once stopped a young mother on Magdalen Bridge to ask, 'Will your baby tell us anything about pre-existence, madam?').[12] His answer is based on certain fundamental scientific facts which he applies to man:

There is in the generative principle of each animal and plant a power which converts the substances by which it is surrounded into a substance homogeneous with itself. That is, the relation[s] between certain elementary particles of matter undergo a change and submit to new combinations. For when we use the words *principle, power, cause*, &c, we mean to express no real being, but only to class under those terms a certain series of co-existing phenomena . . .[13]

It is extremely unlikely that we existed before birth, in the sense of having a conscious existence and a personal identity; it is equally unlikely that such will be the case after our death.

These questions have indicated that Shelley's metaphysical investigations were closely allied to his scientific studies. It is interesting to note that, whereas his strictly scientific approach first causes him to deny that there is any evidence for believing in a future state, it is largely through a scientific understanding of the processes of nature that he finally arrives at the position of sceptical probabilism which informs the note to *Hellas*. Shelley went on asking the same questions throughout his life, but, with the passage of time, the rigorous negatives of his youth were gradually modified into tentative affirmations. In a progression similar to that of his political poetry, he moved through an acknowledgment of the possibilities of despair to an insistence on the paramount duty of hope.

From the writing of *Alastor* in 1815 to the initial conception of *The Triumph of Life* in the spring of 1822, Shelley was haunted by thoughts of mutability which were usually related to his observation of the natural world. Though there were times when the response took place at the level of literary convention ('The flower that smiles to-day / Tomorrow dies' or 'We are as clouds that veil the midnight moon / ...Nought may endure but Mutability') Shelley generally approached the subject with a willingness to encounter its full complexity. In *Alastor*, for instance, his reactions to the death of the protagonist are so diverse, and his own uncertainties about the meaning of death press on him so strongly, that most readers are left in a state of some confusion. It is clear, however, that one of the central issues of the poem is the protagonist's desperate search for a key to the secret of life and death which the natural world denies him. The difficulties of this quest are suggested with imagistic force in the following lines:

> Roused by the shock he started from his trance—
> The cold white light of morning, the blue moon
> Low in the west, the clear and garish hills,
> The distinct valley and the vacant woods,
> Spread round him where he stood ...
> ...His wan eyes
> Gaze on the empty scene as vacantly
> As ocean's moon looks on the moon in heaven.
> (lines 192–6, 200–2)

For all its beauty, nature here is cold and meaningless; its colours are harsh and unwelcoming; behind it there is a void. The insistence on emptiness (*vacant wood, empty scene, vacantly*)[14] is highly significant, and suggests that whatever meaning the protagonist has discovered in nature is the projection of his own desires or fears; there is a close connection with Shelley's final words to Mont Blanc, 'And what were thou, and earth, and stars, and sea, / If to the human mind's imaginings / Silence and solitude were vacancy?'

Later on in this poem, whose landscape is so obviously related to the landscape of the mind, we are led with the poet–protagonist to this grimly symbolic location:

> A pine,
> Rock-rooted, stretched athwart the vacancy

Its swinging boughs, to each inconstant blast
Yielding one only response, at each pause
In most familiar cadence, with the howl
The thunder and the hiss of homeless streams
Mingling its solemn song, whilst the broad river,
Foaming and hurrying o'er its rugged path,
Fell into that immeasurable void
Scattering its waters to the passing winds.

(lines 561–70)

In the context of the rest of the poem, *vacancy* is a word which cannot
be ignored. In these lines Shelley seems to have taken his hero to the
very brink of death, where the river of his life falls into the immeasurable void. Though nature makes some amends by leading the poet to
a more tranquil spot before he dies, there can be no doubt that behind
this passage and behind the whole poem lies the terror of death, the
dreadful suspicion that beyond the colourful display of nature there is
a great emptiness. The feeling is similar to that of the sonnet which
begins with the famous injunction 'Lift not the painted veil which
those who live / Call Life'. The reason why it is better to refrain from
probing into these matters, better not to peer behind the screen of
nature, is starkly expressed: 'behind, lurk Fear / And Hope, twin
Destinies; who ever weave / Their shadows o'er the chasm, sightless
and drear.' Obviously, this chasm can be identified with the immeasurable void of *Alastor*; both passages face the blank wall of despair which
underlies Shelley's rationalist analysis in 'On a Future State'. In *Alastor*
nature itself is dismissed and the narrator, who expresses a 'natural
piety' which carries obviously Wordsworthian resonances, is trapped
by the logic of the story he tells, with the result that his obstinate
questionings receive no comforting answer.

From this dilemma Shelley's inquisitions into nature could never
entirely liberate him: the grave would never release a messenger who
might 'render up the tale / Of what we are'. Neither telescope nor
microscope could satisfy his anxieties concerning a personal life after
death. Yet, it seems that he was increasingly delighted by the processes
of the natural world, to which he responded enthusiastically as evidence, not that he would survive death in the mortal form which he
recognised nor even in a glorified body, but that nature itself was
positive. In particular he displayed a precise interest in the processes
of plant biology; it seems as if the image of 'death's blue vault, with
loathliest vapours hung', the tangible evidence of 'the heart black and
without motion' must be countered and overbalanced by the dispas-

sionate analysis of science. Against the Gothic gloom of the charnel house there stood the radiant gospel of science as embodied, for example, in the works of Humphry Davy.

(iii)

One of Shelley's notebooks provides a good indication of how seriously he studied these matters. It includes nearly twenty pages of detailed notes based on a reading of Davy's *Elements of Agricultural Chemistry*.[15] Some samples will give an idea both of Shelley's concerns and of what he learned from Davy :

1. The sap in plants becomes dense as it ascends and deposits the solid matter which is modified by 'heat light and air' in the leaves and descends through the bark producing the peculiar deposit by which that substance is formed.
2. Sap produced from water, and produces the varieties of substances in plants. Soil, consists of earths—earths are composed of highly inflammable metals and oxygens; are undecomposed by vegetation—(or may be so?)
3. The earth is the laboratory in which the nutriment of vegetables is prepared. Manure is useful and may be converted into organized bodies . . .
4. An exchange is made between carbonic acid gas and oxygen gas; the former the result of the destruction of the principle of life and the latter the food by which it is nourished.
5. The perpendicularity of the growth of plants depends upon gravitation.
6. Chemistry a correct instrument for agricultural improvement.
7. Positive and Negative Electricity. Electricity probably has great effect on plants. Corn sprouted more rapidly in water positively electrified by the Voltaic battery than in negatively. The clouds are usually negative—the Earth therefore positive.

It is instructive to discover the beautiful and ineffectual angel taking notes on the chemical action of manure and its agricultural benefits. No one will be surprised by Shelley's interest in the social improvements resulting from the proper application of scientific principles; the emphasis in 'Chemistry a correct instrument for agricultural improvement' and the reference to quicker methods of germinating corn are entirely characteristic of the man who believed that scientific progress could help to liberate the world. Many of the quotations reveal a system in which everything is meaningful, even 'the destruction of the principle of life'. Behind the appearances of nature are identifiable laws whereby, for example, 'an exchange is made between carbonic acid gas and oxygen gas' or electrical action is based on positive and negative poles.

The main area of interest is the life, growth and structure of plants. The passages on sap concern the relations between plants, the earth in which they grow and the air they breathe; they provide a scientific explanation of the miraculous processes which combine to produce the perfected plant and maintain it in being. Shelley's notes on chapter 3 go into considerable detail on the composition of plants. He records the different parts of trees and flowers and the three divisions of the seed. He notes: 'The tubes of the fibrous parts receive the saps, the cells elaborate its parts and expose it to the action of the atmosphere and the new matter in trees is produced in storing the outer cortical layer of the last year.' Scientifically speaking there is nothing remarkable about these notes but they do tell us a good deal about the workings of Shelley's mind and they relate very closely to some of the poetic concerns of his later years.

Take for example *The Sensitive Plant*, which Shelley wrote early in 1820 and published with *Prometheus Unbound*. This poem confronts the problem of mortality, particularly as it is manifested in the natural world. It focuses on a garden which manifests the mutuality, interchange and interdependence more scientifically recorded by Shelley in his notes on Davy's *Lectures*:

> For each was interpenetrated
> With the light and the odour its neighbour shed,
> Like young lovers whom youth and love make dear,
> Wrapped and filled by their mutual atmosphere.

The personification (perhaps suggested by Erasmus Darwin's example in his versified text-book *The Botanic Garden*) is important to the metaphysical scheme of the poem, which implies a parallel between the state of the flowers in the garden and the human condition. Later, this Eden-like calm is broken by the onset of winter which Shelley describes with morbid extravagance:

> The rose-leaves, like flakes of crimson snow,
> Paved the turf and the moss below.
> The lilies were drooping, and white, and wan,
> Like the head and the skin of a dying man . . .

> For the leaves soon fell, and the branches soon
> By the heavy axe of the blast were hewn;
> The sap shrank to the root through every pore
> As blood to a heart that will beat no more . . .

And under the roots of the Sensitive Plant
The moles and the dormice died for want:
The birds dropped stiff from the frozen air
And were caught in the branches naked and bare.

Most sinister of all, something then goes wrong with the expected resurrection of the spring:

When winter had gone and spring came back,
The Sensitive Plant was a leafless wreck;
But the mandrakes, and toadstools, and docks, and darnels,
Rose like the dead from their ruined charnels.

It is a nightmare version of 'Ode to the West Wind' in which the azure wind of spring does not return driving sweet buds like flocks to feed in air but only the coarser plants rise from their winter graves in a grotesque parody of the new birth. The reluctance to be committed to full affirmation ('O Wind, / If Winter comes, can Spring be far behind?') has been horribly justified. In this grim vision, survival of the fittest is not synonymous with survival of the finest. At the centre of this enigma is the Sensitive Plant (the mimosa) which is set apart from the other flowers of the pre-lapsarian garden in that it has 'no bright flower' and no fragrance; in terms of the basic allegory the plant seems to represent the position of man in the natural world, to which he belongs but from which he is also separated through the possession of mental faculties. The question which Shelley asks himself at the end of the poem is whether the Sensitive Plant is doomed to die like the other flowers of the garden, subject to a harsh natural process which favours only a crude durability; or can there be a more permanent principle which survives the grosser alterations which are visible to the natural eye?

Whether the Sensitive Plant, or that
Which within its boughs like a spirit sate,
Ere its outward form had known decay,
Now felt this change, I cannot say.

     . . . but in this life
Of error, ignorance and strife,
Where nothing is, but all things seem,
And we the shadows of the dream,

It is a modest creed, and yet
Pleasant if one considers it,
To own that death itself must be,
Like all the rest, a mockery.

That garden sweet, that Lady fair,
And all sweet shapes and odours there,
In truth have never passed away :
'Tis we, 'tis ours, are changed; not they.

For love, and beauty, and delight
There is no death nor change : their might
Exceeds our organs, which endure
No light, being themselves obscure.

In this calm and beautifully poised piece of writing the final emphasis
is on the limited scope of human perception, which is 'obscure' and
dull; Shelley has successfully embodied in verse some of the implications
of Locke's discussion of the sensitive plant in *An Essay Concerning
Human Understanding*.[16]

In this poem, then, the final resort is philosophy; if we cannot fully
understand the processes of nature, it is only because of the limitations
of human knowledge and intellect. We may hope (and the imagery of
the poem carefully and subtly leads us towards this possibility) that
the principle or principles of life which animated the Sensitive Plant
and the other flowers of the garden has not been obliterated but merely
obscured; it may be, perhaps, an enduring principle. This final affirmation is all the more acceptable for the tactful and unassertive manner
in which it is advanced : 'It is a modest creed', says Shelley, 'and yet /
Pleasant if one considers it'.

Similar concerns can be found in *The Zucca*, an unfinished poem of
eleven stanzas which Mrs Shelley assigned to January 1822. *The Zucca*
begins by describing the loneliness and unfulfilment of the narrator :

Summer was dead, but I yet lived to weep
 The instability of all but weeping . . .

Like many of Shelley's surrogates, he is seeking for something beyond
the confines of this mortal world, some perception of the ideal not
normally granted to man : 'Thou, whom, seen nowhere, I feel everywhere.'[17] This mysterious ideal to which he addresses himself is beyond
the obscure comprehension of man; to attempt to unveil it is to desire
'More in this world than any understand'. It seems to be an animating

spirit, a principle of life which can be sensed in winds, trees, streams and 'all things common' but also in music, in 'the sweet unconscious tone / Of animals' and in the human voice. It is inconstant, intangible and evanescent and seems to bear some relation to the spirit of Intellectual Beauty, to the unpredictable force of poetic inspiration, to the 'Spirit of Delight' and to the 'Spirit, whose inconstant home / Is in the Spirit of inconstant man'.[18] There is also an obvious connection with *Adonais*, which describes how 'the one Spirit's plastic stress / Sweeps through the dull dense world, compelling there, / All new successions to the forms they wear / . . . And bursting in its beauty and its might / From trees and beasts and men into the Heaven's light'.

After the introductory stanzas where the poet sadly reflects on the intangibility and evanescence of the mysterious and beautiful animating spirit, he makes a discovery:

> And thus I went lamenting, when I saw
>   A plant upon the river's margin lie,
> Like one who loved beyond his nature's law,
>   And in despair had cast him down to die;
> Its leaves, which had outlived the frost, the thaw
>   Had blighted; like a heart which hatred's eye
> Can blast not, but which pity kills; the dew
> Lay on its spotted leaves like tears too true.

This is obviously a very sensitive plant indeed, whose weeping, like that of its predecessor, seems to be a lament for the desolation of the autumnal world. Again, like *the* Sensitive Plant this zucca is the victim of unrelenting nature:

> The Heavens had wept upon it, but the Earth
>   Had crushed it on her unmaternal breast
> Even as the rest who owe their bitter birth
>   To that great mother . . .[19]

Stirred to pity, the narrator takes it home where he watches over it with tender care:

> I bore it to my chamber, and I planted
>   It in a vase full of the lightest mould;
> The winter beams which out of Heaven slanted
>   Fell through the window-panes, disrobed of cold
> Upon its leaves and flowers . . .

The mitigated influences of air
   And light revived the plant, and from it grew
Strong leaves and tendrils, and its flowers fair,
   Full as a cup with the vine's burning dew,
O'erflowed with golden colours; an atmosphere
   Of vital warmth enfolded it anew,
And every impulse sent to every part
The unbeheld pulsations of its heart.

Though there are hints here both of sentimentality and of the weakly fanciful style which Shelley occasionally slipped into ('its flower fair / Full as a cup with the vine's burning dew'), the passage as a whole clearly demonstrates Shelley's ability to relate to the processes of growth. The adjective 'lightest' enables us to participate in the gentle fostering relationship of soil and plant: here we might be reminded of a more tactual realisation of the same experience—'The breath of the moist earth is light / Around its unexpanded buds'.[20] The high point of the second stanza is the final couplet, which shows a delicate sensitivity to the vibrations of plant life allied to a more general realisation of the harmonious and silently integrated functioning of the natural system. After the narrator has watered the plant with his tears much in the manner of Keats's Isabella, the fragment ends with a series of harsh images of the winter world outside the chamber, a natural pathology reminiscent of *The Sensitive Plant*:

The birds were shivering in their leafless bowers,
   The fish were frozen in the pools, the form
Of every summer plant was dead . . .

The unfinished poem seems to be setting up a contrast between the miraculous invisible processes which are involved in sustaining the life of the melon plant and the manifest cruelty which is also part of nature. It would be foolish to speculate as to how Shelley might have resolved this problem; however, we can observe him at work on a similar theme in the unfinished play which he was writing at Pisa early in 1822. This was much the time when he wrote *The Zucca* and it may well be that the play is developing the ideas which he left unconcluded in that poem. The central passage of this play was originally published by Richard Garnett under the title of *The Magic Plant*, which later gave its name to Carl Grabo's influential biography. It concerns a mysterious dream which a Lady recounts to an Indian youth, who is in love with her:

Methought a star came down from heaven,
And rested mid the plants of India,
Which I had given shelter from the frost
Within my chamber. There the meteor lay,
Panting forth light among the leaves and flowers,
As if it lived, and was outworn with speed;
Or that it loved, and passion made the pulse
Of its bright life throb like an anxious heart,
Till it diffused itself, and all the chamber
And walls seemed melted into emerald fire
That burned not; in the midst of which appeared
A spirit like a child, and laughed aloud . . .
Then bent over a vase, and murmuring
Low, unintelligible melodies,
Placed something in the mould like melon-seeds,
And slowly faded, and in place of it
A soft hand issued from the veil of fire,
Holding a cup like a magnolia flower,
And poured upon the earth within the vase
The element with which it overflowed,.
Brighter than morning light, and purer than
The water of the springs of Himalah.

The parallels with *The Zucca* are striking—for instance, the rescue of the plant from the clutches of winter, and the behaviour of the meteor, whose pulse throbs in a manner which might remind us of the 'unbeheld pulsations' of the melon plant. To make the identification even closer, the spirit of the meteor actually deposits 'something . . . like melon-seeds'. The mythologising, of course, is something new; the introduction of the meteor and the spirit like a child adds a fresh, if puzzling, dimension to the narrative.

Here it must be remembered that, according to Shelley's scientific conceptions, meteors were not necessarily confined to the heavens but could be exhaled from the earth rather than descending on it. In particular these meteors breathed up from below were often associated with flowers: in *The Sensitive Plant* Shelley specifically describes the flowers of the garden as 'the meteors of that sublunar heaven'. This is part of the elaborate symbolical patterning by which stars and flowers are often interchangeable, a pattern highly significant for the ultimate transcendence of death in poems such as *Adonais* and *The Sensitive Plant*. Behind this conception of the flower as a meteor of the earth there was a scientific appreciation of the important function of the soil in creating atmosphere. For example, one of Shelley's first teachers, Adam Walker, had written: 'The atmosphere is a thin fluid . . . principally made up of heterogeneous matter exhaled from the earth.'[21] His own notes on Davy included the phrase, 'Plants consist chiefly of carbon and gases' and some detailed analysis of the earth's role as 'the laboratory in which the nutriment of vegetables is prepared'. Thus, on examination, the Lady's dream would appear to be no mere decorative fantasy but a mythological presentation of the essential facts of plant biology. Even the emerald fire would seem to have a precise significance; very probably it should be associated with the 'light, like a green star' which burns on the head of that 'delicate spirit / That guides the earth through Heaven' in *Prometheus Unbound*. These details suggest a connection with electricity, which Adam Walker had identified with light and heat, whose triple force he recognised as 'the grand agents in the order of nature'.[22] We may deduce then that the 'element . . . / Brighter than morning light', if not electricity, is a principle akin to it, the source of life, energy and motion.

Having detailed her dream to the Indian Youth, the Lady goes on to describe the consequences. Coming to the flowerpot, she sees 'two little dark-green leaves / Lifting the light mould at their birth . . .'. Here again the phrasing reminds us of *The Zucca*. The Lady then recounts how the magic plant began to grow:

> And day by day, green as a gourd in June,
> The plant grew fresh and thick, yet no one knew
> What plant it was; its stem and tendrils seemed
> Like emerald snakes, mottled and diamonded
> With azure mail and streaks of woven silver;
> And all the sheaths that folded the dark buds
> Rose like the crest of cobra-di-capel,
> Until the golden eye of the bright flower . . .
> Gazed like a star into the morning light.

The introduction of the snake reflects Shelley's spontaneous delight in the beauty of reptiles, a slightly heretical taste which matches well with his own nickname ('The Snake'). It is also characteristic that Shelley should compare a plant with a cobra-di-capel since, to his eye, the beautiful manifestations of nature were evidence of animating causes which eluded Linnaean classification. It should be noted, too, that this plant which had its origin in a meteor now produces a flower whose eye 'Gazed like a star into the morning light': once again flowers and stars are mysteriously interchangeable. However, for all its beauty,

> It soon fell,
> And to a green and dewy embryo-fruit
> Left all its treasured beauty.

Over this embryo the Lady watches with sentimental affection as it grows, pokes its way out of the lattice and trails across the lawn to a pool where its fruit lies 'like a sleeping lizard / Under the shadows'. Eventually,

> when Spring indeed
> Came to unswathe her infants, and the lilies
> Peeped from their bright green masks to wonder at
> This shape of autumn crouched in their recess,
> Then it dilated . . .

The Lady describes in some detail how it lay in the Elysian calm of its own beauty, a creature of the light which surrounded it :

> . . . it seemed
> In hue and form that it had been a mirror
> Of all the hues and forms around it and
> Upon it pictured by the sunny beams
> Which, from the bright vibrations of the pool,
> Were thrown upon the rafters and the roof
> Of boughs and leaves . . .

Once again, the precise choice of word in *vibrations* indicates that the interest here is more than a simple response to a calm and beautiful scene. *Vibrations* suggests the waves by which light was transmitted;[23] the plant is shown 'Changing light to fragrance' that is receiving the light and, by the process of photosynthesis, transforming it into its own substance. Though this long descriptive passage is sometimes sentimental and sometimes overwritten, it is none the less a remarkable endeavour to represent by poetic means the very essence of the creative process in nature. We cannot tell what Shelley would have done with this passage had he completed his play; nor can we tell how it might have related to the total structure. As it stands, it seems to be of central importance; indeed, like the plant itself, it has trailed its way beyond the limits until it dominates the whole of the play.

A similar interest can be detected in two stanzas of *The Witch of Atlas*. In this case the agent of generation is Love. Following the lead of Mercury in the Homeric *Hymn*, Love escapes from his cradle and steals a strange seed, which he wraps up in mould and sows in his mother's star (presumably, Venus). The results are closely akin to those we have already examined :

The plant grew strong and green, the snowy flower
  Fell, and the large and gourd-like fruit began
To turn the light and dew by inward power
  To its own substance; woven tracery ran
Of light firm texture, ribbed and branching, o'er
  The solid rind, like a leaf's veinèd fan . . .

                         (lines 305–10)

Once again, the process of growth is presented with particular care. Once again, we meet a mischievous child who initiates the mysterious transformation of seed to plant. Though this passage is brief, it is an integral part of the joyful atmosphere of a visionary poem and yet another indication of how Shelley was excited by the everyday miracles of plant life.

(iv)

These passages have shown Shelley rejoicing in the principle and processes of growth, which he sets up against the 'swift and hidden spirit of decay' and the inexorable fact of death. While the miracles of plant biology cannot provide a definitive answer to his obstinate questionings, they seem to suggest two possible solutions. First of all, as science had taught Shelley and as his poetry acknowledges, the process of growth involves innumerable transformations in an ever-shifting chain of natural consequences. Once we have been given this insight, it is possible to see death as merely another shift in structure, another stage in the continuous cycle of transformation. Secondly, it is also possible to deduce that, although specific forms are impermanent, each one of them is given its identity by the animating principle which informs it. Though this principle or power may seem to be withdrawn when the human being, animal, or plant is seen to die, or when the inanimate object alters its form, this may be an illusion due to the imperfect nature of our organs of perception. What we *can* recognise is the existence of an animating principle, its mysteriousness, its power and beauty.

Shelley often associated this mysterious force with a laughing child, as in the case of the *Unfinished Drama*. As a translator from Greek he had turned to the figure of the child-god Mercury as a joyful substitute for the oppressive system of fear and hope which was the foundation of so many religions;[24] however, in his own poetry the child-god is more than a liberating possibility, more than a means of release from the chains of orthodox gloom and self-contempt. It seems likely that it

I

also represents the life-giving principle, which we can recognise but never fully comprehend.

Consider, for example, 'The Cloud'. Most readers now recognise that behind this delightfully fresh and energetic celebration there is a solid basis of scientific fact. Shelley may well have read Luke Howard's famous *Essay on Clouds* which inspired Goethe, Constable, Turner and Wordsworth: in any case, he understood the basic principles involved.[25] Adam Walker had taught him that 'water rises through the air, flying on the wings of electricity', which may have inspired the lines, 'Sublime on the towers of my skiey bowers, / Lightning my pilot sits'.[26] Having identified lightning and electricity, Walker had also taught him how the opposition of positive electricity in the clouds and negative electricity on the earth usually resulted in 'a violent effort to restore equality by a storm of thunder and lightning'.[27] These facts Shelley also found in Davy and wrote out in one of the notebooks in which he drafted 'The Cloud'.[28] It is of no real consequence whether his source was Walker or Davy or even some other authority; what matters is that the apparent luxury of the mythological invention is founded on precise scientific facts. It is important to recognise this, since so many readers and critics have either seen the poem as beautiful but empty or else as an exercise which demonstrates Shelley's 'customary self-concern'.[29] In the face of such blindness it is necessary to adduce the scientific data so carefully assembled by Carlo Grabo, Peter Butter and Desmond King-Hele. However, poetry aspires to a condition beyond the reach of versified meteorology. Thus, to say as Stopford Brooke once did, that if we strip off the 'imaginative clothing from "The Cloud", science will support every word of it', is only a step in the right direction.[50] Admittedly, Shelley deploys his cirrostratus and his cumulonimbus with the dexterity of a meteorologist, but what of the achievement of the poem as a whole? Does it rise beyond the limitations of an Akenside or a Thomson or an Erasmus Darwin?[31]

The answer to this depends not on the accuracy of the scientific observation nor on the incidental felicities of image or phrasing but on the imaginative vitality of the whole poem. This is a criterion which Shelley himself recognised and which he applied to Leigh Hunt's *The Nymphs*, a poem which bears certain similarities to 'The Cloud'. Shelley told Hunt that his poem was 'truly *poetical*, in the intense and emphatic sense of the word'.[32] What he meant by this becomes clearer in another letter where he establishes as his criteria of excellence originality, intensity and the combination of the fullest and most flowing lyrical power with the most intelligible outline of thought and language (a formulation not very dissimilar from Coleridge's 'more than usual state of emotion, with more than usual order').[33] Behind everything there is the informing spirit of imagination which fuses the elements, transcending the limitations of thought and emotion and combining them in a higher unity. Here Shelley makes an interesting distinction between *The Nymphs* and *The Story of Rimini*, a rather thin piece of narration in the vein of the historical-descriptive, where for all his response to the particularities of Italian history and his niceties of detail, Hunt has allowed his own originality to be cramped by the need for verisimilitude.

For the twentieth-century reader, *The Nymphs* is not a completely realised imaginative creation. For the most part it seems to be the product of the fancy rather than the imagination and to lack that very intensity which Shelley considered so essential. It is difficult not to conclude that Shelley must have been aware of this deficiency and to assume that his remarks to Hunt were intended as an encouragement rather than as his ultimate critical judgement. However, his comments are very helpful because they do provide a criterion by which we can measure poems like 'The Cloud'; and *The Nymphs*, because of its very failure to achieve the required standard, also provides a convenient indicator.

Hunt's poem is an attempt to render in verse an account of those animating spirits of nature whom the Greeks personified in the shape of nymphs. It includes an extensive catalogue ranging from Dryads, Napeads, Limniads and Oreads to Ephydriads, Naiads and Nereids. In itself this suggests the essential weakness of the poem, its lack of an original mythological vision. Instead of establishing a fresh relationship with the natural world, Hunt has reverted to the dictionary of mythology and copied out an extensive catalogue. The poem goes nowhere and its length is determined by the number of nymph-species Hunt has been able to discover; it would not be seriously damaged were it shortened or extended, since it has no inner momentum of its own. Thus, while its raw material is derived from mythology, the poem itself is not mythological in any meaningful sense of the word.

The passage which is particularly relevant to 'The Cloud' is that which presents the Nepheliads (or nymphs of the clouds), a passage which bears certain resemblances to Shelley's poem and which, we may reasonably deduce, was one of the influences which helped to shape his own more vital presentation. Hunt's description is inordinately lengthy (one of his obvious weaknesses) so it will only be possible to quote a truncated version :

> . . . every cloud had a bright Nymph to it,—
> Each for a guide; and so those bodies fair
> Obeyed a nobler impulse than the air,
> A bright-eyed, visible thought,—beneath whose sway
> They went, straight stemming on their far-seen way.
> Most exquisite it was indeed to see
> How those blithe damsels guided variously,
> Before, behind, beside. Some forward stood
> As in well-managed chariots, or pursued
> Their trusting ways as in self-moving ones;
> And some sat up, or as in tilted chair
> With silver back seemed slumbering through the air,
> Or leaned their cheek against a pillowy place
> As if upon their smiling, sleepy face
> They felt the air, or heard aerial tunes.

And so it continues, portraying in endless detail the activities of individual nymphs, rather like some over-elaborate Baroque ceiling. Some of the details remind one of Shelley—the guiding spirits in each cloud, and the fluttering attitudes, which bear some resemblance to the behaviour of the Oceanides in *Prometheus Unbound*: yet Shelley's guiding spirits are associated with the power of electricity and, for all their luxury, his Oceanides come closer to the clear-cut outlines of John Flaxman than to Hunt's pictorial extravagance. Here Hunt is illustrating one of the bad habits which alienated Keats—the tendency to treat a poem as if it were a daisy-chain, a beautiful posy of flowers. Here sweetness is all.

Hunt's failure helps to pinpoint the particular strengths of Shelley's poem. What is lacking in Hunt can be demonstrated easily by quoting the first stanza of 'The Cloud':

> I bring fresh showers for the thirsting flowers,
>   From the seas and the streams;
> I bear light shade for the leaves when laid
>   In their noon-day dreams.
> From my wings are shaken the dews that waken
>   The sweet buds every one,
> When rocked to rest on their mother's breast,
>   As she dances about the sun.
> I wield the flail of the lashing hail,
>   And whiten the green plains under,
> And then again I dissolve it in rain,
>   And laugh as I pass in thunder.

There is a directness and a lack of hesitation about this initial self-announcement which reminds one of the gods and heroes of Greek literature. (This quality of unselfconscious egotism can be found in Shelley's own 'Hymn of Apollo', which is closely connected with the composition of 'The Cloud'.[34]) This impression is sustained by the speed and confidence of the verse, based on an anapaestic measure which Shelley seems to have borrowed from Herrick.[35] Nature itself becomes animated, as in the lines: 'When rocked to rest on their mother's breast / As she dances about the sun', with the stress so perfectly falling on *dances*. What gives unity to this stanza (as to the whole poem) is Shelley's conception of the spirit of the cloud. In Hunt's poem the Nepheliads are introduced to us descriptively, so that, long before they are able to sing for themselves, we are reacting to them in pictorial terms; in contrast, the nature of Shelley's cloud is bodied forth in the vitality of its own words. What is more—the principle of change is satisfyingly introduced in terms of the mythological scheme: 'And then again I dissolve it in rain, / And laugh as I pass in thunder.' Here Shelley has attempted to reconcile his conflicting feelings about the natural world in the image of the divine child, who is capricious and ultimately beyond the range of human comprehension. In this imaginative creation is centred the life of the poem; it is the laughing child-god who gives unity and meaning to 'The Cloud'.

What is the cause of this divine laughter? At times it seems to be the result of sheer delight in the joyous appearances of the universe:

> ... The stars peep behind her, and peer;
> And I laugh to see them whirl and flee
>   Like a swarm of golden bees ...

More often, it seems to be related to a kind of self-content, which in a mortal would be complacent but which in a divinity seems to suggest a superior knowledge of the workings of the universe: 'And I all the while bask in Heaven's blue smile, / Whilst he is dissolving in rains'. Compare to this the behaviour of the Witch of Atlas:

> 'This,' said the wizard maiden, 'is the strife
> Which stirs the liquid surface of man's life.'
>
> And little did the sight disturb her soul.

In both cases, it is impossible for the nature which is more than human to involve its affections in the imperfect world of humanity. This is not cruelty; the divine nature is gifted with a different perspective (as *convex* so delicately insists, since from the point of view of a merely terrestrial observer the earth's atmosphere bends the rays of sunlight into concaves).[36] The Spirit of the cloud partakes of the divine nature in the sense that, although she is intangible, she is gifted with a permanence to which no human being can aspire. The individual cloud may be dispersed or dissolved but the informing principle which creates one cloud can just as easily create another. She laughs presumably because, being immortal, she is not subject to the harsh process of time and because, behind the apparent surface of transience, she can see the principles of permanence. There is, too, a suggestion of caprice which may be due to the limitations of human perception. Through the murk of our epistemological twilight the spirit of the cloud may appear to taunt us, to behave like a naughty child; if we could see everything clearly, we would realise that the apparently capricious laughter is the sign of an immortal delight, what Homer calls the 'unquenchable' laughter of the gods.[37]

Much of this is nicely illustrated by the last stanza of 'The Cloud':

> I am the daughter of Earth and Water,
>   And the nursling of the sky;
> I pass through the pores of the oceans and shores;
>   I change, but I cannot die—
> For after the rain, when with never a stain
>   The pavilion of Heaven is bare,
> And the winds and sunbeams, with their convex gleams,
>   Build up the blue dome of air,
> I silently laugh at my own cenotaph,
>   And out of the caverns of rain,
> Like a child from the womb, like a ghost from the tomb,
>   I arise, and unbuild it again.

The whole stanza celebrates permanence in impermanence: behind the dissolving cloud and the evaporating water-particles we are shown the pavilion, the blue dome and the cenotaph, all images of architectural solidity. The essence of the meaning is usually located in the cloud's simple but poignant assertion, 'I change, but I cannot die'. However, the last four lines are equally important, particularly the paradoxical 'I silently laugh at my own cenotaph', where Shelley crystallises the whole meaning of the poem in the rhyme which opposes *laugh* to *cenotaph*. The apparent tomb is empty and the resurrected spirit laughs at the illusion of death. The same triumphant spirit characterises the last three lines with their opposition of the womb and the tomb, of the child and the departed spirit, and their image of energetic childish activity. The child's caprice, its rebelliousness, is manifested in its mischievous delight in unbuilding: but the unbuilding is the unbuilding of a cenotaph, an empty tomb, so that the child is performing a kind of celestial conjuring trick. In this world both positive and negative are part of a higher unity just as, in an earlier stanza, the positive and negative poles of electricity enact complementary roles (lines 21–30). Thus, although they are difficult, the final lines of this poem achieve a metaphysical complexity which satisfyingly embodies the paradox of the cloud.

(v)

Finally, we come to *Prometheus Unbound*. In the last act we are presented with two visions, one of the moon and one of the earth, each of which is centred on a presiding spirit imaged in the form of a child. After an introduction which is imaginative but rooted in realities which are recognisably visual we penetrate to the Spirit which sits within the chariot of the moon:

> Within it sits a winged infant—white
> Its countenance, like the whiteness of bright snow;
> Its plumes are as feathers of sunny frost ...

This wingèd infant obviously bears some relation to the guiding spirit of 'The Cloud' but its appearance is closely related to its specific function as the Spirit of the Moon. It is white not only because that is the first impression which the moon would make on the eye of an observer but to differentiate it from the variegated and colourful earth, the 'Green and azure wanderer / Happy globe of land and air' (MS. draft). The insistence on absence of colour (*white ... whiteness ... white ... white ... white ... white*) supported by analogy (*snow ... frost ... pearl ... light*) is obviously intentional: as Shelley knew, the moon has no atmosphere to break the light of the sun into its constituent colours.[38] Later, under the redeeming influence of love, it acquires an atmosphere, gives life to vegetation and substitutes pied beauty for the monotony of white. The passage ends with an image of harmony, which hints at the music of the spheres and which is taken up and developed in the next speech.

This speech is devoted to the second vision, Panthea's image of the earth. Like Ione's vision of the moon, it falls into two parts, the first being a general description and the second focusing briefly but significantly on the Spirit of the Earth:

Panthea.   And from the other opening in the wood
    Rushes, with loud and whirlwind harmony
    A sphere, which is as many thousand spheres,
    Solid as crystal, yet through all its mass
    Flow, as through empty space, music and light:
    Ten thousand orbs involving and involved,
    Purple and azure, white and green, and golden,
    Sphere within sphere; and every space between
    Peopled with unimaginable shapes,
    Such as ghosts dream dwell in the lampless deep,
    Yet each inter-transpicuous; and they whirl
    Over each other with a thousand motions,
    Upon a thousand sightless axles spinning,
    And with the force of self-destroying swiftness,
    Intensely, slowly, solemnly roll on,
    Kindling with mingled sounds and many tones
    Intelligible words and music wild.
    With mighty whirl the multitudinous orb
    Grinds the bright brook into an azure mist
    Of elemental subtlety, like light;
    And the wild odour of the forest flowers,
    The music of the living grass and air,
    The emerald light of leaf-entangled beams,
    Round its intense yet self-conflicting speed
    Seem kneaded into one aërial mass
    Which drowns the sense. Within the orb itself,
    Pillowed upon its alabaster arms,
    Like to a child o'erwearied with sweet toil,
    On its own folded wings and wavy hair
    The Spirit of the Earth is laid asleep;
    And you can see its little lips are moving
    Amid the changing light of their own smiles,
    Like one who talks of what he loves in dream.

Ione.   'Tis only mocking the orb's harmony.

Perhaps the most intriguing feature of this whole vision is the discovery of the sleeping child. This is not to be dismissed as a pretty piece of mythologising in the vein of Leigh Hunt or of Akenside's *The Naiads* or even of Flaxman's designs; the figure of the child is central to Shelley's conception. There is some doubt as to whether *mocking* was intended to mean making fun of or simply imitating, as it often does in Shelley. The second meaning may seem more likely since Ione puts forward an explanation of the child's behaviour which is intended to be reassuring ('Tis only mocking . . .'); if this interpretation is correct, the expression of the child's face is an imitation of the harmony-in-flux of the earth itself. Yet, however one interprets this word, there can be no doubt that the child represents a principle in nature which is mischievous and above all, inexplicable.

Shelley's intentions become clearer if we examine *The Wisdom of the Ancients*, a book in which Shelley's much-admired Francis Bacon attempts to explicate the basic meaning of thirty-one Greek myths. These include 'Prometheus, or the State of Man' and 'Proteus, or Matter' which Shelley makes use of in a reference to Bacon himself in *The Triumph of Life* (lines 270–1). The seventeenth essay is entitled 'Cupid, or an Atom'—a surprising conjunction which bears a striking similarity to the components of Panthea's vision in *Prometheus Unbound*. Bacon writes:

This fable tends and looks to the cradle of Nature, Love seeming to be the appetite or desire of the first matter, or (to speak more plain) the natural motion of the atom, which is that ancient and only power that forms and fashions all things out of matter of which there is no parent—that is to say, no cause, seeing every cause is as a parent to its effect. Of this power or virtue there can be no cause in Nature (as for God, we always except Him), for nothing was before it, and therefore no efficient cause of it. Neither was there anything better known to Nature, and therefore neither genus nor form. Wherefore, whatsoever it is positive it is, and but inexpressible. More-over, if the manner and proceeding of it were to be conceived, yet it could not be any cause, seeing that (next unto God) it is the cause of causes, itself only without any cause. And perchance there is no likelihood that the manner of it may be contained or comprehended within the narrow com-pass of human search. Not without reason, therefore, is it feigned to come of an egg which was laid by Nox ... For the principal law of nature, or power of this desire, created by God in these parcels of things, for con-curring and meeting together (from whose repetitions and multiplications all variety of creatures proceeded and were composed), may dazzle the eye of men's understandings, and comprehended it can hardly be.

The emphasis here on the limitations of human understanding would have been sympathetically endorsed by Shelley. Bacon goes on to ex-plain that Cupid is a peculiarly appropriate symbol to represent the basic principles of matter:

Now, as concerning his attributes: he is elegantly described with perpetual infancy or childhood, because compound bodies they seem greater and more stricken in years; whereas the first seeds of things or atoms, they are little and diminute, and always in their infancy.

He is also well feigned to be naked, because all compound bodies to a man rightly judging seem to be apparelled and clothed, and nothing to be properly naked but the first particles of things.

Concerning his blindness, the allegory is full of wisdom; for this Love or desire (whatsoever it may be) seems to have but little providence, as directing his pace and motion by that which it perceives nearest, not unlike blind men that go by feeling. More admirable, then, must that chief divine providence be, which from things empty and destitute of providence, and, as it were, blind, by a constant and fatal law, produceth so excellent an order and beauty of things.

Though his eyes are closed in sleep, Shelley's Spirit of the Earth is not blind like Bacon's Cupid; in both cases, however, there is an obvious contrast between the apparent childishness of the behaviour and the importance of the great laws of nature which are represented. Though the Spirit of the Earth cannot be equated with Cupid, it is clear that they have much in common; the Spirit even exhibits a precocious tendency to amorousness for which he is is reproved by Asia ('Peace, wanton! thou are yet not old enough'). And, as we have seen, in *The Witch of Atlas* the child-god Love is directly associated with the creative process in plants. Given these connections, it is not perhaps unreasonable to see Shelley's playful child as both a bodying-forth of the basic mysteries of nature and a personification of the tantalising restrictions of philosophical or scientific enquiry.

With the help of Bacon, we may conjecture that Panthea's vision is, in part at least, a mythological representation of the behaviour of matter and 'The first particles of things'. There is no doubt that Shelley was well informed on the subject of atomic theory, notably from his reading of Davy, who may well have provided a direct influence in the following passage:

Since all matter may be made to fill a smaller volume by cooling, it is evident that the particles of matter must have space between them; and since every body can communicate the power of expansion to a body of lower temperature, that is, can give an expansive motion to its particles, it is a probable inference that its own particles are possessed of motion; but as there is no change in the position of its parts as long as its temperature is uniform, the motion if it exists, must be a vibratory or undulatory motion, or a motion of the particles round their axes, or a motion of particles round each other.[39]

This comes very close to the behaviour of Shelley's orbs (which may have been influenced also by Adam Walker, Laplace, Lucretius and others).[40]

Even more important is Davy's discussion of the chemical processes of plant life which, as we have seen, was an obsession to Shelley in his later years. Here, for example, Davy projects an image of energetic activity which is not random and wasteful, of change which is part of a greater stability:

And by the influences of heat, light, and electrical powers, there is a constant series of changes; matter assumes new forms, the destruction of one order of beings tends to the conservation of another, solution and consolidation, decay and renovation, are connected, and whilst the parts of the system continue in a state of fluctuation and change, the order and harmony of the whole remain unalterable.[41]

This provides another helpful clue for the understanding of Panthea's vision. For, while the 'Ten thousand orbs involving and involved' seem to suggest a universe of almost astronomical severity, the world of Newton rather than the world of Davy, the 'sphere, which is as many thousand spheres' possesses a fluidity, a subtlety, a rapidity of change which indicates a chemical interpretation of matter. The mystical dance of Milton and Dante, the geometrical ballet of the orbs, is included here but it is given a new flexibility, a new dimension of permanence in impermanence, by Shelley's assimilation of the writings of Davy and the other founders of chemistry. Shelley's vision of matter is highly complex and also very simple. It is solid and yet punctuated by spaces; it is one, yet many; its swiftness is 'self-destroying', its speed 'self-conflicting'—the rapidity of the many orbs within is countered by the slow, solemn movement of the great sphere itself. The correspondence with Davy's description of how 'the destruction of one order of beings tends to the conservation of another' is clear enough, as is the parallel with his system whose parts 'continue in a state of fluctuation and change' while 'the order and harmony of the whole remain unalterable'.

Yet, even if science can support many of the facts and even if it provided much of the inspiration, it is Shelley's poetic compression and imaginative force which make them significant and memorable. Consider, for instance, his use of colour. The ten thousand orbs are described as 'Purple and azure, white and green and golden', a formulation which caused Shelley some difficulty, as the draft reveals. None of the scientists who had investigated the behaviour of molecules would have endorsed Shelley's colour-scheme: and yet, in the wider sense, his vision is neither imprecise nor inaccurate. In these lines he is attempting to present the molecular activity of matter as an essential part of the behaviour and identity of the earth we live on. Some of the most striking images in Shelley's poetry are the result of his tendency to project himself to an external point of vantage from which he can observe our planet. Thus, he can visualise the earth projecting a conical shadow

('I spin beneath my pyramid of night'), or he can imagine it as a traveller through space, variegated and colourful ('Thou art speeding round the sun, / Brightest world of many a one, / Green and azure sphere . . .'). What distinguishes the earth from the other planets is its own atmosphere which produces such refreshing and alluring colours; recent pictures taken in space have shown that the 'Green and azure sphere' stands out like an oasis against the black interstellar background and the monotony of the other planets.

If Shelley's list of colours characterises a welcoming planet which can sustain human and animal life, the range of his spectrum probably indicates that he was alert to the new possibilities for poetry opened up by Newton's discoveries of light and colour.[42] One important predecessor, James Thomson, had been fascinated by the colours of the spectrum and had experimented with a description of a summer's day in which he proceeded through all the colours, beginning and ending with white, the undifferentiated source from which all colours are derived (see Shelley's 'Life, like a dome of many-coloured glass, / Stains the white radiance of Eternity'). This may explain the central position of white in Shelley's list; in any event, Shelley's inheritance from science and eighteenth-century poetry was greatly increased by his own experience of light and colour during the years in Italy and by a sensitivity and responsiveness to these details which marks him as the contemporary of Turner (who actually visited Rome at much the time when Shelley was completing the Third Act of *Prometheus Unbound* in the Baths of Caracalla). In particular, Shelley was excited by the colours of the Italian sky which was sometimes azure, a colour used by Thomson 'to describe the clarity of ethereal light in which there is a minimum of refraction by moisture',[43] but more often purple (see for example Shelley's references to 'The purple noon's transparent might' and 'The inmost purple spirit of light').[44] Green and golden are not specifically Italian though they do occur in Italian settings, sometimes together when they seem to suggest hope and the vernal resurrection; on other occasions, they may represent the dappled effect of sunlight falling on leaves. Thus, Shelley's list of colours does not refer specifically to the dance of matter which is the ostensible subject of the description but to the earth itself, which is continuously constituted and reconstituted by means of this joyful *perpetuum mobile*. In these lines Shelley has employed his metaphorical powers to 'mark the before unapprehended relations of things' and to fuse his materials by poetic means.

The same applies to the synaesthetic effect which Shelley attributes to the vision as a whole.[45] Among others, Newton, Darwin and Adam

Walker had all written about the connection between the spectrum bands and the intervals of the octave; yet Shelley transcends the range of science and approaches the realm of mystical exeeperience when he suggests that the earth is actually participating in the music of the spheres, 'Kindling with mingled sounds, and many tones, / Intelligible words and music wild'.

Here in fact Shelley is an heir to the great tradition of European religious literature. Panthea's vision has its analogues in Ezekiel, in Dante and, more specifically perhaps, in the mystical dance of the planets and the fixed stars in *Paradise Lost*, with its 'mazes intricate, / Eccentric, intervolv'd, yet regular / Then most, when most irregular they seem' (v. 618–25). Shelley, too, discovers a pattern which includes and transcends disharmonies; he, too, rejoices in the movements of the universe. Of course, Dante, Milton and the Biblical prophets all present their visions in the service of orthodoxy, while Shelley intimates a faith which is personal and which depends on his own poetic imagination; yet, although he acknowledges neither God nor his Church, his vision is remarkably similar to that of his predecessors. Like them he finds in a moment of visionary insight the hidden beauties of life; like them he celebrates a universe which is not only harmonious but beautiful.

Finally, we may return to the sleeping Spirit of the Earth. It is no accident that the Spirit is 'laid asleep', 'Like to a child o'erwearied with sweet toil'. Shelley makes notable use of a similar image in the *Defence of Poetry* where he describes the vivifying powers of poetry: 'it strips the veil of familiarity from the world, and lays bare the naked and sleeping beauty, which is the spirit of its forms'.[46] This, indeed, is what Shelley is attempting to do in his evocation of the dance of matter; the sleeping child is the secret principle of life which lies concealed beneath the appearances of nature. Indeed, this image might serve as an emblem of Shelley's whole poetic enterprise. In his eyes, life is essentially positive and the world is endlessly potential. Underneath the moist earth the flowers are as yet unexpanded, while above the ground the forest still waits for the animating breath of spring; man is still in bondage to his tyrants and Prometheus, not yet unbound, is chained to his rock; but if we could only see into the heart of things, exercise the prophetic intuition of the poet, we would realise that a slow, gradual, silent change is now in process, that, however delayed, the spring will come and man will ultimately be delivered from his imprisonment. In this energetic vision which 'marries . . . eternity and change' and 'subdues to union, under its light yoke, all irreconcileable things', Shelley both celebrates the facts of life and pays his homage to hope. Here mythology and science, tradition and innovation, reason and imagination are all at work together; the result is difficult but rewarding, a vigorously realised vision of all that life has to offer us, a sustaining and enduring image of hope and possibility.

Notes to chapter eight

1   *Letters*, II. 16.
2   *Letters*, II. 25.
3   *Letters*, II. 56.
4   'Not one among the many seemed to know / His way, but as gray moths when grass is mown / Go blindly fluttering from the moving heap ...' (Draft of *The Triumph of Life*, printed by Reiman, p. 240).
5   *The Witch of Atlas*, l. 173.
6   'Evening: Ponte al Mare, Pisa', l. 3.
7   Kathleen Raine, *Defending Ancient Springs*, Oxford University Press, 1967, p. 147.
8   *Letters*, I. 192–3.
9   *P.W.*, pp. 478–9.
10   Clark, *Prose*, p. 176. A similar interest can be detected in some of Shelley's best-known lyrics (e.g. 'Music, when soft voices die').
11   Clark, *Prose*, p. 177.
12   *Life*, I. 73.
13   Clark, *Prose*, p. 177.
14   Cf. l. 662.
15   Shelley's notes on Davy can be found in Bod. MS. Shelley adds. e. 6, pp. 155–72. The notebook appears to have been used in 1819–1821 (though Shelley's interest in Davy goes back as far as July 1812 when he ordered *Elements of Chemical Philosophy* in advance of publication; *Letters*, I. 319). The notes are followed immediately by a draft of part of 'Arethusa', usually dated to 1820. Claire Clairmont's *Journal* also indicates an interest in Davy in 1820 (entries for 8 and 10 April), while on 13 April Shelley himself wrote, 'I have been thinking & talking & reading Agriculture this last week' (*Letters*, II. 182). The notes are taken from Davy's *Elements of Agricultural Chemistry* and include direct quotations and summaries.
16   Immediately after dismissing the claims of sensitive plants to the faculty of perception ('I suppose it is all bare *mechanism*'), Locke goes on to say: 'Perception, I believe, is, in some degree, in all sorts of animals; though in some possibly the avenues provided by nature for the reception of sensations are so few, and the perception they are received with *so obscure and dull*, that it comes extremely short of the quickness and variety of sensation which is in other animals; but yet it is sufficient for, and wisely adapted to, the state and condition of that sort of animals who are thus made' (Book II, ix. 11–12: my italics). The sensitive plant is discussed by Davy in *Elements of Agricultural Chemistry*, London and Edinburgh, 1813, pp. 217–18, where he states that 'Such a doctrine is worthy only of a poetic form'. For the eighteenth-century fascination with this subject, see Robert M. Maniquis, 'The Puzzling *Mimosa*: Sensitivity and Plant Symbols in Romanticism', *Studies in Romanticism*, VIII (1969), pp. 129–55.
17   These lines come from a rejected introduction to *The Revolt of Islam* in

Bod. MS. Shelley adds. e. 19, pp. 4–6. The whole passage can be found conveniently in Wasserman, *Shelley*, pp. 188–90.

18 Bod. MS. Shelley adds. e. 12, p. 117.

19 Text from Bod. MS. Shelley adds e. 17, p. 189.

20 'Stanzas Written in Dejection', ll. 5–6.

21 Cited by Peter Butter, *A.P.A.*, p. 270. Walker's influence is discussed by Butter in *Shelley's Idols of the Cave*, pp. 143–53.

22 *Shelley's Idols of the Cave*, p. 143.

23 'Light consists either of vibrations propagated through a subtle medium, or of numerous minute particles repelled in all directions from the luminous body [the sun]' (*P.W.*, p. 800).

24 See, too, my discussion of Mercury in *The Violet in the Crucible*, pp. 70–9; see also my 'Shelley and the Religion of Joy', *Studies in Romanticism*, xv (1976), pp. 357–82.

25 I owe this suggestion to Desmond King-Hele, *Shelley: his Thought and Work*, 2nd ed., Macmillan, 1971, which includes an interesting discussion of Shelley's poem from a scientific point of view.

26 King-Hele, *Shelley*, p. 222.

27 Butter, *A.P.A.*, p. 330.

28 See p. 236. In a passage which Shelley noted in his summary, Davy writes: '... experiments made upon the atmosphere shew that clouds are usually negative; and as when a cloud is in one state of electricity the surface of the earth beneath is brought into the opposite state, it is probable that in common cases the surface of the earth is positive' (*Elements of Agricultural Chemistry*, p. 37).

29 *The Penguin Companion to Literature*, Penguin Books, Harmondsworth, 1971, I. 474.

30 Introduction to *Selections from Shelley*, n.d., pp. xli–xlii.

31 The same applies to F. H. Ludlam, 'The meteorology of Shelley's Ode'. *T.L.S.*, 1 September 1972, pp. 1015–16. While it is important to recognise the accuracy of Shelley's observation, accuracy does not necessarily constitute poetic merit.

32 *Letters*, II. 2–3.

33 *Letters*, II. 152. For Shelley's account of the effect of *The Story of Rimini*, see 'A gentle story of two lovers young' (*P.W.*, p. 584).

34 Bod. MS. Shelley adds. e. 6, p. 22 shows that lines 5–6 of 'The Cloud' had originally been part of the adjacent 'Hymn of Apollo' in a slightly different form. See Wassermann, *Shelley*, pp. 243–5.

35 For Shelley's debt, see James E. Cronin, ' "The Hag" in "The Cloud" ', *Notes and Queries*, cxcv (1950), pp. 341–2.

36 King-Hele, *Shelley*, p. 225. Contrast this typical eighteenth-century perspective: 'th' aerial concave without cloud, / Translucent ...'.

37 See 'Shelley and the Religion of Joy'.

38 A traditional allusion is detected here by Harold Bloom (*Shelley's Mythmaking*, pp. 141–2) who proposes two apocalyptic references: one to Ezekiel, 1: 27 and the other to Revelation, 1: 14 ('His head and his hairs were white like wool, as white as snow; and his eyes were as a flame of fire ...'). See also *Paradiso*, xxxi. 14–15.

39 Quoted in Carl Grabo, *A Newton Among Poets*, p. 142.

40 For Shelley's possible debt to Laplace and others, see Thomas A. Reisner, 'Some Scientific Models for Shelley's Multitudinous Orb', *K.-S.J.*, 23 (1974), pp. 52–9. Whatever the source, the image was important to Shelley. It occurs, rather surprisingly, in a political context in the *Essay on Christianity*: 'The great community of mankind had been subdivided into ten

thousand communities each organised for the ruin of the other. Wheel within wheel the vast machine was instinct with the restless spirit of desolation' (Clark, *Prose*, p. 205).

41   *Elements of Agricultural Chemistry*, p. 8.
42   Marjorie Hope Nicolson, *Newton Demands the Muse*, Princeton University Press, Princeton, 1946.
43   *Newton Demands the Muse*, p. 44.
44   'Stanzas Written in Dejection', l. 4; *Julian and Maddalo*, l. 84.
45   For a detailed account, see Glenn O'Malley, *Shelley and Synaesthesia*, Northwestern University Press, Chicago, 1964.
46   *Defence*, p. 56.

SELECT BIBLIOGRAPHY

Abrams, M. H., *Natural Supernaturalism: Tradition and Revolution in Romantic Literature*, Oxford University Press, 1971.

Bagehot, Walter, 'Percy Bysshe Shelley' (1856) in *Literary Studies*, 2 vols., Dent, 1951.

Barnard, Ellsworth, *Shelley's Religion*, University of Minnesota Press, Minneapolis, 1937.

Bloom, Harold, *Shelley's Mythmaking*, Yale University Press, New Haven, 1959.

Bloom, Harold, *The Visionary Company: A Reading of English Romantic Poetry*, revised ed., Cornell University Press, Ithaca and London, 1971.

Butter, Peter, *Shelley's Idols of the Cave*, University Press, Edinburgh, 1954.

Cameron, Kenneth Neill, *Shelley: The Golden Years*, Harvard University Press, Cambridge, Mass., 1974.

Cameron, Kenneth Neill, *The Young Shelley: Genesis of a Radical*, Macmillan, New York and London, 1951.

Chernaik, Judith, *The Lyrics of Shelley*, Case Western Reserve University Press, Cleveland and London, 1972.

Curran, Stuart, *Shelley's Annus Mirabilis: The Maturing of an Epic Vision*, Huntington Library, San Marino, California, 1975.

Curran, Stuart, *Shelley's Cenci: Scorpions Ringed with Fire*, Princeton University Press, Princeton, 1970.

Davie, Donald, 'Shelley's Urbanity' in *Purity of Diction in English Verse*, reissue with additions, Oxford University Press, 1967.

Fogle, Richard Harter, *The Imagery of Keats and Shelley: A Comparative Study*, University of North Carolina Press, Chapel Hill, 1949.

Grabo, Carl, *A Newton Among Poets*, University of North Carolina Press, Chapel Hill, 1930.

Holmes, Richard, *Shelley: The Pursuit*, Weidenfeld & Nicolson, 1973.

Hughes, A. M. D., *The Nascent Mind of Shelley*, reprinted ed., Clarendon Press, Oxford, 1971.

Johnson, R. Brimley (ed.), *Shelley–Leigh Hunt: How Friendship Made History*, Ingpen and Grant, 1928.

MacNiece, Gerald, *Shelley and the Revolutionary Idea*, Harvard University Press, Cambridge, Mass., 1969.

Mills, Howard, *Peacock, his Circle and his Age*, Cambridge University Press, Cambridge, 1969.

Norman, Sylva, *Flight of the Skylark: The Development of Shelley's Reputation*, University of Oklahoma Press, Norman, 1954.

Notopoulos, James A., *The Platonism of Shelley: A Study of Platonism and the Poetic Mind*, Duke University Press, Durham, N.C., 1949.

Pulos, C. E., *The Deep Truth: A Study of Shelley's Scepticism*, University of Nebraska Press, Lincoln, 1954.

Redpath, Theodore, *The Young Romantics and Critical Opinion 1807–1824*, Harrap, 1973.

Reiman, Donald H., *Percy Bysshe Shelley*, St Martin's Press, New York, 1969.

Robinson, Charles E., *Shelley and Byron: The Snake and Eagle Wreathed in Fight*, Johns Hopkins Press, Baltimore and London, 1976.

Rogers, Neville, *Shelley at Work: A Critical Inquiry*, 2nd ed., Clarendon Press, Oxford, 1967.

Wasserman, Earl, *Shelley: A Critical Reading*, Johns Hopkins Press, Baltimore and London, 1971.

Wasserman, Earl, *The Subtler Language: Critical Readings of Neoclassic and Romantic Poems*, Johns Hopkins Press, Baltimore, 1959.

Webb, Timothy, *The Violet in the Crucible: Shelley and Translation*, Clarendon Press, Oxford, 1976.

White, Newman Ivey, *Shelley*, 2 vols., Knopf, New York, 1940.

White, Newman Ivey, *The Unextinguished Hearth: Shelley and his Contemporary Critics*, Duke University Press, Durham, N. C., 1938.

Wilson, Milton, *Shelley's Later Poetry: A Study of his Prophetic Imagination*, Columbia University Press, New York, 1959.

Woodman, Ross G., *The Apocalyptic Vision in the Poetry of Shelley*, University of Toronto Press, Toronto, 1964.

Yeats, W. B., in *Essays and Introductions*, Macmillan, 1961.

INDEX

Abrams, M. H., 176, 180
Academy, 222, 225
Acropolis, 203, 222–3
Addison, Joseph: *The Spectator*, 83
Aeschylus, 4, 58, 59, 132, 142, 144, 194, 199, 200, 206–7, 208, 210, 226; Oresteian trilogy, 200; *Persae*, 199; *Prometheus Bound*, 142–4, 171, 176, 206–7, 210
Agamemnon, 149
Agathon, 117
Ahrimanes, 137, 140
Akenside, Mark, 246; *Hymn to the Naiads*, 252
Alps, 140, 142
Amphitryon, 218
Antisthenes, 198
Apollo, 209, 210, 211
Ariel, 15, 19, 20
Aristotle, 60, 62, 221; *Ethics*, 65; *Poetics*, 59
Arno, 1, 3, 82
Arnold, Matthew, 21, 95, 196
Asia, 118, 119, 148, 149, 163–4, 173, 176, 180, 181, 186, 200, 207, 210, 220, 254
Athenaeus, 225, 226, 227
Athene, 151
Athenians, 24, 119–20, 151, 184, 194, 195
Athens, 151, 193, 194, 197, 199, 203, 222–4
Auden, W. H., 53–4, 124

Bacchus, 212–13
Bacon, Francis, 63, 184, 253; *Advancement of Learning*, 184; *The Wisdom of the Ancients*, 253
Bagehot, Walter, 75
Bagni di Lucca, 192, 229
Bamford, Samuel, 101
Barnard, Ellsworth, 33–4

Barthélemy, Abbé J. J.: *Anacharsis*, 194
Basho, 59
Bateson, F. W., 75–6
Beatrice, 41, 186
Beaumont, Sir George, 223
Benevento, 49
Berkeley, George, 57
Bible, 45, 78, 82, 102, 106, 127, 128, 129, 130–1, 158, 162, 165, 168, 176, 179–80, 215, 257; New Testament, 130, 170, 179; Old Testament, 130, 131, 144; Acts, 151, 180, 184; Apocrypha, 130; Corinthians, 174, 178–9, 181; Ezekiel, 130, 257, 259; Genesis, 180; Isaiah, 130, 158–9, 179, 180; James, 172, 174; Job, 58, 59, 130, 177, 180, 195; Luke, 130, 153; Matthew, 153, 159, 168–9; Psalms, 38–9, 71, 130, 142, 176, 177; Revelation, 45, 172, 176, 179, 180, 259; Sermon on the Mount, 90, 121, 159, 161–2, 172, 176, 182, 187; Tobit, 153; The Wisdom of Solomon, 130, 153, 170
Blackwood's Edinburgh Magazine, 5, 28, 63, 82
Blake, William, 18, 22, 77, 94, 97, 121, 153, 157, 169, 180; *The Everlasting Gospel*, 153
Bologna, 188
Boscombe Manor, 15
Bostetter, Edward, 31, 40, 71
Bradley, A. C., 22
Brandreth, Jeremiah, 107, 134
Bridehead, Sue, 28
Bristol Channel, 109
Brooks, Cleanth, 25, 33, 35–6, 59
Browning, Robert, 22
Brun, Friederika, 141
Burdett, Sir Francis, 106; *Address to the Prince Regent*, 106
Burns, Robert, 178

263